Global Agricultural Policy Reform and Trade

Global Agricultural Policy Reform and Trade

Environmental Gains and Losses

Edited by

Joseph Cooper

Economist and Deputy Director
Resource Economics Division
Economic Research Service
United States Department of Agriculture
Washington, DC, USA

Edward Elgar

Cheltenham, UK • Northampton, MA, USA

Published by
Edward Elgar Publishing Limited
Glensanda House
Montpellier Parade
Cheltenham
Glos GL50 1UA
UK

Edward Elgar Publishing, Inc.
136 West Street
Suite 202
Northampton
Massachusetts 01060
USA

A catalogue record for this book
is available from the British Library

Library of Congress Cataloguing in Publication Data

Global agricultural policy reform and trade : environmental gains and losses /
    edited by Joseph Cooper.
        p. cm.
        Includes bibliographical references (p.).
            1. Agriculture—Environmental aspects. 2. Agriculture and
        state—Environmental aspects—International cooperation. 3. International
        trade—Environmental aspects—International cooperation. I. Cooper, Joseph.

S589.75.G59 2004
338.1'81—dc22
                                                                    2004047957

ISBN 978 1 84376 887 6

Printed and bound by CPI Group (UK) Ltd, Croydon, CR0 4YY

Contents

Part I ENVIRONMENTAL IMPACTS OF
TRADE LIBERALIZATION

Part II TRADE IMPACTS OF
AGRI-ENVIRONMENTAL PROGRAMS

Part III IMPLICATIONS FOR RESEARCH AND POLICY

List of figures

List of tables

List of boxes

List of contributors

Jason Bernstein is an economist at the United States Department of Agriculture's Foreign Agricultural Service in Washington, DC, USA.

Jean-Christophe Bureau is a professor at the Institut National Agronomique, Paris Grignon, and UMR Economie Publique INRA-INAPG, Paris.

Roger Claassen is an economist at the United States Department of Agriculture's Economic Research Service in Washington, DC, USA.

Joseph Cooper is an economist and deputy director of the Resource Economics Division at the United States Department of Agriculture's Economic Research Service in Washington, DC, USA.

Kevin Ingram is an economist at the United States Department of Agriculture's National Resource Conservation Service in Washington, DC, USA.

Jonathan Kaplan is an assistant professor at California State University, Sacramento.

Robert Johansson is an economist at the United States Department of Agriculture's Economic Research Service in Washington, DC, USA.

Mark Peters is an economist at the United States Department of Agriculture's Agricultural Marketing Service in Washington, DC, USA.

Mark Smith is an economist at the United States Department of Agriculture in Washington, DC, USA.

John Sullivan is an economist at the United States Department of Agriculture's Economic Research Service in Washington, DC, USA.

Utpal Vasavada is an economist and branch chief in the Resource Economics Division at the United States Department of Agriculture's Economic Research Service in Washington, DC, USA.

Preface

Economic theory suggests that, in the absence of market imperfections, free trade policies increase economic welfare. In practice, the World Trade Organization's (WTO) recent attempts at agricultural trade liberalization have encountered resistance from groups who believe that the current movement towards globalization fails to adequately address environmental concerns. Agricultural trade liberalization is likely to affect the environment in a variety of ways, some positive and others negative. Even in developed countries, such as the US, where agriculture at the farm level represents less than 2 per cent of gross domestic product, agriculture is a major user of land and water resources and a major source of water degradation. Hence, trade-induced changes in agricultural production levels could have notable environmental effects. In principle, if socially optimal environmental policies were in place in all trading countries, then opposition to trade liberalization on environmental grounds would be minimal. Despite significant challenges from private interest groups as well as from governments, agricultural negotiations that were started with the Uruguay Round Agreement on Agriculture have continued more recently with the 2001 WTO ministerial conference in Doha, Qatar, and the 2003 WTO Ministerial in Cancun, Mexico, opening opportunities for multilateral examinations of the interactions between agricultural trade and the environment. Within the context of ongoing trade negotiations, this book provides an objective overview of the environmental implications of liberalized trade.

Not only may changes in trade policy effect the environment, but environmental policy can also effect trade. Consequently, this book also examines the rise of multilateral environmental agreements (for example, the Cartagena Protocol on Biosafety) and the challenges of coordinating trade agreements with them. Many physical and economic interactions are possible between trade and the environment. Trade liberalization can change both production in the aggregate as well as shift production between countries and between commodities. Production of various commodities can increase or decrease. Technologies used in the production process can change as well. A priori, not only is it impossible to determine whether the net environmental effect of trade liberalization is positive or negative, but it also likely varies by sector and region. In the process of achieving some environmental goals, a domestic agri-environmental policy can decrease production (for example, as does a land set-aside program such as the Conservation Reserve Program in the US) and decrease the country's contribution to world production for some commodities, thereby increasing world prices. Alternatively, some domestic agri-environmental programs could actually increase production (either intentionally or not) of traded commodities, thereby decreasing world prices. A hypothetical, but not inconceivable example of such a program is one that pays a farmer to use an environmentally friendly farm management practice regardless of whether or not the farmer was already using it prior to joining the program.

The overall aim of this book is to lay out an overview of potential economic consequences of trade and environment linkages in one document. This book is targeted to a wide audience, including policymakers, policy analysts, environmental groups, commercial agriculture interests, and anyone else interested in exploring the linkages between agricultural trade and the environment. The book is intended to serve as a single reference source that readers can turn to when they have questions on this subject.

Under this overall goal, this book has several objectives. One is a prospective empirical examination of the potential environmental impact of agricultural trade liberalization in the US as well as globally. A second objective is to examine the potential impact of domestic (US) agri-environmental policies on trade. Third, the book pays special attention to conceptual and policy issues on the relationship of agricultural trade to unintentional environmental by-products, transboundary concerns, and multilateral environmental agreements.

PRELIMINARY ANALYSIS OF DOMESTIC ENVIRONMEN-TAL EFFECTS OF TRADE LIBERALIZATION

We evaluate some of the environmental impacts on the US of a trade liberalization scenario involving the elimination of all agricultural policy distortions (that is, agricultural subsidies and tariffs) in all trading countries (and no new environmental policies) that were in place in the year 2000. This empirical simulation of a total trade liberalization scenario provides an extreme example of the possible market effects of more probable scenarios of partial trade liberalization. We find that for the US:

- Due to predicted changes in trade flows between countries resulting from the trade liberalization scenario, overall agricultural commodity production is anticipated to increase, but by less than 1 per cent. Even for this extreme case scenario for trade liberalization, the estimated change is well within the bounds of normal seasonal variation in US agricultural commodity production as observed over the last 35 years.
- Corn production is likely to increase in all US regions (by 2.5 per cent overall), with most changes being marginal. Wheat production increases in some

regions and decreases in others, with a 3.7 per cent decrease overall. Soybean production is likely to fall marginally in all regions, with an overall decrease of less than 1 per cent.

- Potential changes in the livestock and feed sectors are expected to be marginal overall, with some variation at the regional levels. For example, while dairy production falls overall by less than 0.5 per cent, many regions exhibit potential increases in production. Swine, beef, and poultry production increases are small as well, with the biggest overall increase being for poultry, at 1.5 per cent. The changes vary by region, but they are small as well.

Given the relatively small predicted changes in agricultural production, would the adverse environmental impacts, including runoff from erosion, fertilizers, pesticides, and animal manure, be small as well? Empirical analysis confirms this expectation.

- The change in potential environmental impacts associated with increased production is less than 1 per cent for the US as a whole. However, while the environmental impacts are small, they are not uniform across the US. Some regions will have increases in potential environmental impacts, while others will see reductions in environmental impacts.
- Adverse environmental impacts would increase in the Midwest and East regions, and decrease in the South and West. Soil erosion would increase by 1.6 per cent in the Midwest and by 0.4 per cent in the East, while decreasing by less than 1 per cent in the South and West.
- Many changes in cropping patterns and production interact to produce these environmental changes. One reason for the increases in environmental impacts in the Midwest and East regions is that the projected increase in cropped acres, albeit small, is greater than in the South and West.
- In addition, conventionally tilled acres, which are associated with higher levels of sheet and rill erosion, in the Midwest and East regions are expected to increase by a greater extent (2.3 and 1.8 per cent, respectively) than the increases in total acreage (0.9 and 0.6 per cent, respectively).

PROSPECTIVE GLOBAL ENVIRONMENTAL EFFECTS OF AGRICULTURAL TRADE LIBERALIZATION

We supplement our detailed US analysis with an illustration of a process for estimating the global environmental impacts of world agricultural trade liberalization. The global model is more aggregated than the US-specific model, and addresses more general changes in input use, from which one can surmise possible environmental impacts. The center of attention for our analysis is the impact in the EU (European Union), US, and Southeast Asia, while the rest of the world is an aggregation of notably smaller agricultural economies. Simulating a 30 per cent across-the-board reduction in subsidies and tariffs, we find that:

- For the EU, the percentage reduction in crop production is much larger than the percentage decrease in cropland because the EU also experiences relatively large reductions in the use of water, labor, and capital. These results suggest beneficial impacts on the environment.
- Southeast Asia shows increases in crop production and cropland, with the percentage increase in crop production roughly double the percentage increase in cropland. This difference may signal a potential area for concern, in that pollution impacts are associated with both increased land conversion for cropping and a more intensive use of all cropland. The region experiences increases in water, labor, capital and cropland, and decreases in pasture land, forestland, and other land uses, but the changes are small.
- Results for the US are consistent with the US-specific analysis, although in many instances the two are not directly comparable. As do the US-specific results, the global model results show increases in both cropland and crop production across most of the US. These increases imply that, barring major changes in technologies, farm management practices, or types of crops, pollution associated with crop production could increase, but with the US-specific analysis suggesting these changes to be marginal.
- In the US, since the percentage increase in crop production is generally greater than the percentage increase in cropland in all areas, the intensity of cropland use is likely to increase. This increase implies that water-borne pollutants from cropland are likely to become more concentrated, with the US-specific analysis suggesting these changes to be marginal.
- With regard to grazing land in the US, the global model indicates that, although some grassland habitats increase in the West, grazing pressure on these lands increases as well. Other grassland habitats decrease, but grazing pressure decreases in these habitats as well.

ANALYSIS OF PROSPECTIVE IMPACT OF DOMESTIC AGRI-ENVIRONMENTAL POLICIES ON TRADE

A comprehensive assessment of the linkages between trade and environment requires not only examination of the impacts of trade agreements on the environment, but examination of the impacts of agri-environmental policies on trade. In many OECD (Organization for Economic Cooperation and Development) member countries, including the US, interest in developing agri-environmental programs is strong. The trade impacts of such policies are uncertain, but potentially significant within the WTO context.

Agri-environmental policies can take many forms and address multiple objectives. Our analysis compares and contrasts various options for reducing nitrogen or sediment losses to waterways. Using an empirical simulation of taxes on nitrogen fertilizer, subsidy payments to the farmer in return for reducing erosion and nitrogen loss to water, hypothetical regulations mandating reductions in activities that contribute to erosion and nitrogen loss, and land retirement, we find that:

- With respect to the goal of reducing nitrogen loss to water, the nitrogen fertilizer tax policy as modeled in our study is the most cost-effective, followed in order by the regulatory, agri-environmental subsidy, and land retirement approaches to achieving this goal.
- For erosion reduction, the regulatory policy is the most cost effective, followed in order by agri-environmental subsidies and land retirement.
- Evaluating the policies by their trade effects results in a different ranking, but one that is consistent across the two environmental objectives. The agri-environmental subsidy policy has the least effect on trade, followed by regulation, tax (where relevant), and land retirement policies. This ranking with respect to trade impact is determined by the policy's impact on production. Not surprisingly, the policy with the least impact on production (that is, agri-environmental payments) has the least impact on trade volume, while the policy with the greatest impact on production (land retirement) has the greatest impact on trade.

In many OECD countries, agri-environmental subsidies (for example, incentive payments and cost sharing in exchange for the farmer adopting more environmentally benign management practices) represent the agri-environmental policy approaches that are of particular interest to policymakers. As small differences in the details of agri-environmental subsidy programs may have notably different market implications, we take an in-depth look at the trade implications of alternative designs for such programs. In this context, we examine the trade impacts of three generic agri-environmental schemes that provide farmers with incentive payments to encourage farm management activities that reduce erosion.

We find that, for the three agri-environmental payment scenarios evaluated, the maximum change in exports ranges from a 7 per cent decrease (wheat) to a 1 per cent increase (soybeans). One requirement for the inclusion of an agri-environmental program in the WTO's "green box" is that it has no more than "minimal" trade-distorting impacts on production. With regard to the scenario predicting a decrease in production, the reality is that no country is likely to challenge agri-environmental programs (for example, the Conservation Reserve Program in the US) that decrease production.

MULTILATERAL AGRI-ENVIRONMENTAL ACCORDS AND THEIR LINKAGES TO AGRICULTURAL TRADE

Multilateral environmental agreements (MEAs) can complement trade agreements to mitigate potential adverse environmental or trade impacts. Linking MEAs with trade agreements may increase the potential for success of an MEA. However, because MEAs can restrict the free flow of goods between countries, they can also potentially conflict with WTO trade rules. Recent history suggests that MEAs can be linked to agricultural trade either formally (albeit rarely) through explicit trade provisions in the MEAs, or indirectly through jurisdictional overlaps. Of the approximately 200 MEAs in place today, 20 of these contain trade provisions. The linkages and jurisdictional overlaps between MEAs and trade agreements suggest that trade will be affected not only through multilateral trade negotiations, but potentially also through multilateral environmental negotiations. Hence, those interested in agricultural trade policy may need to keep abreast of environmental negotiations.

One of the functions of MEAs is to support the conservation of global public goods, including those that are threatened by the globalization of trade. Our analysis suggests that environmental indicators for the value of these goods are necessary for the optimal management of the financial contributions supporting conservation. While no ideal indicators exist, one may be able to obtain, for a number of developed and developing countries, some reasonable proxies for the value of a number of environmental and public goods.

Continuing our examination of environmental goods, we address the "multifunctionality of agriculture" concept. This concept embodies one of the most explicit acknowledgements that agriculture sometimes provides secondary benefits – environmental and otherwise – that are incidental to production of agricultural commodities. Multifunctionality is a trade issue as it may be used by some countries to justify production-linked agricultural support. The central question in the multifunctionality debate is whether or not agri-environmental policy can conserve or even enhance the supply of these multifunctions without distorting trade. In addressing this question, we find that:

- Empirical analysis to date on the environmental impacts of agricultural trade liberalization is of little help as it does not address these positive multifunctions (that is, amenities), perhaps due to insufficient demand until recently for conserving amenities as well as to particular difficulties in obtaining data on them.

- For influencinging the level of amenities, and disamenities (negative by-products) of agricultural production, policies that target these by-products directly are likely to be more effective in terms of allocating resources and increasing social welfare than policies that directly target agricultural production and, therefore, are less likely to violate WTO commitments.
- However, while the negative consequences of a policy may decrease with better targeting, the trade-off is that transaction costs (for example, costs associated with formulating and administering the policy) increase.
- Economic efficiencies may be achieved by coordinating policies targeted at inter-related by-products rather than targeting each by-product independently.

ACKNOWLEDGEMENTS

The authors gratefully acknowledge the input provided by Chantal Line Carpentier, Andrea Cattaneo, Mary Bohman, David Brooks, Mary Burfisher, Judy Dean, Joseph Dewbre, George Frisvold, Mark Gelhlar, Paul Gibson, Jason Hafenmeister, Rachel Hodgetts, Mark Manis, Fred Nelson, Mark Ribaudo, Jim Shortle, Agapi Somwaru, Carol Stillwagon, Jim Stoudt, John Wainio, Marca Weinberg and Alix Peterson Zwane. Layout and design by Victor Phillips, Jr. and Wynnice Pointer-Napper.

DISCLAIMER

The views presented herein are those of the authors, and do not necessarily represent the views or policies of the Economic Research Service or the United States Department of Agriculture.

1. Introduction

Joseph Cooper[1]

MOTIVATION

While economists have long argued that free trade is economically optimal from the viewpoint of world welfare, recent attempts at agricultural trade liberalization by the World Trade Organization (WTO) have encountered resistance on environmental grounds. Some environmental non-governmental organizations (NGOs) and WTO member nations fear that "globalization" can contribute to environmental degradation. Opposition has also come from interest groups seeking to associate environmental amenities with agricultural production, as embodied in the so-called "multifunctionality of agriculture" notion that is embraced by a number of OECD (Organization for Economic Cooperation and Development) member countries, and is a concept that some critics believe is a tool for justifying production-linked agricultural support.[2] Despite these significant challenges to the trade liberalization agenda, agricultural negotiations continue at the WTO, spurred by the 2001 ministerial conference held in 2001 in Doha, Qatar.

Within the context of these ongoing efforts, this book provides a much needed objective assessment of the environmental implications of liberalized trade, an area that continues to be of significant policy concern.[3] For example, environment and agricultural trade are listed as priority policy areas by the US Department of Agriculture (US Department of Agriculture, 2001), which in 2002 initiated an intra-departmental task force specifically tasked with addressing trade and environment issues. The Commission on Environmental Cooperation, an international organization created by Canada, Mexico and the United States under the North American Free Trade Agreement's (NAFTA) environmental side agreement, has focused its efforts on examining the environmental impacts of agricultural trade liberalization.[4] The recent US Executive Order 13141 and the Trade Act of 2002 mandate that environmental assessments of all proposed trade agreements be performed. Because affected Federal departments have little experience to date in quantifying the environmental consequences of agricultural trade agreements, this book also seeks to provide background material that could be useful to such assessments.

With a focus on agriculture, one of the goals of this book is to empirically assess the potential environmental impact of agricultural trade liberalization in the US and abroad. *A priori*, it is not only impossible to determine whether the net environmental effect of trade is positive or negative, but it also likely varies by sector and region. A second goal of this book is to examine the impact of domestic agri-environmental policies on trade. The WTO's treatment of domestic agricultural support allows countries to provide unlimited support for agri-environmental policies that meet certain over-riding criteria, including that the program shall have no, or minimal, trade-distorting effects on production. If not now, at least in the near future, the inclusion of agri-environmental programs with trade-distorting effects in the WTO's "green box" could be challenged in principle by WTO member countries. The third goal is to lay out agri-environmental policy issues that may have pertinent linkages to agricultural trade.

The following section presents a conceptual framework to analyze linkages between trade and environment. The next section of this chapter provides a roadmap to the rest of this book. The analysis of agri-environmental issues follows in the subsequent chapters.

TRADE LIBERALIZATION AND THE ENVIRONMENT: DECOMPOSITION OF EFFECTS

In principle, trade liberalization offers the prospect for improved environmental outcomes. Through the utilization of differences in comparative advantages between countries, international trade can improve the allocative efficiency of resources worldwide. This process creates greater incomes in all trading nations and increases the demand not just for material goods but also for environmental amenities, such as cleaner air and water. To the extent that government policies reasonably reflect the underlying preferences of a country's population, stricter environmental regulations will be voluntarily enacted and enforced when incomes rise. However, as long as per capita incomes (and perhaps social and cultural values) vary across countries, different environmental demands are likely to persist. A combination of freer trade, globally mobile capital, and diverse environmental preferences may result in the export of some pollution problems from developed countries (DCs) to less developed countries (LDCs) as LDCs specialize in the production of more pollution-intensive goods (Copeland and Taylor 1994). Nonetheless, increasing worldwide incomes should also concurrently create conditions under which all countries, including the LDCs, raise their environmental standards.

Many economists argue that trade enhances welfare even if it temporarily increases pollution. The elimination of policies that distort markets will lead to domestic prices accurately reflecting the opportunity cost of supplying the goods in question. Economic theory suggests that, as long as domestic and world prices differ in this situation, there are efficiency gains from trade.[5] Furthermore, the gains from trade are not contingent on the source of these price differences. For instance, even if the source of a country's comparative advantage is the operation of polluting factories, the economic gains from trade remain undiminished and international harmonization of pollution standards should be rejected (Krugman 1997). These economic gains increase per capita gross domestic product (GDP), which in turn increases the demand not just for material goods but for environmental amenities as well. This increase in demand provides the motivation for countries to adopt increasingly stringent environmental regulations as their wealth increases. Forced upward harmonization of environmental standards, however, is unlikely to be successful.

Chichilnisky (1994) counters the free trade position with the argument that if the LDCs lack the institutional capacity to define property rights, the illusion of a comparative advantage may be created when one does not exist. Such a situation can result in the over-exploitation of the environment in LDCs both in terms of excessive consumption of underpriced natural resources as well as pollution associated with over-production, which may be inconsistent with public preferences in developed as well as developing countries. Trade liberalization exacerbates these distorting effects. Bhagwati (1996) points out that there are many imperfections in the world economy and market failures abound, which is an argument for improving the efficiency of markets, and not for protectionist policies.

One concern regarding trade liberalization frequently expressed by governments is that this process creates an incentive for countries to lure capital by lowering environmental standards, which in turn may cause other countries to respond in kind, a process commonly referred to as the "race-to-the-bottom" hypothesis. Little evidence has been found for this effect in practice (for example, Fredriksson and Millimet, 2000; Xu, 1999), and based on the evidence provided, the concept appears to apply more to manufacturing than to agriculture. A related concept is that of the "pollution haven" hypothesis, which says that some countries with low demand for environmental quality will adopt lax environmental standards that attract investment and export pollution-intensive goods. Countries with a high demand for environmental quality will adopt high standards and import pollution-intensive goods. One of the differences between the race-to-the-bottom hypothesis and the pollution haven hypothesis is that the former implies an overall world level of environmental regulation that is less than optimal, while the latter does not (Frankel and Rose, 2002). Namely, in a "pollution haven," the level of environmental regulation may well reflect the public's preferences for environmental quality.

Even if efficiency gains from trade liberalization exceed trade-induced pollution costs, this increase in net welfare begs the question of how trade liberalization might affect environmental outcomes. As an aid to understanding the sources of these outcomes, the environmental impact of trade liberalization may be decomposed into a technique effect, scale effect, and composition effect (Cole, Rayner and Bates 1998), although slightly different alternative decompositions are feasible (for example, Abler and Shortle, 2001).

Technique Effect. Trade liberalization may have environmental impacts due to producers altering production methods to adopt either cleaner or dirtier production technologies in response to trade impacts. This change can occur for several reasons:

1. Increases in consumer income or changes in consumer preferences may precipitate stricter environmental restrictions (Grossman and Krueger 1995);
2. Changes in relative prices may create incentives to alter production technologies (Anderson 1992);
3. International diffusion of clean technologies, perhaps through foreign direct investment, could reduce pollution emissions (Leonard 1998; Wheeler and Martin 1992); and
4. Lowered environmental standards to attract industry could result in increased emissions of pollutants (Barrett 1994a).

Scale Effect. Empirical evidence has long linked open economies to economic growth (Edwards 1992; Harrison 1996). Increased output and scale of production are generally associated with economic growth and may generate additional pollution emissions and accelerate the depletion of natural resources.

Composition Effect. Trade liberalization may also affect the composition of output (types and relative proportions) produced in an economy, as resources formerly devoted to protected inefficient industries will be utilized elsewhere. For instance, Cole, Rayner and Bates (1998) suggest that the phasing-out of the Multi-Fiber Agreement under the Uruguay Round will cause textile production in LDCs to increase and heavy manufacturing to contract. Since textile production may be less pollution-intensive than heavy industry, there may be a positive composition effect, although a negative scale effect may offset it.

These three distinct effects may interact to create an inverted-U relationship between income and pollution, although it is not clear how robust this relationship is (Dasgupta *et al.*, 2002) or whether it applies to agriculture. In honor of Simon Kuznets, who proposed a similarly-shaped relationship between income and income inequality, this hypothetical relationship has come to be known as the environmental Kuznets curve (EKC) (*ibid.*; World Bank, 1999). The stylized EKC in Figure 1.1 illustrates this phenomenon. The argument is that, when a country develops from an initially low level of income, the scale effect dominates, as there is an increase in the demand for all inputs, including the environment as a sink for waste. Rising incomes, however, increase the willingness to pay for environmental amenities (for example, cleaner air and water). Regulations are enacted, forcing a shift to cleaner production processes, as the technique effect reduces harmful emissions and environmental damage. Furthermore, trade liberalization may facilitate the international diffusion of cleaner technologies, as Wheeler and Martin (1992) find in the case of wood pulp production. As resources are shifted out of polluting industries and rising incomes shift preferences to cleaner goods, the composition and technique effects eventually dominate the scale effect.

Although Stern, Common and Barbier (1996) criticize the estimation and usefulness of the EKC, Grossman and Krueger (1995) provide empirical support for this hypothesis. They find that, for most pollutants, mean air and water concentrations increase as per capita GDP initially increases from a low level of income, but that concentrations begin to decline before per capita GDP reaches $11 000 in 1999 dollars.[6] In 1999, examples of Latin American per

Figure 1.1 Stylized environmental Kuznets curve

Level of Pollutant

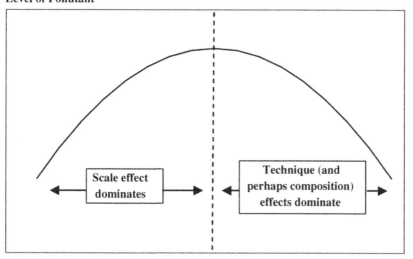

GDP per capita

Source: Figure is loosely based on that in World Bank (1999).

capita GDPs are $5080, $3570, and $4600 for Mexico, Brazil, and Chile, respectively. Canadian and US per capita GDP were $19 999 and $31 915, respectively (World Bank, 2000a, 2000b). The relevance of the EKC to agricultural trade liberalization will be discussed in Chapter 8 of this book.

Another possible way to achieve environmental gains from trade besides the international diffusion of cleaner technologies (environmental goods) discussed above is through technological and managerial innovation. According to Esty and Gentry (1997), multinational corporations, which generally originate from countries of origin that have higher environmental standards, have a tendency to bring to a lower-standard host country the cleaner production techniques used in the originating country.[7] They may do so for reasons of efficiency in maintaining uniform production practices across countries and concerns over their high visibility (*ibid.*). The relevance to the agricultural sector of this path to environmental gains is unknown, but may have some applicability to food-processing industries, for example. Of course, whether or not the introduction of multinationally-based production facilities to a country indeed results in a net decrease in adverse environmental impacts in that country depends on a number of factors, including the change in the composition of goods produced in the country after the introduction, as well as technological and managerial spill-over effects on the rest of the economy associated with this introduction.

Yet another possible way to achieve gains in environmental standards may be through trade liberalization leading to a *de facto* increase in these standards. That is, private inspectors from importing firms representing an importing country with higher environmental standards (country A) may demand that the exported goods (from country B) be produced under the higher environmental standards of country A. Such higher quality standards may spill over to production intended for country B's own domestic market (Lopez, 2002).

The schematic in Figure 1.2 (derived from Frankel and Rose, 2002) represents a visual summary of the linkages between the concepts addressed in this section. Path 1 represents the economic gains from trade, while Path 2 is the reverse impact from income to trade. Path 3 is the environmental Kuznets curve. The effects of environmental policy (for example, regulation, voluntary incentives) on production (and wealth) can be either negative (as one may usually expect) but may even be positive, and are represented by Path 4. Path 5 is the effect of commodity production on the environment (the combination of scale, composition, and technique effects), and can be positive or negative. Path 6 denotes linkages between environment and trade policy, including impacts such as those suggested by the "race-to-the- bottom" hypothesis. Linkage 7 represents a government system, presumably democratic, that translates public preferences into environmental policy.

Figure 1.2 Hypothesized relationships between trade and the environment

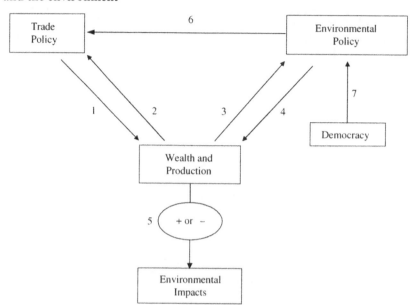

Note: The path numbers are referenced in the text

OBJECTIVES AND ROADMAP FOR THIS STUDY

Figure 1.3 is a graphical outline of the relationship between the chapters in this book that draws the linkages between agricultural trade and environmental policy and production and environmental impacts. Chapter 2 specifically addresses conceptual and policy issues regarding the unintended environmental by-products provided by agriculture, and their linkages to agricultural trade, and provides the general premise for the development of the specific indicators (that is, measures of environmental impacts) used in the subsequent chapters. The chapter addresses both the environmental amenities and disamenities provided by agriculture. While the concerns over environmental impacts of liberalizing trade generally focus on the potential for increasing negative environmental consequences, some interest groups argue that liberalizing trade may diminish the positive environmental consequences of agriculture. For example, one of the challenges for trade policy involves a host of issues arising from a desire to protect the environmental amenities provided by agriculture, as embodied in the "multifunctionality of agriculture," and their relationship to trade negotiations.

Figure 1.3 Book outline: Issues and chapter linkages

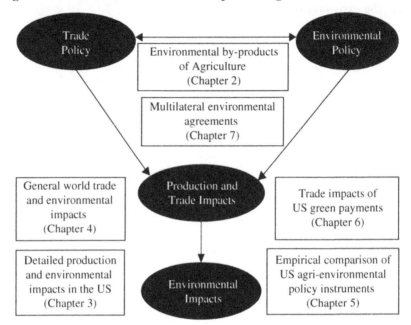

Chapters 3 and 4 empirically explore the effects of trade policy on the environment, with the former focusing on domestic impacts and the latter on global impacts. Conversely, agri-environmental policy, through its influence on farm management practices, can have impacts on trade. Chapters 5 and 6 empirically explore the effects of environmental policy on production, and consequently, on trade, with the former focusing on alternative agri-environmental policies designed to achieve set objectives and the latter extending this line of analysis with an in-depth look at agri-environmental payment programs.

Chapter 7 rounds out this book by paying special attention to transboundary issues covered by multilateral environmental agreements (MEAs), and their linkages to agricultural trade. One of the challenges facing trade policy is the rise of MEAs and the challenges of coordinating trade agreements with them. Some of the environmental consequences of trade liberalization agreements may be addressed by linking these agreements to MEAs. Conversely, some MEAs have provisions that could restrict agricultural trade.

The assessment of environmental impacts in Chapters 3 and 4 presumes that some set of environmental measures has been chosen for analysis. The discussion in Chapter 7 of the availability and relevance of environmental indicators on a worldwide basis provides linkages to Chapters 3 and 4.

NOTES

1. The views presented herein as those of the authors, and do not necessarily present the views or policies of the Economic Research Service or the United States Department of Agriculture.

2. See Chapter 2 for the definition of the "multifunctionality of agriculture."

3. In this book, the word "environment" is defined broadly to include the physical, biological, and human environments.

4. For example, the Commission on Environmental Cooperation held a conference "Assessing the Environmental Effects of Trade Liberalization: Lessons Learned and Future Challenges," in Montreal, Canada in January 2002.

5. "Economic efficiency" refers to strategies that could optimize society's overall welfare, including the taking into account of externalities.

6. The 1985 prices in the original source of Figure 1.1 are re-expressed in 1999 dollars using the implicit price inflator from US Department of Commerce, Bureau of Economic Analysis (2000). GDP data is from World Bank (2000a).

7. On the other hand, multinational corporations may relocate production to countries with lower environmental standards so that they can use dirtier production techniques than are allowed in the home country.

FOR FURTHER READING

Anderson, Kym and Anna Strutt, "On Measuring the Environmental Impact of Agricultural Trade Liberalization," in Maury Bredahl *et al.* (eds), *Agriculture, Trade, and the Environment: Discovering and Measuring the Critical Linkages*, HarperCollins Boulder and Westview Press: London, 1996: 151–72.

Anderson, Kym, "Effects on the Environment and Welfare of Liberalizing World Trade: The Cases of Coal and Food," in Kym Anderson and Richard Blackhurst (eds), *The Greening of World Trade Issues*, University of Michigan Press: Ann Arbor, 1992: 145–72.

Anderson, K., "The Standard Welfare Economics of Policies Affecting Trade and the Environment," in Kym Anderson and Richard Blackhurst (eds), *The Greening of World Trade Issues*, University of Michigan Press: Ann Arbor, 1992.

Antweiler, W., B. Copeland and M. Taylor, "Is Free Trade Good for the Environment?," *American Economic Review*, Sept. 2001: 877–908.

Barbier, Edward, "Trade in Timber-Based Forest Products and the Implications of the Uruguay Round," in *The Economics of Environment and Development: Selected Essays*, Edward Elgar: Cheltenham, UK and Northampton Massachusetts, 1998: pages 476–90.

Barbier, Edward, "Links between Economic Liberalization and Rural Resource Degradation in the Developing Regions," *Agricultural Economics* 23(3), Sept. 2000: 299–310.

Barbier, Edward and Michael Rauscher, "Trade, Tropical Deforestation and Policy Interventions," in *The Economics of Environment and Development: Selected Essays*, Edward Elgar: Cheltenham, UK and Northampton Massachusetts, 1998: 427–43.

Dean, J. M., *International Trade and the Environment*, Aldershot: Ashgate, 2001.

Dean, J. M., "Does Free Trade Harm the Environment? A New Test," *Canadian Journal of Economics*, Vol. 35, No. 4, November 2002: 819–42.

Kreuger, A., *Growth, Distortions and Patterns of Trade Among Many Countries*, International Finance Section, Princeton University: Princeton, New Jersey, 1997.

Leamer, E. E., "Paths of Development in the Three Factor, n-Good General Equilibrium Model," *Journal of Political Economy* 95 (October, 1987): 961–99.

Strutt, A. and K. Anderson, "Will Trade Liberalization Harm the Environment? The Case of Indonesia to 2020," *Environmental and Resource Economics* 17(3), Nov. 2000: 203–32.

Tyers, R. and K. Anderson, "Liberalising OECD Agricultural Policies in the Uruguay Round: Effects on Trade and Welfare," in G.H. Peters (ed.), *Agricultural Economics*, Elgar Reference Collection, International Library of Critical Writings in Economics, vol. 55, Edward Elgar: Aldershot, UK and Brookfield, Vermont, 1995: 470–89.

2. The environmental by-products of agriculture: International policy responses

Joseph Cooper, Jason Bernstein,
Utpal Vasavada and Jean-Christophe Bureau[1]

I. INTRODUCTION

Producing agricultural commodities simultaneously produces many unintentional environmental by-products, some desirable and some not. Examples of those impacts include changes in soil erosion, nitrogen run-off, and landscape amenities. Judging from the relatively high levels of government expenditures on agri-environmental issues in many OECD countries, the public is indeed concerned with agriculture's impacts (both positive and negative) on the environment, a concern that does not appear to be abating. In fact, proposed conservation funding was slated to increases by 80 per cent under the 2002 US Farm Bill as compared to the previous 1996 Farm Bill (Economic Research Service, 2002a). Most research and policy attention to date on the externalities of agriculture has focused on negative externalities, such as soil erosion and water contamination. In fact, given limitations in currently available information, all the environmental impacts measured in the subsequent chapters are negative by-products of agriculture.[2] However, policy in a number of developed country members of the WTO is increasingly giving attention to the positive by-products of agriculture, such as scenic views and open space. One of the most explicit acknowledgements that agriculture provides desirable secondary benefits—environmental and otherwise—is embodied in the normative concept of the "multifunctionality of agriculture."[3]

Chapter 1 provided a general overview of the economics of trade and the environment. In this chapter, we turn to agriculture-specific issues in trade and the environment. Namely, we raise the economic implications of domestic policies in WTO member countries that target the unintended by-products of agriculture for agricultural trade and the WTO. In the first of the sections that cover this area, we address the economics of the multifunctionality of agriculture concept. We next highlight the differences in agri-environmental policy between the US and other countries that have a substantial body of agri-environmental policy. We then address how WTO rules on domestic support might bring changes in agri-environmental policies among its members. Next, we address policy alternatives for adjusting the level of these by-products in a minimally trade-distorting manner. While this chapter focuses on examples drawn from OECD countries as most policy related to these by-products of agriculture is found in these countries, our last section before the conclusion highlights why the environmental impacts of agricultural trade liberalization could vary between low and high income countries.

As a foundation for our discussion of environmental issues in relationship to agricultural trade, we begin by providing an overview of the economic and policy issues surrounding the environmental externalities of agriculture. For instance, what are these externalities, why do they occur, and how can we quantitatively assess their economic impacts?

II.   OVERVIEW OF THE NEGATIVE UNINTENDED CONSEQUENCES OF AGRICULTURAL PRODUCTION

Agricultural activities constitute the most pervasive nonpoint-source pollution problem in the US (EPA, 1984). In particular, agriculture is one of the leading sources of pollution of rivers and streams (EPA, 1998). Negative by-products of agricultural production can include sediments, nutrients (nitrogen and phosphorus), pesticides, pathogens, and salts.[4] While farmers do not intend for these materials to move from the field or enterprise, they often do, carried by rainfall, snowmelt, or irrigation water. Nutrients applied to cropland, chiefly nitrogen and phosphorus, can cause water quality problems when they enter surface- and groundwater systems. Box 2.1 overviews the basic economic concepts for why socially nonoptimal quantities of unintended by-products of market activities (or externalities) may be produced.

Nitrogen and phosphorus from agriculture are concerns for surface water quality because they promote algae in receiving surface waters (known as eutrophication), resulting in clogged pipelines, decreased oxygen levels, fish kills, and reduced recreational opportunities. The EPA reports that nutrient pollution is the leading cause of water quality impairment in lakes and is the third leading cause in rivers. Harmful algal blooms in coastal waters have been attributed to nutrients from manmade sources, including fertilizers. Whether nitrogen actually contaminates surface or groundwater depends on the amounts of nitrogen applied to agricultural land, other management practices, and the leaching characteristics of the soil, and on precipitation (factors which are in fact accounted for in the model used for the analyses in Chapters 3, 5 and 6).

Sediment can damage water resources. For instance, accelerated reservoir siltation reduces the useful life of reservoirs. Sediment can clog roadside ditches and irrigation canals, block navigation channels, and increase dredging costs. By raising streambeds and burying streamside wetlands, sediment increases the probability and severity of floods. Suspended sediment can increase the cost of water treatment for municipal and industrial water uses. Sediment can also destroy or degrade aquatic wildlife habitat, reducing diversity and damaging commercial and recreational fisheries. However, note that while we focused this discussion on water quality issues—the area that is historically a major focus of agri-environmental policy, not all environmental impacts of agricultural activities are water-related. For instance, agriculture contributes to both methane and nitrous oxide emissions to the atmosphere.

Table 2.1 provides a count of the frequency of citation of various disamenities in papers submitted by consultants from various OECD countries at an OECD conference on multifunctionality in 2001 (Abler, 2001).[5] The table provides a simple indication that many countries accept the existence of the same negative externalities associated with agricultural production. Water pollution is the most frequently cited externality and threats to animal welfare the least cited. Papers by consultants from four countries made no mention of negative externalities at all. The specific environmental indicators used in the empirical models whose results are expressed in Chapters 3, 5, and 6 fall into the "Water Pollution from Nutrients and Erosion" column in the table. Chapter 4 has indicators that fall in the irrigation category of the table. Research is ongoing at ERS in including into these models the indicators that fall into the biodiversity column of the table.

III. OVERVIEW OF THE POSITIVE BY-PRODUCTS
     OF AGRICULTURAL PRODUCTION

While most agri-environmental policy is focused on reducing the negative environmental by-products of agriculture, agricultural activity does produce positive environmental by-products as well. For instance, a primary function such as milk production often produces scenic pastures, a positive externality, or amenity. Hellerstein *et al.* (2002) provides an extensive overview of rural amenities, while this chapter takes an international perspective on the closely related, but more specific subject of the environmental amenities provided by agriculture, given that rural amenities may encompass nonagriculturally related activities as well.

Broadly defined in the spirit of Hellerstein *et al.* (2002), the environmental amenities provided by agriculture encompass a variety of goods that result from agricultural activities and that cannot be reduced to a market commodity.

Box 2.1 Externalities, market failure, and public goods

Economists use the term "*externality*" to describe a harmful or beneficial side effect that occurs in the production, consumption, or distribution of a particular market good. Production of an agricultural good may generate an environmental externality, for instance. To produce the market good, a producer chooses a technology and input mix (land, labor, machinery, and chemicals). In the production process, either wastes and/or amenities may be produced as a by-product. These are externalities if they affect the well-being of others in a way that is not transmitted by market prices; that is, the producer does not bear the costs of the waste cleanup or receive compensation for the benefits of the amenity provided.

Externalities often arise when there is no market for a product. Ill-defined or poorly enforced property rights (for example, when resources such as ground and surface water or air over a city are owned either by the community or by no one) can generate the lack of market. Externalities also tend to occur when those affected are widely dispersed and difficult to identify. The cost to the community of water pollution or air pollution is not reflected in the market—economists refer to this as *market failure*.

Market failure occurs when the market price of a good does not include the costs or benefits of the externality. Producers or consumers may have little incentive to alter activities that contribute to pollution, for example, or to adopt environmentally beneficial technologies because these external costs do not enter their private costs of production. Often, government policies in the form of regulations (such as standards, bans, and restrictions on input use) and incentive-based mechanisms (such as taxes, subsidies, and marketable permits) are implemented as corrective measures. The basic idea behind these policies is to require people who create (or consume) externalities to take their costs (or benefits) into account. While these policies may meet environmental (or other) goals, they also affect production, trade, investment, technological change, and consumption.

Public goods are goods or, more commonly, services that are nonrival and nonexcludable. National defense is a good example. It is nonrival because one new citizen does not reduce the defense benefits enjoyed by all other citizens. It is nonexcludable because it is impossible to prevent a citizen from receiving the services. When a service is nonexcludable markets do not work well: there is no incentive to pay for the service, and it cannot be withheld for nonpayment. No incentive to pay means that no private firm would be willing to supply the service. In such cases, governments provide the service and collect taxes to cover the cost.

Markets work well for *private* goods because they are rival and excludable: there is an incentive to pay and prices can be determined. In practice, the world is not neatly divided into public and private goods. Between purely private and purely public goods exist a spectrum of goods. For example, large numbers of tourists visiting a rural area can cause congestion and reduce the enjoyment of the visit by all, that is, the good is nonexcludable but not nonrival.

This "nonmarket" feature refers to the value of an amenity as a function of things that are not reflected in its market price (which is zero), but has positive economic value to society. Since these values are not reflected in market prices, like the value of the negative by-products discussed in the previous section, farmers have little incentive to consider how the provision of these non-market public goods (see Chapter 1 for a discussion of public goods) may be affected by agricultural production. Hence, while this market failure may result in the overproduction of the negative by-products, it can also result in the underproduction of the positive by-products.

Table 2.2 provides a count of the frequency of citation of various amenities in papers submitted by consultants from various OECD countries at the same OECD conference as for Table 2.1. The table provides a very simple indication that many countries recognize the existence of the same amenities (noncommodity outputs). Interestingly enough, a comparison of Tables 2.1 and 2.2 indicates that the papers by consultants from two countries that addressed the greatest number of amenities categories listed in Table 2.2 did not address any disamenities of agriculture.

The most frequently cited environmental amenity category in Table 2.2, "landscape and open space" amenities, tends to be somewhat abstract in comparison to the environmental disamenities discussed in the previous section. Economic valuation of such intangible goods can be difficult, as pointed out in Chapter 1. At present, none of our empirical models in the chapters so far can analyze amenities falling in any of the categories in Table 2.2. We address the difficulty of doing so in the conclusion to this chapter.

IV. WHEN IS A DISAMENITY AN AMENITY OR VICE-VERSA? DIFFICULTIES IN CATEGORIZING THE ENVIRONMENTAL BY-PRODUCTS OF AGRICULTURE

Tables 2.1 and 2.2 list some of the positive and negative environmental by-products of agriculture. A given farm operation may provide different levels (including zero) of these by-products. However, whether a by-product is considered to be an amenity or disamenity is partially subjective.[6] Determining whether agriculture is a superior means of providing an amenity requires comparison with all alternative uses of the land. Box 2.2 juxtaposes two columns listing the environmental impacts of agriculture to demonstrate that agriculture may have positive or negative impacts compared to an alternative land use. Compared to urban land use as an alternative, agriculture is probably generally a positive contributor to each of the factors in the first column. One overview of the relationship between farming and flood control claims that linkages

Table 2.1 Synthesis of negative environmental by-products of agriculture

Country	Loss of biodiversity	Water pollution from nutrients & erosion	Threats to animal welfare	Irrigation over use, salinization	Greenhouse gas emissions	Total negative externalities
Australia	✓	✓		✓		3
Austria	✓	✓		✓	✓	4
Belgium		✓		✓		2
Canada	✓	✓		✓	✓	4
Czech Rep						0
Finland	✓	✓			✓	3
France	✓	✓	✓			3
Greece		✓				1
Japan						0
Korea						0
Netherlands	✓	✓			✓	3
New Zealand	✓	✓		✓		3
Norway						0
Spain	✓	✓		✓		3
Switzerland	✓	✓				2
UK	✓	✓				2
USA	✓	✓				2
Total	11	13	1	6	3	35

Source: Abler (2001)

between these two are quite strong and positive under the Asian monsoon rice production system (Kada, 2001). On the other hand, compared to land in a wild state, agriculture likely contributes greater nutrient runoff. Farmland likely provides more wildlife or flood control than urban development, but may or may not provide less than woodland or other natural states. Agriculture is not

"Valley of the Caffarella" provides open space and agricultural scenery adjacent to a high density urban neighborhood within the city of Rome, Italy (photo © Joseph Cooper).

the unique source of rural or environmental amenities, but advocates of agriculture as the provider of these amenities can make it appear so by excluding all but inferior alternatives. When considering policy design, the analyst should determine whether agriculture provides more or less of the amenity than the land use pattern that would likely exist without the policy.

The broad agri-environmental policy difference in addressing a negative externality versus a positive externality is that for the former, an agri-environmental program would be designed to encourage or require that the farmer undertake activities that reduce the level of the externality while for the latter, an agri-environmental program would be designed to encourage or require the farmer to undertake activities that increase the level of the externality. Furthermore, while the production of negative externalities is a result of market failure, an excess supply of positive externalities is not necessarily an issue that policy needs to address.

V.   ECONOMIC VALUATION OF ENVIRONMENTAL IMPACTS OF TRADE: AN OVERVIEW

To make a full economic assessment of the change in the unintended environmental by-products (or externalities) resulting from trade liberalization, these

Table 2.2 Synthesis of positive environmental by-products of agriculture

Country	Landscape & open space amenities	Prevention of natural hazards	Ground water resource recharge	Enhancement of biodiversity	Total positive externalities
Australia					0
Austria	✓	✓		✓	3
Belgium	✓			✓	2
Canada	✓			✓	2
Czech Rep	✓			✓	2
Finland	✓				1
France	✓				1
Greece	✓	✓		✓	3
Japan	✓	✓	✓	✓	4
Korea	✓	✓	✓	✓	4
Netherlands	✓	✓	✓		3
New Zealand					0
Norway	✓			✓	2
Spain	✓			✓	2
Switzerland	✓			✓	2
UK	✓			✓	2
USA	✓				1
Total	15	4	3	11	34

Source: Abler (2001)

impacts need to be valued. However, numerous empirical obstacles need to be overcome in the quest to make these assessments. The inherent obstacle to valuing many of these positive externalities is that they have a public good nature (see Box 2.1).

For the reasons outlined in Box 2.1, public goods and negative externalities tend not to be priced in the market. For example, if a scenic agricultural panorama is nonexcluable, a tourist is not charged a fee to view it. Does this imply that there is no value to this view? Certainly not. The view does have a value to society even if it is a "nonmarket" value. Economists have separated these nonmarket benefits into different categories according to whether the goods have *use* or *nonuse* values. A use value is one the individual derives from

---

Box 2.2 Side-by-side comparison of the positive and negative environmental by-products of agriculture

Possible impacts

By-Product	Positive	Negative
Water quality	Watershed protection	Nutrient/pesticide runoff
Water quantity	Flood control	Reduced flood control
Siltation/sedimentation	Soil conservation	Soil erosion
Landscape	Scenic vistas	Odor and noise
Biodiversity	Biodiversity gain	Biodiversity loss
Ecosystem impacts	Wildlife habitat gain	Wildlife habit loss

---

coming into direct contact with the environmental good, for example, recreational fishing and bird-watching. A nonuse value is more intangible as it is the value given to the existence of an environmental good even though it is not currently used. Nonuse values can be subdivided into three categories: (i) *existence value*—the value of simply knowing that the environmental good exists; (ii) *bequest value*—the value an individual holds for knowing that the good will be preserved for future generations; and (iii) *option value*—the value of conserving the good so that the option is maintained of being able to use it sometime in the future.

Because of the difficulties inherent in valuing these nonmarketed environmental by-products of agricultural activities, the valuation exercises in Chapters 3, 5, and 6 encompass only a portion of the physical environmental impacts assessed. All the empirical valuations assessed in these three chapters fall into the use value category. As nonuse values tend to be quite intangible, incorporating them into an empirical model of the agricultural sector would be difficult at best. No valuation measures are undertaken for the model of the world agricultural sector in Chapter 4 given the broad definitions and geographic scope of the environmental measures in the model, although some attempts have been made to value general environmental resources (for example, an acre-foot of fresh water) on a global basis. Costanza *et al.* (1997) remains a controversial study for its efforts in valuing global ecosystem functions.

In conventional economics, the indicator of economic value is based on what individuals want. Specifically, the maximum amount of one thing a person is willing to give up to get more of something else is considered a fair measure of the relative "value" of the two things to that person. Money is a universally accepted measure of economic value because the amount that people are "willing to pay" (WTP) for something reflects how much of all other for-sale goods and services they are willing to give up to get it.

For purposes of assessing the economic value of the environmental externalities of agricultural activity, it is important to note that measuring their dollar value does not require an explicit market in which they are bought and sold. For assessing the value of the environmental amenities of agricultural activity, the measurement only requires estimating how much purchasing power (dollars) people would be willing to give up to obtain them (or would need to be paid to give them up), if they were forced to make a choice. Similarly, for assessing the costs of the environmental disamenities of agricultural activity, the measurement only requires estimating how much purchasing power (dollars) people would be willing to give up to reduce them, if they were forced to make a choice.[7] Table 2.3 lists the basic methods for valuing nonmarketed goods. The environmental valuations in the model used in Chapters 3, 5, and 6, with one exception, use the change in production costs approach to calculate environmental benefits/damages (see Appendix 3).

Because both agricultural amenities and disamenities do not have market prices, measuring the WTP for their conservation or reduction requires special economic techniques. These techniques are outlined in Table 2.3. The hedonic method makes use of the fact that while an amenity such as open space may not be explicitly priced in the market, housing prices may be positively affected by proximity to the open space in the same way that housing price is positively correlated with the number of bedrooms. Statistical regression techniques allow the values of these attributes of the house to be separately identified and estimated. Similarly, the travel cost method (TCM) uses the statistical relationship between the number of trips to an area and the level of amenities in that area to estimate the changes in economic benefits due to a change in the level of the amenities. The hedonic and TCM approaches are revealed preference techniques, in which values are inferred from people's actions. The main stated method approach is the contingent valuation method (CVM), in which survey techniques essentially ask individuals how much they are willing to pay for a good. The contingent valuation method is the only available economic tool for valuing nonuse agricultural amenities or disamenities.

Why is it important to know these economic values? In general, a rationale is created for government intervention by the provision or reduction of environmental by-products given that markets do not exist for the positive by-products nor do they account for the negative by-products. While the lack of a market mechanism to account for the costs of negative by-products is a motivation for government intervention, a lack of a market for positive by-products is not necessarily grounds for government intervention. It is possible that socially optimal levels of some environmental amenities are being provided without any government intervention. Determining the appropriate levels of the amenities requires a tradeoff between all benefits and all costs to the point that the benefits from providing an additional unit of the amenity equal the costs of doing so. Usually, the policy costs for providing amenities (reducing disamenities) are easier to measure than the benefits; for the provision of some amenities (disamenities), the market may provide the costs, while benefits estimation usually require nonmarket valuation techniques.

VI. THE MULTIFUNCTIONALITY OF AGRICULTURE

Is the protection of the environmental amenities associated with agriculture a reason or an excuse for government intervention? For a number of developed countries, in the greater context of the negotiations addressing the "multifunctionality of agriculture," this contentious question has been high on the list of topics they have sought to include in recent rounds of agricultural trade negotiations. The 1994 Uruguay Round Agreement on Agriculture (URAA) liberalized trade in agricultural products. It also placed enforceable limits on the agricultural policies and trade regimes of World Trade Organization (WTO) members. Article 20 of the URAA encourages WTO member countries to make "substantial progressive reduction in support and protection ... [while] taking into account ... nontrade concerns." Agricultural officials in some countries argue that policies designed to meet nontrade concerns should be exempt from the Uruguay Round's limits on agricultural protection. Others contend that, while Article 20 recognizes the importance of nontrade concerns, it does not create a loophole for protection and domestic support.

These nontrade concerns are sometimes vaguely specified, but can include legitimate (that is, widely accepted) domestic policy objectives like preserving family farms and rural landscapes or ensuring food safety, food security, and animal welfare. These concerns reflect a fear that freer markets and globalization may undermine the provision of valued nonmarket amenities and cultural traditions associated with agriculture. These anxieties have coalesced and are often generalized using the term "multifunctionality." Multifunctionality has been a relatively controversial subject. Some see it as a veiled attempt at protectionism. According to Article 13 of the WTO's Doha Ministerial Declaration, the goals of the agricultural trade negotiations are "substantial improvement in market access; reductions of, with a view to phasing out, all forms of export subsidies; and substantial reductions in trade-distorting domestic support." The basic trade issue over multifunctionality is not whether legitimate multifunctions exist, but whether nontrade concerns can be allowed to negate the goal of the agricultural negotiations.

Table 2.3 Methods of valuing environmental by-products of agriculture

Method	Value assessed	Description
Averting or defensive expenditures	Use value	Measuring expenditures made by individuals to reduce loss of amenities (e.g., purchasing a field to prevent its development) or to protect against disamenities (e.g., purchase of drinking water filters to combat nitrate contamination). This method estimates values of ecosystem services based on either the costs of avoiding damages due to lost services, the cost of replacing environmental assets, or the cost of providing substitute services.
Changes in production costs	Use value	Infer the cost of a positive or negative externality by observing changes in firm profits, input costs or output prices due to changes in environmental quality.
Revealed preference	Use value	Observe individual behavior and infer the demand for environmental quality. For example, the travel cost method uses recreational trips to measure the demand for environmental quality, with the travel cost serving as the price. Conventional demand equations are then estimated to determine the value of environmental quality. Hedonic models can break the price of a market good down among its individual attributes, among which can be environmental quality.
Stated preference	Use value and nonuse value	Directly ask individuals questions about their willingness to pay for a change in environmental quality (contingent valuation method), or ask them to order scenarios involving varying prices and levels of environmental quality (conjoint contingent valuation analysis).

Source: Feather *et al.* (1999)

Multifunctionality refers to the many secondary functions of agriculture (Bohman *et al.*, 1999; Cahill, 2001; Mullarkey, Cooper and Skully, 2001; OECD, 1998), including the environmental amenities discussed earlier. Multifunctionality in the normative sense (as it has often been used in trade negotiation circles) refers to only the positive secondary functions, and as such, can also suggest an attitude or a policy position supporting domestic agricultural production as a means to a variety of nontrade ends. Use of the term appears to have originated in the late 1980s and then spread into policy conversations among various OECD countries during the early 1990s. Some of the general categories of frequently cited multifunctions of agriculture include environmental, social, rural development, and food security functions.

Several countries have used multifunctionality arguments to push for exemptions to Uruguay Round constraints. Countries such as Japan, the Republic of Korea, and Norway place "a lot of emphasis on the need to tackle agriculture's diversity as part of these nontrade concerns" (WTO, 2002b). An "informal" EU discussion paper notes: "safeguarding [the] existing multifunctional character of agriculture, as well as enhancing its multifunctional role for the future, is a … nontrade concern" (EC, 2001).

However, current (2002) EU policy does appear to suggest an approach to addressing multifunctional concerns that fits the existing WTO rules for "green" payments (see Box 3.2, Chapter 3, and Appendix 4). According to a WTO post-Doha conference summary of the agricultural negotiations, "The EU's proposal says nontrade concerns should be targeted (for example, environmental protection should be handled through environmental protection programs), transparent and cause minimal trade distortion" (WTO, 2002b). At least with regard to current EU policy proposals, support for multifunctionality may not in fact be a pretext for supporting agricultural output-coupled subsidies. Regardless, multifunctionality is still a relevant concept even if it is addressed only in the green box, as it provides a basis for increasing or creating direct subsidies for supporting positive externalities.

VII. CONTRASTING PARADIGMS ON AGRI-ENVIRON-MENTAL POLICY

US Federal level agri-environmental programs are best described as conservation programs. That is, US programs are directed at preventing or alleviating specific environmental problems (disamenities) that are a direct result of agricultural production, such as soil erosion, water pollution, destruction of wildlife habitats, or overproduction on wetlands and highly erodible land. Prior to the 2002 Farm Bill, US Federal agri-environmental policy did not address the provision of the environmental amenities of agriculture, such as open space, scenic vistas, organic production methods, or small scale farms. Historically, such environmental goals were left to other US Federal or State programs.[8] However, with the 2002 Farm Bill, US Federal policy appears to be moving in the direction of directly addressing the environmental amenities of agriculture. Namely, the new version of the Farmland Protection Program (FPP) extends eligibility to land with "historical or archaeological resources." The Grassland Reserve Program (GRP) is similar in concept to State level agricultural land preservation programs (see Appendix 6 for a description of FPP and GRP).

Like the US, the EU also uses a broad array of policy tools to address environmental concerns. However, the EU has an official set of agri-environmental objectives that go beyond those voiced at the US Federal level. Namely, the "European model" of agriculture goes beyond promoting the development of a competitive agricultural sector and environmentally friendly production methods with the objectives of ensuring that "agriculture is multifunctional, sustainable, competitive and spread throughout Europe, including regions with specific problems." Specifically, agriculture should be "capable of maintaining the countryside, conserving nature, and making a key contribution to the vitality of rural life, and that it responds to consumer concerns and demands as regards food quality and safety, environmental protection and the safeguarding of animal welfare" (European Commission, 2000b). In other words, as a matter of theory if not practice, government support of agriculture in the EU is not intended merely to maintain agricultural production, aid farmers, and reduce the disamenities of agriculture, but also to support the provision of agricultural amenities and social goals, especially the viability of rural communities, in a significantly more aggressive manner than at the US Federal level.

The EU identifies and subsidizes a broad range of measures such as organic farming, maintenance of the countryside and landscape features, and improvements to public access that are believed to promote agriculture's positive amenities (European Commission, 1998, p. 38). The comprehensive agricultural, environmental, and farm income aims of EEC 2078/92 (commonly referred to as the "agri-environmental" regulation) and its successor (EC 1257/99) rules make it difficult to separately identify social and rural development goals from environmental goals in EU agricultural policy. The EU may further strengthen the connections between the environment and agricultural support during the Agenda 2000 mid-term review in 2003.[9]

In some respects, Japan's model for agriculture overlaps with the EU's. For example, in 2000 a measure was introduced that uses subsidy payments to maintain agricultural production activity in hilly and mountain areas, with the goal of preventing the abandonment of such land. In fiscal year 2000, the agreements concluded under this measure covered around 567 000 hectares in 1 700 municipalities (Nakashima, 2001). In another example, because paddy fields that are left unplanted as a result of set-aside programs are considered unsightly, the planting of "landscape crops (non-saleable flowers such as sunflower or cosmos)" on such fields is subsidized (*ibid.*). With similar landscape preservation motives, in a Sicilian program that conforms to Agenda 2000, cultivation on walled terraces can be subsidized up to 450 euros per hectare per year, with a requirement that there be at least 200 meters of wall per hectare not less than 0.5 meters high. Qualifying walls cannot be made of concrete or concrete blocks, that is, they must be old-fashioned (Regione Siciliana, undated).

Perhaps to a large extent, the divergence in views between various OECD countries on the role of agri-environmental policy may be due to the difference in relative weights that the public places on the amenities of agriculture. For instance, while it is difficult to pin down exactly what the public values in maintaining land in agriculture, one of the American public's concerns over farmland loss is that it could be turned over to urban uses. While this is a concern of a large number of residents of Europe and Japan as well, anecdotal evidence suggests that many Europeans and Japanese appear to be concerned about farmland abandonment itself, namely, from seeing run-down farm buildings, overgrown hedges, and ill-kept fields; occurrences that are increasingly frequent in these countries as agricultural activities diminish in locations (for example, hillsides) not favorable to modern production techniques. Also, exactly what tends to constitute amenities in the EU and the US may differ. In the former, many consider abandoned and overgrown farms to be eyesores and government funds may be used to forestall their occurrence, while in the US, such land may simply be considered open space. Agriculture has been practiced in the EU for so long, and so much wilderness was removed long ago, that agriculture, and in particular small scale agriculture, is part of the natural scene. Some farming areas within the EU, such as those in the Tuscany region of Italy, are major tourist destinations and are recreational alternatives to national parks in the US. Surveys of Europeans on the valuation of agricultural amenities show that the existence of a diversified (in terms of crops and animals) family farm ranks high among the criteria on which tourists decide the location of a house to rent for vacation (Mahé and Ortalo-Magné, 2001). In addition, cultural values associated with small farms are quite high in the EU. The reasons that Europeans have an especially close affinity to the farm may be due to the high population densities that promote a closer intermingling of urban and farming areas than in the US, and the fact that Europeans have closer demographic ties to agriculture. A generation ago, a significantly larger percentage of Europeans than Americans were engaged in agriculture, and hence, a large number of Europeans still have family ties with a (frequently retired) farmer, and by extension, may see themselves as peasants by inheritance.

VIII. TRADE AND THE ENVIRONMENT: WTO RULES ON DOMESTIC SUPPORT MIGHT BRING CHANGES IN AGRI-ENVIRONMENTAL POLICIES IN MEMBER COUNTRIES

While there are important differences between both the goals of EU, Japan, and US agri-environmental policies and how they are implemented, the future of agri-environmental policy in these regions may be shaped by WTO rules on domestic support. Future debates about the liberalization of international trade will likely have large impacts on agri-environmental policies.

The Uruguay Round Agreement on Agriculture (URAA) formalized the long run goal of achieving significant reductions in domestic support measures that directly influence production decisions. Such measures are commonly referred to as "amber box" policies (see Box 3.2 in Chapter 3 and Appendix 4). At the same time, countries are exempt from reducing support for policies that have no, or a minimal effect, on production or trade, the so-called "green box" policies. Since 1995, both the EU and the US have placed many of their agri-environmental policies in the green box.[10] If the EU's traditional methods (for example, production-linked support) for maintaining a more managed countryside come under increasing pressure in trade negotiations, then the EU will have to increasingly rely on decoupled "green box" policies to support their goals.[11] One can speculate that this is the reason that the EU has insisted on the recognition of the multifunctional role of agriculture in its WTO negotiating proposals, with an interpretation of the green box that includes measures for poverty alleviation and promotion of animal welfare in addition to measures for protecting the environment (European Commission, 2000b). Such measures will likely include supporting rural development and less favored areas, preventing land abandonment, and managing the landscape for the promotion of tourism and biodiversity. With such a broad definition of the green box, however, it becomes harder to distinguish between policies whose goal is to protect the environment and have a minimal effect on production or trade and those policies that are more likely to act as disguised support to production. At least after the "Peace Clause" of the WTO's Agreement on Agriculture (see Chapter 6) expires, the claim of such policies having a "minimal effect" on production could be potentially challenged in the WTO. In such an event, resolution of the issue would depend on the recommendations of the panel of experts established by the WTO's Dispute Settlement Body (DSB). One would expect that the EU's recent stand that policies addressing nontrade concerns should "cause minimal trade distortion" (WTO, 2002b) places a limit on how broadly the green box can be interpreted.

A requirement for agri-environment programs to be included in the WTO green box is that they have not more than minimally distorting trade effects. Current US cost-sharing, incentive payment, and technical assistance programs likely have a minimal effect on production (for example, Burfisher and Hopkins, 2003), given that the focus of such programs is on environmental improvements rather than altering production.

However, it is difficult to ascertain the effects of both actual US and EU agri-environmental programs on production and trade. Payments under EU agri-environmental technical assistance or cost-sharing programs would likely have a minimal impact on production similar to the effect of US programs. In addition, payments that are used for cosmetic environmental improvements such as expanding public access, maintaining woodland areas, or building fences and hedgerows should also have no effect on production. However, agri-environmental payments that are used for the early retirement of farmers, preventing land abandonment, and for some rural development goals, may affect production by raising the opportunity cost of selling farmland to nonfarm uses. Such measures may also conflict with the additional condition of green box policies, which states that payments must be limited to subsidizing the added cost or lost income from the environmental measure adopted or technology shift accomplished. If either EU or US environmental payments are not tied to specific environmental practices or if there is little evidence that such practices will result in environmental benefits, then such payments may not be considered exempt from reduction. WTO rules and standards are in place to prevent a wholesale repackaging of production and trade-distorting measures to environmental green box measures without significant changes. However, more research is needed to quantify the production and trade effects of specific agri-environmental programs.

IX. JOINTNESS AND POLICY TARGETING

Chapters 5 and 6 empirically address some of the possible environmental and economic impacts of agri-environmental policy instruments and environmental instruments. This section provides a foundation for these empirical simulations by presenting a general discussion of agri-environmental policy design and the targeting of policy to specific environmental issues.

In general, the by-products of agriculture are externalities that are not fully accounted for in markets. Farmers do not bear all the costs associated with agricultural production, such as soil erosion, water depletion, surface and groundwater pollution, and loss of wildlife habitat. Nor do they generally reap all the benefits of recreational amenities, open space, and flood control. Many of the externalities have characteristics of public goods—no one can be excluded from enjoying the amenity, and use by one individual does not preclude use by any other individual. Further, some of these amenities, like wildlife, open space and sustaining cultural heritage, may generate nonuse values. Some people value the continued existence of these amenities whether or not they actually use them.

These amenities and disamenities of agriculture are often the target of domestic agricultural policy because conventional markets will not usually provide them at the desired levels. Appropriate policies can foster the development of markets for previously unvalued goods. Markets for pollution permits and wetlands mitigation banks may encourage producers to generate more positive externalities and fewer negative externalities. However, government intervention can also unintentionally increase the severity of negative externalities. A production subsidy that encourages producers to make more intensive use of fixed resources (for example, conversion of wetlands to crop production), may increase negative externalities. Developing appropriate policy depends on the characteristics (such as the extent to which it is a public good, the potential for nonagricultural supply, and nonuse values) of the amenity or disamenity being targeted.

For instance, one challenge facing WTO negotiators is how to allow for legitimate nontrade objectives without compromising the progress made in reducing trade-distorting policies. The central question remains, "How can agri-environmental policy conserve or even enhance the supply of the multifunctions of agriculture without distorting trade?" It is possible that many nontrade objectives can be achieved by minimally distorting trade. However, in some cases this may require abandoning agricultural production as the means to the nontrade end.

Many environmental amenities or disamenities of agricultural production affect society as a whole and have a social benefit or cost much greater than the private benefit or cost affecting farmers. In such cases, there is an economic rationale for the government to subsidize the environmental amenity (or tax the environmental disamenity) in order to produce the socially desired level of environmental protection. Indeed, as discussed earlier, both the United States and the European Union have a series of Federal and/or State agri-environmental programs to encourage the provision of environmental amenities and the reduction of environmental disamenities associated with agriculture, although they do have divergences in agri-environmental goals and programs.

Central to the discussion of multifunctionality is the concept of jointness between agricultural production and the multifunctions of agriculture. Joint products are those that can only be produced simultaneously. Hides and meat are joint products of cattle. Some countries argue that various multifunctions of agriculture are joint products of agricultural production. This claim is significant because countries may argue that production subsidies are needed to maintain the jointly produced desirable multifunctions of agriculture.

On the surface, jointness seems to be a logical characterization of the multi-functionality of agriculture. Close scrutiny reveals a different story. It is true that many multifunctions are by-products of agricultural production. However, this does not mean that agriculture is *required (or is required in its present form)* in order to provide them. Bohman *et al.* (1999) contend that virtually all of the desirable functions of agriculture are not unique to production agriculture; there are almost always other, less trade-distorting means of supplying the amenities and other goals sought under multifunctionality. For example, the restoration and maintenance cost of historic farm structures could be directly subsidized.

Moreover, increased agricultural production does not necessarily increase the supply of amenities. A scenic landscape may be no more lovely with 40 cows than with 30. Thus jointness is not a generally accurate or complete explanation of the relationship between agriculture and amenities, and production subsidies will not guarantee the desired level of amenities. In addition to jointness between the production of agricultural commodities and its by-products, some level of jointness exists between the by-products. For instance, a site's scenic views may be a composite of a number of its characteristics, including plants, animals, slope of the terrain, architectural details of the farm structures, and so on.

Interestingly enough, it does appear that while it is difficult to make a case that many of the amenities of agriculture (scenic vistas, stone walls, picket fences, old fashioned barns) are highly correlated with agricultural production levels, it appears to be the case that at least some of the significant disamenities of agriculture (for example, sediment erosion, nitrogen runoff) do have a strong link to production and acreage. This is, after all, the reason for the environmental concerns associated with subsidies that increase agricultural production. Indeed, the empirical simulation analyses in Chapters 3, 4, 5, and 6 would not have been possible without this link to production. Of course, a direct link between some amenities and agricultural production cannot be completely discounted. For instance, an acre of a row crop is an acre of open space. Even so, if what society mainly wants is to preserve open space, there may be cheaper alternatives than preserving it through agricultural production.

Bohman *et al.* (1999) discuss the wide range of policy alternatives to commodity-linked subsidies that may be available. In general, economic efficiency increases as the policy instrument is more precisely *targeted* to the externality of interest (for example, Bhagwati, Panagariya and Srinivisan, 1998). Although targeted policy instruments potentially have some impacts on production and trade, these instruments would be expected to be more effective and less trade-distorting than indirect policies such as price supports and production subsidies (Bohman *et al.*, 1999; Randall, 2002). Note however, that even if it may be more economically efficient to pay farmers directly to main-

tain rural amenities, practical implementation of such programs aimed directly at the amenities may meet with some resistance from the farm sector. For
example, a strong lobby of farmers in the EU is strongly opposed to the idea
of being paid as "gardeners of landscape." They want to be producers and
receive "decent prices" that cover their costs of production.[12]

When making the generalization that targeting the policy instrument directly to the externality is the economically efficient decision, we assume that the
transaction costs in targeting the policies are zero. Transaction costs include
the efforts required to meet information requirements, formulating the policy,
and monitoring and enforcing contracts. Vatn (2002) notes that transaction
costs may increase with increasing precision in the targeting of the policy.
Given a goal of promoting the production of the multifunctional goods, Vatn
argues that when agricultural production and provision of the multifunctions
are jointly related and the transaction costs in directly targeting the multifunctions are positive, it may be more reasonable to subsidize agricultural production than to target the multifunctions directly. However, Vatn does not consider that the decreased transaction costs associated with less precise targeting of
the commodity production-linked instrument have to be weighed against their
possible negative consequences. These negative consequences include
increased impacts on taxpayers, commodity markets, imports, exports, world
prices, as well as possible increased production of negative externalities and
excess production of positive externalities. Hence, the extent of negative consequences of a policy may be decreasing with the increasing precision of its
targeting, even if transaction costs increase. Further complicating the mission
of targeting a specific amenity for protection is that provision of this amenity
could be correlated, either as a substitute or complement, with the provision of
other amenities. For instance, a policy that maintains a scenic vista may also
result in biodiversity benefits. Efficiencies may be achieved by coordinating
the policies targeted at such interrelated amenities rather than targeting each
amenity independently.

X.   POTENTIAL "NORTH–SOUTH" AGRI-
ENVIRONMENTAL CONSIDERATIONS AND
TRADE LIBERALIZATION

In this chapter we focus on agri-environmental issues in developed countries,
as these are where most policy related to these by-products of agriculture
occurs. However, before we move to the conclusion to this chapter, it could be
useful to briefly highlight how the environmental impacts of agricultural trade
liberalization could vary according to a country's wealth.

The environmental impacts of agricultural trade liberalization may vary between the developed countries (DCs) and the less developed countries (LDCs). Agriculture tends to constitute a larger portion of the economy in the LDCs than in the DCs. Hence, the economic impacts of agricultural trade liberalization may be more significant as a percentage of GDP in the former than in the latter. Consequently, in LDCs, the share of the total environmental impact of trade liberalization that is associated with the agriculture sector may be proportionally greater than in DCs. Over time, as an LDC's wealth increases, some share of the labor force in agriculture may shift to other sectors, such as manufacturing and services. This shift may have environmental implications. For instance, the pressure to farm on marginal land may decline.

In addition, the relative importance of agricultural externalities (that is, unintended by-products of production) may differ according to a country's wealth. For example, the prevalence of extensive methods of agricultural production, in which output is increased primarily by expanding area planted, possibly to marginal lands, may be greater in poorer countries. In contrast, wealthier countries may be more likely to employ intensive methods, in which output is increased primarily by expanding the use of inputs other than land. Extensive and intensive methods are associated with different types of externalities. In extensively farmed areas, soil erosion and deforestation may be the environmental impacts of particular concern. In intensively farmed areas, nutrient runoff, pesticide runoff, and the loss of agricultural genetic diversity may be of greater concern. Agricultural genetic diversity loss is discussed in detail in Chapter 7. Agricultural trade liberalization may affect the overall level of environmental degradation, but it may also cause shifts between the different types of effects. Of course, this comparison of the environmental impacts of extensive versus intensive agriculture is a generalization, but it may help to characterize some of the differences in "North–South" agri-environmental issues. Of course, issues related to the type and scale of agriculture, the sensitivity of the environment to agriculture, and the value of environmental degradation are relevant to all regions.

XI. CONCLUSION

In the absence of markets for agricultural externalities, governments, facing pressure to protect domestic agriculture, yet constrained by international trade agreements to reduce protection of the agricultural sector, may be concerned with finding effective ways to promote the production of the amenities of agriculture (and inhibit production of disamenities) that may otherwise be lost. Among the challenges in designing policies to promote socially optimal levels of the multifunctions of agriculture is how to define, measure, and economically value these multifunctions. The list of potential amenities and disamenities is long, and it is likely that all countries will not agree on what should be considered a legitimate multifunction.

Determining the appropriate level of production of the environmental amenities of agriculture requires a balancing of all benefits and all costs, including impacts on trade. The efficient amount of environmental amenities occurs when the benefits from further increase in the amenity are just offset by the costs of providing any further increase.

The costs of implementing policies aimed at either positive or negative externalities are generally easier to measure than their benefits. Measuring the benefits requires putting a value on amenities and attributes that are not specifically valued in the market, requiring use of the costly economic approaches discussed earlier to obtain these values. Compounding the difficulty of these valuations efforts is that many of the amenities are likely quite local in nature. Site-nonspecific externalities can be cheaper to economically value than site-specific ones. For example, a person would be expected to have the same value for avoiding a liter of water with a given level of nitrate contamination regardless of its source; nitrates are nitrates. Hence, it is possible that the value of avoiding nitrate contamination that was estimated for one region can be applied—with adjustments for demographic differences (for example, Crutchfield, Cooper and Hellerstein, 1997)—to another region. At the other extreme, it would seem most unlikely that one would hold the same viewing value for every agricultural vista. If values are site-specific and are functions of attributes that are difficult to measure, a value estimated from a study of one scenic area may not then be reasonably applied to other scenic area, thereby necessitating a new study for that area. Not surprisingly then, little empirical information exists on the demand for the environmental functions of agriculture. Kline and Wichelns (1996) have provided some estimates in the United States and Drake (1992) has done the same in Europe. The recent OECD publication on multifunctionality (OECD, 2001b) and the ERS report on rural amenities (Hellerstein *et al.*, 2002) may prompt increased research in this area.

NOTES

1. The views presented herein are those of the authors, and do not necessarily represent the views or policies of the Economic Research Service or the United States Department of Agriculture.

2. Chapter 4 provides an analysis of changes in more general measures, such as irrigation levels, from which environmental impacts may be inferred.

3. The basic notion of the "multifunctionality of agriculture" is that agriculture is more than just producing and selling commodities; it also produces many unintended by-products. Frequently cited by-products encompass a broad range and include, for example, preservation of rural landscapes, flood prevention, and cultural heritage (see section VI of this chapter for more detail).

4. This section provides only a brief overview of these issues. For more information on the environmental impacts of agriculture, please see Economic Research Service (2000a) and Economic Research Service (2001).

5. The workshop "Multifunctionality: Applying the OECD Analytical Framework Guiding Policy Design" was held at OECD, Paris, 2–3 July 2001, *http://www1.oecd.org/agr/mf/*.

6. Of course, definition of the amenity itself is nontrivial. For example, the notion of "open space" is surely context sensitive and somewhat subjective. In an area that is heavily urbanized, people may consider both forested land and cleared (farm) land to be open space. In an area that is heavily forested, people may only consider cleared land to be open space. In fact, one would expect that in a heavily forested region, the marginal amenity value of an additional acre of cleared land would be higher than the marginal amenity value of an additional acre of forested land.

7. See Cooper (2001, 1995) or Feather, Hellerstein and Hansen (1999) for more detailed discussion of WTP and of methods to determine this value.

8. See Hellerstein *et al.* (2002) for a list of US State agri-environmental programs.

9. The EC's 2002 mid-term review of CAP (Commission of the European Communities, 2002) calls for a strengthening of cross-compliance requirements for receiving direct payments.

10. Bernstein, Cooper, and Claassen (2004) provide a more detailed discussion of this topic. Also, note that the countries themselves, and not the WTO, decide which programs to report as "green box."

11. Decoupled payments are lump sum income transfers to farm operators that do not depend on current production, factor use, or commodity prices (Burfisher and Hopkins, 2003).

12. Opinions of this nature are demonstrated by Jean-Michel Lemétayer, president of the French farmers' union Fédération Nationale des Syndicats d'Exploitants Agricoles (FNSEA), in a speech in February 2002 (Lemétayer, 2002).

FOR MORE INFORMATION

Anderson, K., "Agriculture's 'Multifunctionality' and the WTO," *Australian Journal of Agricultural and Resource Economics* 44(3), September 2000, 475–94.

European Commission, "State of application of regulation (EEC) No 2078/92: Evaluation of Agri-environment Programmes," DG AGRI FII.2, 1998.

European Environment Agency, "Environmental Themes: Agriculture," *http://themes.eea.eu.int.*

Heimilich, R. and R. Claassen, "Conservation Compliance in the US and Europe: An International Comparison," presentation, USDA–ERS, 2001.

Potter, C., "Against the Grain: Agri-Environmental Reform in the United States and the European Union," CAB International: Oxford, 1998.

PART I

Environmental Impacts
of Trade Liberalization

3. Some domestic environmental effects of US agricultural adjustments under liberalized trade: A preliminary analysis

Joseph Cooper, Robert Johansson and Mark Peters[1]

I.   INTRODUCTION

US legislation requiring formal environmental reviews, or environmental assessments, of major Federal activities significantly affecting the environment dates back 30 years. Within the last decade, nongovernmental organizations (NGOs) and other interested parties have called for extending these environmental reviews to trade agreements (WWF, 2001). In 2002, the first relatively in-depth environmental review of a trade agreement (US–Chile Free Trade Agreement) was conducted for legislative review.[2] Many interest groups and policymakers may desire a more rigorous analysis for further-reaching trade agreements, such as that which might occur under multilateral trade liberalization between all WTO member nations. The goals of this chapter are to discuss as well as quantify some of the possible US environmental impacts of a hypothetical agricultural trade liberalization scenario in the WTO context.

To motivate this change in trade policy, consider the declaration on agricultural trade from the Fourth WTO Ministerial Conference held in Doha, Qatar in November 2001 (the ministerial is the highest level meeting of the WTO). Here the WTO affirms its commitment to "correct and prevent restrictions and distortions in world agricultural markets." The WTO commits itself "to comprehensive negotiations aimed at: substantial improvements in market access; reductions of, with a view to phasing out, all forms of export subsidies; and substantial reductions in trade-distorting domestic support."[3] Given that agriculture is the leading source of pollution in 57 per cent of river miles, 30 per cent of lake acres (excluding the Great Lakes), and 15 per cent of estuarine waters that were found to be impaired in the US (ERS, 2001), changing agricultural production levels following a post-Doha trade agreement could have observable environmental effects in the US.

The next section of the chapter provides a literature review of empirical assessments of the environmental impacts of agricultural trade liberalization. Next, we describe the modeling framework used in obtaining our results. The third section presents the results.

II.   TRADE LIBERALIZATION AND AGRICULTURE: REVIEW OF EMPIRICAL EVIDENCE

A broad empirical literature examines the links between trade and the environment, although little of it is explicitly linked to agriculture. For example, Frankel and Rose (2002) statistically examine the impacts of trade liberalization on various air pollution measures. In their analysis, they found little evidence that trade had a detrimental effect on the levels of their indicators of air pollution in the US, and one indicator (sulfur dioxide, or SO_2) actually decreases significantly with increasing openness to trade. Another study, also using a statistical analysis (Antweiler, Copeland and Taylor, 2001), likewise finds that SO_2 levels exhibit net decreases with freer trade. However, it is uncertain whether or not lessons relevant to agriculture trade can be drawn from a literature that does not explicitly model the impacts of agriculture on the environment. Returning to an earlier example, Antweiler, Copeland and Taylor observed that rural areas (including agricultural production regions) tend to be associated with lower SO_2 than urban areas, a finding that may be relevant to a discussion on the environmental impacts of agricultural trade liberalization. Hitherto, few empirical studies have specifically examined the environmental effects of agricultural trade liberalization. Several notable exceptions (detailed below) include research on the environmental effects of trade between OECD countries and on the potential environmental effects of NAFTA (US, Mexico, and Canada).

Using a simulation model, Abler and Shortle (1992) analyzed restrictions on agricultural chemicals in the United States and the European Community (EC) under various farm commodity policy scenarios. Their model had three regions (US, EC, rest of the world) and four commodities (wheat, maize, coarse grains, soybeans). Given the farm programs existing at the time of the analysis, they found that US farmland owners gained economically from chemical restrictions while EC farmland owners generally lost. Given bilateral elimination of farm programs, both US and EC farmland owners benefited economically from restrictions on chemical use. They found that bilateral farm program elimination without chemical restrictions induced a shift in chemical usage from the EC to the United States.

Another detailed simulation analysis of 22 agricultural subsectors in Mexico indicates that unilateral trade liberalization by Mexico would decrease both agricultural output and pollution, as measured by 13 indicators of water, air, and soil effluents (Beghin et al., 1997). Overall Mexican real GDP, however, increases significantly (*ibid.*). Using a simulation model of the agricultural economy in conjunction with statistical analysis, Williams and Shumway (2000) examine the impact of NAFTA, economic growth, research investment, and farm policy. Due to the combined effects of these factors, real farm income is projected to increase in both the United States and Mexico, and dramatically so in the latter. Williams and Shumway's simulation model predicts that both fertilizer and pesticide usage in the United States will increase substantially and, although pesticide usage will decrease in Mexico, there will be substantial increases in Mexico's fertilizer usage.

The Commission for Environmental Cooperation (CEC), created by NAFTA's environmental side agreement, the North American Agreement on Environmental Cooperation (NAAEC), also conducts original research on the environmental effects of NAFTA.[4] In particular, two case studies sponsored by CEC focus on the environmental impacts of NAFTA-induced changes in agricultural market structures. One of these agricultural case studies concerns Mexican corn production (Nadal, 1999). As corn producers in Mexico adjust to changing price dynamics, their responses could generate important environmental effects. Potential responses include the modernization of production techniques or the substitution of corn for other crops. Modernization involves capital-intensive production technologies such as irrigation, the intensive use of agro-chemicals, and the increased use of mechanized equipment. Many of these technologies are water-intensive. Thus, their adoption could place increased pressure on water resources that may already be imperiled by overuse. The study indicates some loss of crop genetic diversity, as farmers shift from local varieties of corn to hybrids with higher yields. This loss is limited by heterogeneous soil qualities, climates, and local pests, which limit the performance of high yield hybrids.

On the other hand, a shift from corn to feed grains (for example, sorghum, barley) may have positive environmental outcomes, because plowing and water usage would most likely decrease. Since the implementation of NAFTA, total area harvested in Mexico has remained fairly stable, but the area devoted to sorghum production has reached record levels and the area devoted to barley has increased slightly. These increases in feed grains, however, have not come at the expense of corn area, which has fluctuated due to a series of droughts. In the case of sorghum, the increase in area planted may have been driven by increased beef production in Mexico. Trade liberalization undoubtedly reinforces a shift to crops for which a country possesses a comparative advantage, but predicting this shift and its environmental impact poses a significant challenge.

Taken as a whole, the limited number of existing studies in conjunction with their limited scope do not allow us to draw generalizations from their results. As such, they certainly leave room for further empirical studies that provide a reasonably comprehensive examination of the environmental impacts of trade liberalization. Our empirical examination includes an integrated assessment of the major commodities in the agricultural sector to account for production, consumption, and price changes between commodities and regions. Such an integrated assessment is necessary to form a reasonably comprehensive assessment of the potential effects of trade policy on the environment.

III. SOME ENVIRONMENTAL IMPACTS OF AGRICULTURAL TRADE LIBERALIZATION ON US AGRICULTURAL AREAS: RESULTS OF THE EMPIRICAL SIMULATION

In this section, we simulate the environmental impacts on the US of estimated agricultural production changes associated with the trade liberalization scenario. Our methodology employs three components: a trade equilibrium model for world agriculture, a spatial equilibrium model for US agriculture (that is, production is disaggregated regionally), and a spatial environmental simulation model based on US agricultural production technologies (see Box 3.1 for graphical linking of the topics and models). Note that the introductory chapter to this publication provides the theoretical background for our empirical analysis. Appendix 3 discusses the details of these models.

Trade Impacts

The first model component estimates the changes in world production resulting from lifting all trade restrictions on agricultural products between WTO member nations, including US production changes. To do this we employ the results from a multiple commodity, multiple country model of agricultural policy and trade, the ERS/PSU World Trade Model, which simulated the agriculture sector's response to a scenario in which all countries eliminate their border protections and trade-distorting domestic support for all commodities.[5] To do so, US tariffs, fixed payments per unit of output and per unit of intermediate output, as well as any direct and whole-farm payments that are based on area or that otherwise affect crop mix were eliminated. Payments that are not linked to production of specific crops (for example, production flexibility contracts) therefore do not factor into this set of simulation models. In sum, all WTO blue and amber box forms of support (see Box 3.2) are excluded in both the model of US agriculture and the world model.

**Box 3.1 Methodology used to map
the impacts of trade liberalization on the environment**

Agricultural Trade Liberalization
(post-Doha Scenario)
⇓
Change in world prices
(estimated by the ERS/PSU World Trade Model)
⇓
Changes in production practices, input use and outputs
(estimated by the US Regional Agricultural Model [USMP])
⇓
Changes in physical measures of environmental impacts
(estimated by the US Regional Agricultural Model [USMP])
⇓
Changes in economic measures of environmental impacts
(estimated by the US Regional Agricultural Model [USMP])

We present the resulting production shocks and changes in gross returns in Table 3.1, assuming 2000 as the base year. For the most part, US agricultural production marginally increases with trade liberalization. Several notable impacts are increases in corn production by 2.4 per cent and substantial decreases in the production of several dairy commodities (for example, butter, nonfat dry milk, and whole dry milk). Furthermore, many of these changes are accompanied by a countervailing domestic price effect, which serves to temper the effects of reduced production on gross returns (price times quantity) and to augment the effects of production increases on gross returns. Estimated gross returns to agriculture increase by approximately $10.8 billion US, or 4.2 percent. However, because of higher prices, US consumers would spend more (an estimated $12.2 billion) and get less (2.3 million metric tons less) of agricultural produce. On the other hand, costs of the subsidies on taxpayers will decrease.

Placing these changes in the context of historical experience, we note from Figure 3.1 that these percentage changes in production levels are well within the bounds of past changes in production levels.[6] Nevertheless, the changes in production may be more pronounced at the regional production level, which is where we turn to next.

**Box 3.2 Treatment of domestic agricultural support in the
Uruguay Round Agreement on Agriculture (URAA)**

Category	General criteria	Examples of policies
Exempt support (green box)	Measures must be financed by the government rather than consumers and must not provide price support to producers Specific criteria are defined for general government services, public stockholding, domestic food aid, direct payments, payments under agri-environmental programs, and other programs	Green box programs include direct payments to farmers that do not depend on current production decisions or prices, disaster assistance, and government programs on research, extension, pest and disease control, and agri-environmental subsidy programs such as the Conservation Reserve Program and the Environmental Quality Incentives Program
Exempt direct payments (blue box)	Direct payments under production-limiting programs must be based on fixed area or yields, and cover 85 percent or less of the base level of production or head of livestock	Blue box policies are direct payments to producers, linked to production of specific crops, but which impose offsetting limits on output
Nonexempt support (amber box)	Market price support, nonexempt direct payments and any other subsidies not specifically exempted are subject to reduction commitments	Amber box policies include market price supports, and output and input subsidies

Source: Uruguay Round Agreement on Agriculture, WTO (with modifications
by the authors).

Regional Changes in US Agricultural Production

The next step is to impose the aggregate US production shocks from Table 3.1
into the spatial equilibrium model for the US (the US Regional Agricultural
Programming Model, or USMP).[7] This model uses a multicommodity, spatial
equilibrium approach of the type described in McCarl and Spreen (1980).

Table 3.1 Simulated changes in US production and gross returns to producers resulting from the elimination of all agricultural trade distortions[1]

Commodities	Change in production (%)	Change in consumer price (%)	Change in gross returns (%)
Rice	−1.2	13.2	−0.8
Wheat	−0.1	4.8	2.5
Corn	2.4	16.5	13.9
Other coarse grains	1.7	13.5	10.9
Soybeans	−0.7	7.5	3.9
Cotton	0.0	4.5	2.1
Beef & veal	−0.1	10.6	8.1
Pork	0.0	7.5	5.0
Poultry meat	1.6	13.0	10.5
Butter	−15.0	−12.0	−12.0
Cheese	−0.6	−1.9	−1.9
Non-fat dry milk	−15.0	−1.6	−1.6
Fluid milk[2]	1.7	−1.2	−1.2
Whole dry milk	−31.6	−13.4	−13.4
Other dairy[2]	1.9	−1.1	−1.1
Total	0.27	9.19	4.23

[1] The year 2000 is assumed to be the base year for this analysis.

[2] Not treated as an internationally traded commodity in the model.

Source: ERS/Penn State World Trade Model

USMP allocates production practices regionally based on relative differences in net returns among the production practices (differentiated by rotation, tillage, and fertilizer rates) by region. As such, USMP can be used to simulate how changes in agricultural trade policy (via production changes) will manifest themselves in a spatial equilibrium across 45 production subregions (for the tables, we aggregate the results up to the 10 US Department of Agriculture Farm Production Regions). Variables in the model include regional commodity supplies, commodity prices, commodity demands, farm input use, farm income, government expenditures, and participation in farm programs. In response to changes in economic incentives, the USMP model allows for scale effects, some composition effects, such as a changing product mix, and technique effects, such as changing management practices. For instance, nitrogen fertilizer use in USMP can be reduced by decreasing acreage planted (scale effect), shifting to production of crops that use less nitrogen fertilizer (composition effect), or by reducing nitrogen fertilizer application rates on a given crop mix (technique effect).

Figure 3.1 Annual aggregated percentage changes in production from pervious year: corn, soybeans, rice, wheat, poultry and pork

Percent change

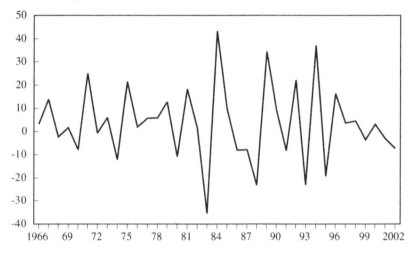

Percentage change by commodity

Statistics	Corn	Wheat	Soybeans	Rice	Poultry	Pork
Mean %change	4.91	1.53	4.39	4.34	4.14	1.06
Median	1.63	0.82	4.47	2.34	4.30	1.10
Range	133.11	61.49	62.46	74.30	13.22	33.16
Minimum	-49.31	-27.46	-25.32	-35.10	-2.32	-17.80
Maximum	83.80	34.03	37.15	39.20	10.89	15.36

Source: Derived from the USDA's Production, Supply, and Distribution
database (http://www.ers.usda.gov/data/psd/)

The estimated regional changes in primary crop and livestock commodities are presented in Tables 3.2a and 3.2b, corresponding to crop and livestock production, respectively. Corn production is predicted to increase in all regions, especially in the Lake, Corn Belt, and Northern Plains regions. The estimated changes in wheat production are fairly homogenous across regions. Soybean production is likely to fall in all regions. Other notable changes include a predicted 9 per cent increase in sorghum production in the Southern Plains and a 17 per cent decrease in rice production in the Corn Belt.

Changes in the livestock and feed sectors are also expected to be marginal overall, with some variations at the regional levels. For example, while dairy

Figure 3.2 US regional aggregations for the trade and environment simulation (USDA production regions)

production falls in general there are many regions that have potential increases in production: Northeast, Appalachia, Southeast, Southern Plains, Delta, and Mountain regions. Swine production is likely to remain relatively unchanged following agricultural trade liberalization. The changes in the beef sector differ by region: decreases in the Northeast, Lake, Corn Belt, and Appalachia regions; increases in the Northern Plains, Delta, Mountain, and Pacific regions (zero changes are estimated for the Southeast and Southern Plains regions). Poultry production is expected to increase marginally in most regions (zero changes are estimated in the Delta and Mountain regions).

In addition to scale effects, we also note potential changes in technique effects in the cropping sectors (Table 3.2c). By and large, these changes are of the same magnitude as the scale effects discussed above. The Northern Plains region would experience the greatest changes in acreage and tillage practices: a 5.1 and 14.7 per cent increase in conventional tillage and no-till acres respectively, and a 6.4 and 6.1 per cent decrease in mulch tillage and ridge-till acres respectively. Total cropping acreage is likely to remain relatively constant following agricultural trade liberalization, with an increase of 2 million acres, or 0.6 percent. At least at the national level, as the per cent increase in total crop production is only slightly larger than the per cent expansion in crop acreage, the increase in intensification of production appears minimal.

Table 3.2a Simulated regional changes in US crop production under the agricultural trade liberalization scenario

Region[1]	NT	LA	CB	NP	AP	SE
Corn			*(Million bu)*			
Base	377.4	1467.0	6285.7	1939.9	538.5	195.2
New Level	383.3	1498.6	6358.7	2056.4	564.7	199.9
Change	5.9	31.6	73.1	116.5	26.1	4.7
% Change	1.6	2.2	1.2	6.0	4.8	2.4
Sorghum			*(Million bu)*			
Base	0.0	0.0	60.8	322.7	3.6	0.8
New Level	0.0	0.0	60.7	330.0	3.5	0.8
Change	0.0	0.0	–0.1	7.2	–0.1	0.0
% Change	0.0	0.0	–0.1	2.2	–3.1	1.1
Barley			*(Million bu)*			
Base	7.9	36.8	0.0	136.9	2.3	0.0
New Level	7.9	37.0	0.0	140.1	2.3	0.0
Change	0.0	0.2	0.0	3.1	0.0	0.0
% Change	–0.3	0.5	0.0	2.3	0.2	0.0
Oats			*(Million bu)*			
Base	8.1	51.2	48.8	37.0	1.7	0.0
New Level	8.2	51.6	49.3	38.3	1.7	0.0
Change	0.1	0.5	0.6	1.4	0.0	0.0
% Change	1.0	1.0	1.2	3.8	0.8	0.0
Wheat			*(Million bu)*			
Base	33.2	155.3	347.7	903.3	68.3	14.2
New Level	33.2	153.8	346.6	899.6	69.0	14.1
Change	0.1	–1.5	–1.0	–3.7	0.7	0.0
% Change	0.2	–1.0	–0.3	–0.4	1.0	–0.3
Rice			*(Million cwt)*			
Base	0	0	1.8	0	0	0
New Level	0	0	1.4	0	0	0
Change	0	0	–0.3	0	0	0
% Change	0	0	–17.7	0	0	0
Soybeans			*(Million bu)*			
Base	44.5	367	1908.7	361.2	205	95.4
New Level	44.2	365.9	1902.4	358.5	199.8	93.8
Change	–0.3	–1.1	–6.3	–2.7	–5.2	–1.6
% Change	–0.6	–0.3	–0.3	–0.7	–2.5	–1.7
Cotton			*(Million bales)*			
Base	0	0	0.4	0	1.5	1.6
New Level	0	0	0.4	0	1.5	1.6
Change	0	0	0	0	0	0
% Change	0	0	–0.1	0	0	0.1

Continued—

Table 3.2a Simulated regional changes in US crop production under the agricultural trade liberalization scenario—Continued

Region[1]	SP	DL	MN	PA	US
Corn			*(Million bu)*		
Base	63.8	146.1	161.6	60.1	11,235.4
New Level	66.8	149.7	164.5	61.7	11,504.2
Change	3.0	3.5	2.9	1.6	268.9
% Change	4.7	2.4	1.8	2.6	2.4
Sorghum			*(Million bu)*		
Base	23.6	243.2	13.9	0.0	668.5
New Level	25.7	245.5	13.9	0.0	680.1
Change	2.2	2.3	0.1	0.0	11.6
% Change	9.2	1.0	0.4	0.0	1.7
Barley			*(Million bu)*		
Base	0.0	0.2	137.7	43.3	365.1
New Level	0.0	0.2	140.8	43.2	371.4
Change	0.0	0.0	3.1	-0.1	6.3
% Change	0.0	0.7	2.2	-0.1	1.7
Oats			*(Million bu)*		
Base	0.0	2.6	0.0	0.6	149.9
New Level	0.0	2.7	0.0	0.6	152.5
Change	0.0	0.0	0.0	0.0	2.6
% Change	0.0	1.7	1.1	1.1	1.7
Wheat			*(Million bu)*		
Base	16.9	560.9	312.4	133.1	2545.1
New Level	17.2	562.3	312.0	133.4	2541.4
Change	0.3	1.5	-0.3	0.3	-3.7
% Change	1.9	0.3	-0.1	0.2	-0.1
Rice			*(Million cwt)*		
Base	141.9	9	0	41.5	194.2
New Level	140	9	0	41.3	191.8
Change	−1.8	0	0	-0.3	-2.4
% Change	−1.3	−0.3	0	-0.6	-1.3
Soybeans			*(Million bu)*		
Base	251.9	11.3	0	0	3245
New Level	247.7	11.2	0	0	3223.6
Change	−4.2	−0.1	0	0	-21.4
% Change	−1.7	−0.8	0	0	-0.7
Cotton			*(Million bales)*		
Base	5	5.7	1.3	2	17.5
New Level	5	5.7	1.3	2	17.5
Change	0	0	0	0	0
%Change	0.2	−0.2	0.2	0	0

See footnotes at end of table 3.2c.

Table 3.2b Simulated regional changes in US livestock and feed production under the agricultural trade liberalization scenario

Region[1]	NT	LA	CB	NP	AP	SE
Silage			*(Million tons)*			
Base	19.8	21.3	12.4	23.2	10.3	2.9
New level	20.2	21.7	12.6	23.5	10.5	3
Change	0.4	0.4	0.2	0.4	0.2	0
% Change	1.9	1.9	1.5	1.5	2	1.7
Hay			*(Million tons)*			
Base	17.9	22.6	27.6	21.5	19.2	2.3
New level	17.9	22.5	27.4	21.9	19.1	2.3
Change	-0.1	-0.1	-0.1	0.4	-0.1	0
% Change	-0.3	-0.3	-0.5	1.8	-0.3	-0.1
Dairy			*(Million animal units)*			
Base	1.800	2.536	0.930	0.315	0.608	0.224
New level	1.840	2.510	0.912	0.303	0.629	0.227
Change	0.040	-0.026	-0.018	-0.012	0.021	0.003
% Change	2.222	-1.025	-1.935	-3.810	3.454	1.339
Swine			*(Million animal units)*			
Base	0.541	2.110	6.136	2.457	7.961	0.156
New level	0.542	2.110	6.137	2.457	7.955	0.156
Change	0.001	0.000	0.001	0.000	-0.006	0.000
% Change	0.185	0.000	0.016	0.000	-0.075	0.000
Beef			*(Million animal units)*			
Base	0.060	1.383	3.905	14.113	0.199	0.000
New level	0.059	1.375	3.886	14.141	0.198	0.000
Change	-0.001	-0.008	-0.019	0.028	-0.001	0.000
% Change	-1.667	-0.578	-0.487	0.198	-0.503	0.000
Poultry			*(Million animal units)*			
Base	0.050	0.049	0.110	0.017	0.162	0.080
New level	0.051	0.050	0.112	0.017	0.165	0.081
Change	0.001	0.001	0.002	0.000	0.003	0.001
% Change	2.000	2.041	1.818	0.000	1.852	1.250

Continued—

Table 3.2b Simulated regional changes in US livestock and feed production under the agricultural trade liberalization scenario—Continued

Region[1]	SP	DL	MN	PA	US
Silage		*(Million tons)*			
Base	0.7	1.3	3.6	0	95.6
NewLevel	0.7	1.4	3.7	0	97.3
Change	0	0	0.1	0	1.7
% Change	1.7	1.6	1.6	0	1.7
Hay		*(Million tons)*			
Base	1.7	1.6	27.1	14.1	155.6
NewLevel	1.7	1.6	27.1	14.1	155.7
Change	0	0	0	0	0.1
% Change	0.1	-0.1	0.1	0	0.1
Dairy		*(Million animal units)*			
Base	0.109	0.439	0.920	1.780	9.661
NewLevel	0.110	0.461	0.967	1.660	9.619
Change	0.001	0.022	0.047	-0.120	-0.042
% Change	0.917	5.011	5.109	-6.742	-0.435
Swine		*(Million animal units)*			
Base	0.163	0.357	0.341	0.112	20.334
NewLevel	0.163	0.357	0.341	0.112	20.330
Change	0.000	0.000	0.000	0.000	-0.004
% Change	0.000	0.000	0.000	0.000	-0.020
Beef		*(Million animal units)*			
Base	0.104	9.368	5.259	1.852	36.243
NewLevel	0.104	9.396	5.273	1.856	36.288
Change	0.000	0.028	0.014	0.004	0.045
% Change	0.000	0.299	0.266	0.216	0.124
Poultry		*(Million animal units)*			
Base	0.070	0.042	0.003	0.060	0.643
NewLevel	0.071	0.042	0.003	0.061	0.653
Change	0.001	0.000	0.000	0.001	0.010
% Change	1.429	0.000	0.000	1.667	1.555

See footnotes at end of table 3.2c.

Table 3.2c Simulated regional changes in tillage practices under the agricultural trade liberalization scenario

Region[1]	NT	LA	CB	NP	AP	SE
Conventional			*(Million acres)*			
Base	3.2	15.6	45.4	32.2	7.8	6.9
New level	3.2	15.7	45.7	33.9	8	6.9
Change	0.1	0.1	0.2	1.6	0.2	0
% Change	2.2	0.8	0.5	5.1	2	0
Mold-Board			*(Million acres)*			
Base	8.2	11.9	12.3	14.6	6.3	1.1
New level	8.2	12	12.4	14.4	6.3	1.1
Change	0	0.1	0	–0.2	–0.1	0
% Change	0.1	0.8	0.3	–1.4	–0.9	–0.1
Mulch			*(Million acres)*			
Base	1.2	7.2	20.6	13.8	1.7	0
New level	1.2	7.4	20.8	12.9	1.8	0
Change	0	0.1	0.2	–0.9	0.2	0
% Change	–0.7	1.8	1.1	–6.4	9	0
No-Till			*(Million acres)*			
Base	2.1	3.2	20.7	4.7	3.4	0
New level	2.1	3.1	20.5	5.4	3.3	0
Change	0	–0.1	–0.2	0.7	–0.2	0
% Change	–0.8	–2.3	–0.8	14.7	–4.9	0
Ridge-Till			*(Million acres)*			
Base	0	0.1	0	1.3	0	0
New level	0	0.1	0	1.2	0	0
Change	0	0	0	–0.1	0	0
% Change	0	–1.4	0	–6.1	0	0
Total			*(Million acres)*			
Base	14.6	38	99	66.7	19.3	7.9
New level	14.7	38.3	99.3	67.9	19.4	7.9
Change	0.1	0.3	0.3	1.2	0.1	0
% Change	0.4	0.7	0.3	1.8	0.4	0

Continued—

Table 3.2c Simulated regional changes in tillage practices under the agricultural trade liberalization scenario—Continued

Region[1]	SP	DL	MN	PA	US
Conventional		*(Million acres)*			
Base	16.6	23.9	11.5	4.5	167.6
New Level	16.6	23.9	11.6	4.5	170
Change	0	0.1	0.1	0	2.4
% Change	–0.1	0.3	1.2	0.1	1.4
Mold-Board		*(Million acres)*			
Base	0.8	5.7	9	3.4	73.4
New Level	0.8	5.7	9	3.4	73.3
Change	0	0.1	0	0	–0.1
% Change	0.1	1.1	–0.2	0	–0.1
Mulch		*(Million acres)*			
Base	0	1.6	2.4	0.2	48.8
New Level	0	1.6	2.4	0.2	48.3
Change	0	–0.1	0	0	–0.5
% Change	0	–3.3	–1.8	–0.2	–1
No-Till		*(Million acres)*			
Base	0.7	0	0	0	34.8
New Level	0.6	0	0	0	35
Change	–0.1	0	0	0	0.2
% Change	–15.1	0	0	0	0.5
Ridge-Till		*(Million acres)*			
Base	0	0	0	0	1.4
New Level	0	0	0	0	1.3
Change	0	0	0	0	–0.1
% Change	0	0	0	0	–5.7
Total		*(Million acres)*			
Base	18.1	31.2	22.9	8.1	326
New Level	18	31.3	23	8.1	327.9
Change	–0.1	0.1	0.1	0	1.9
% Change	–0.6	0.3	0.3	0	0.6

[1] Region definitions: NT = North East; LA = Lake States; CB = Corn Belt; NP = Northern Plains; AP = Appalachia; SE = South East; SP = Southern Plains; DL = Delta States; MN = Mountain; PA = Pacific; US = United States.

Change in Physical Environmental Measures

As we noted above, the predicted percentage changes in production levels are well within the bounds of past changes in production levels. Because these percentage changes in production are quite small at the aggregate level, the corresponding changes in aggregate environmental indicators are also expected to be small. Note that we are not suggesting that there will likely be no increase in environmental effects, but simply that the estimated increases are likely to be small. We use the USMP model to assess the hypothesis that the environmental impacts are in fact small.

While the current version of USMP contains a range of environmental indicators that link agricultural production to environmental quality, only a small subset is presented here.[8] We focus our analysis on the indicators in USMP that may be the most direct measure of environmental implications beyond the edge of the field. The indicators examined are nitrogen, phosphorus and pesticide loss to water; sheet, rill, and wind-related soil erosion; and manure nutrient production (Tables 3.3a and 3.3b).[9]

The estimated changes in environmental impacts are generally small, simply because the changes in commodity production anticipated under agricultural trade liberalization are, as discussed above, also quite marginal. However, regional changes in crop and livestock production will be associated with subsequent regional changes in the relevant environmental indicators. For example, cropping increases likely to occur in the Northern Plains result in potential increases in pesticide loading to ground and surface waters in that region (by 3.3 million lbs). Other notable changes include reductions in pollutant loading to ground and surface waters observed in the Southern Plains region from crop production, but increases in the potential damages from livestock production (an increase in manure nitrogen and phosphorus production of 3 million lbs and 1.3 million lbs, respectively).

Monetary Valuation of Production and Environmental Changes

Assigning monetary values to these production and environmental changes (as introduced in Chapter 1) is necessary to assess the costs and benefits of agrienvironmental policies. However, while researchers are still in the early stages of assessing the environmental impacts of agricultural activities beyond the edge of the field, even fewer attempts have been made to assign monetary values to these impacts. In USMP, economic values are linked to regional net returns in the cropping and livestock sectors and to several of the environmental indicators. These potential changes are expected to have differential effects across farm production regions. For example, agricultural productivity loss is an on-site cost of agricultural soil erosion. The loss of productivity stems primarily from the loss of topsoil and nutrients. The soil depreciation indicator is the discounted value of long term yield changes due to this loss, and is based on current output prices. Wind erosion and water pollution are off-site costs of wind and soil erosion.

We derive estimates of the monetary value of off-site damages from sediment and nitrogen damage indices developed by the US Department of Agriculture (Claassen *et al.*, 2001; Feather *et al.*, 1999; Hansen *et al.*, 2002; Ribaudo, 1986; and other work in progress at ERS). The economic impacts of these outputs include those on municipal water use, industrial uses, irrigation ditch maintenance, road ditch maintenance, water storage, flooding, and soil productivity, fresh water-based recreation, navigation, and estuary-based boating, swimming, and recreation. This set is by no means an exhaustive list of all activities affected by sediment and nitrogen runoff. Furthermore, the impacts of environmental indicators other than erosion and nitrogen loading remain to be monetized. Hence, the monetized estimates of off-site damage calculated by USMP here—the value of nitrogen loss to water and the value of sheet and rill erosion damages—are viewed as a lower bound on total off-site damages.[10]

The monetary estimates of potential production and environmental changes resulting from liberalized agricultural trade are summarized across regions in Table 3.3a and Figure 3.3. We note in general that changes in the dollar value of the environmental damages attributed to these production changes are positive in the aggregate, albeit relatively small, less than 1 per cent. However, several regions (Southeast, Southern Plains, and the Pacific) show environmental benefits, as denoted by negative signs in Table 3.3a and Figure 3.3. To put these changes in context, we note that the value of the aggregate increases in damages to the environment for our narrow set of externalities exceeds $16 million, and represents approximately 1 per cent of the expected gains from trade liberalization as measured by the net change in gross producer receipts and gross consumer expenditures for agricultural products.

IV. CONCLUSIONS

Agricultural trade liberalization under a post-Doha trade liberalization scenario is likely to affect the environment in a variety of ways, some positive and others negative. Trade liberalization will likely produce environmental impacts as a result of scale, technique, and composition effects in production. For the US, our preliminary analysis suggests that the environmental impacts would be small in aggregate at less than 1 per cent with respect to the baseline, but with some potentially important variation across the ten US subregions of our analysis. For example, sheet and rill erosion is likely to increase in the Northern Plains (1.6 per cent) and Northeast (0.8 per cent) regions, while

Table 3.3a Simulated environmental changes and some associated quantified monetary values under the agricultural trade liberalization scenario[1]

Region[2]	NT	LA	CB	NP	AP	SE
Sheet and Rill Erosion			*(Million tons)*			
Base	46.17	92.11	424.51	152.82	71.73	49.988
New Level	46.55	92.67	425.78	155.20	71.79	49.87
Change	0.38	0.57	1.27	2.38	0.06	–0.12
% Change	0.82	0.62	0.30	1.56	0.09	–0.24
Off-Site Sheet & Rill Eronsion Damages			*($Million US)*			
Base	623.80	541.80	1040.80	216.00	233.10	190.90
New Level	629.10	546.10	1044.20	218.80	233.20	190.40
Change	5.30	4.30	3.30	2.80	0.20	–0.50
% Change	0.85	0.79	0.32	1.30	0.09	–0.26
Wind Erosion			*(Million tons)*			
Base	0.97	113.36	41.59	119.97	0.53	0.00
New Level	0.97	112.39	41.96	131.23	0.54	0.00
Change	0.00	–0.97	0.37	11.27	0.01	0.00
% Change	0.34	–0.86	0.90	9.39	2.43	0.00
Soil Depreciation			*($Million US)*			
Base	15.10	11.00	97.90	99.40	42.50	1.20
New Level	15.30	10.50	99.30	99.70	43.40	1.30
Change	0.20	–0.50	1.50	0.30	1.00	0.10
% Change	1.32	–4.55	1.53	0.30	2.35	8.33
Nitrogen Lost to Water from Crop Production			*(Million tons)*			
Base	0.24	0.44	1.93	1.01	0.49	0.17
New Level	0.24	0.45	1.93	1.03	0.50	0.17
Change	0.00	0.01	0.01	0.02	0.00	0.00
% Change	0.51	2.31	0.27	1.72	0.56	0.12
Nitrogen Loss to Water Damages			*($Million US)*			
Base	30.60	0.70	6.20	0.60	43.00	36.10
New Level	30.70	0.70	6.20	0.60	43.40	36.20
Change	0.10	0.00	0.00	0.00	0.30	0.00
% Change	0.33	0.00	0.00	0.00	0.70	0.00

Continued—

Table 3.3a Simulated environmental changes and some associated quantified monetary values under the agricultural trade liberalization scenario[1]—Continued

Region[2]	SP	DL	MN	PA	US
Sheet and Rill Erosion			*(Million tons)*		
Base	92.28	70.26	54.22	35.60	1089.68
New Level	91.56	70.44	54.23	35.58	1093.67
Change	–0.72	0.18	0.01	–0.02	3.99
% Change	–0.78	0.26	0.01	–0.06	0.37
Off-Site Sheet &			*($Million US)*		
Rill Eronsion Damages					
Base	328.80	258.50	84.50	110.50	3628.70
New Level	326.20	259.30	84.50	110.50	3642.40
Change	–2.50	0.80	0.00	–0.10	13.70
% Change	–0.76	0.31	0.00	–0.09	0.38
Wind Erosion			*(Million tons)*		
Base	0.00	185.32	227.04	28.82	717.59
New Level	0.00	185.48	225.97	28.79	727.34
Change	0.00	0.16	–1.07	–0.03	9.75
% Change	0.00	0.09	–0.47	–0.10	1.36
Soil Depreciation			*($Million US)*		
Base	49.00	2.30	7.30	35.00	360.60
New Level	49.00	2.30	7.20	35.00	363.10
Change	–0.10	0.00	–0.10	0.00	2.50
% Change	–0.20	0.00	–1.37	0.00	0.69
Nitrogen Lost to Water			*(Million tons)*		
from Crop Production					
Base	0.51	0.56	0.15	0.09	5.60
New Level	0.51	0.56	0.15	0.09	5.64
Change	0.00	0.00	0.00	0.00	0.04
% Change	–0.48	0.29	0.27	–0.40	0.65
Nitrogen Loss to Water Damages		*($Million US)*			
Base	17.30	21.20	1.90	14.30	172.00
New Level	17.20	21.30	1.90	14.20	172.50
Change	–0.10	0.10	0.00	–0.10	0.50
% Change	–0.58	0.47	0.00	–0.70	0.29

See footnotes at end of table 3.3b.

Table 3.3b Simulated environmental changes without associated quantification of monetary values under the agricultural trade liberalization scenario[1]

Region[2]	NT	LA	CB	NP	AP	SE
Phosphorus Lost to Water from Crop Production		*(Million tons)*				
Base	0.04	0.04	0.21	0.12	0.06	0.03
New Level	0.04	0.04	0.22	0.12	0.06	0.02
Change	0.00	0.00	0.00	0.00	0.00	0.00
% Change	0.53	0.76	0.25	1.13	0.33	−0.07
Pesticides Lost to Water from Crop Production		*(Million tons)*				
Base	12.53	43.72	144.47	50.10	27.78	12.41
New Level	12.64	44.41	145.59	53.46	29.25	12.39
Change	0.11	0.69	1.12	3.36	1.46	−0.02
% Change	0.88	1.58	0.77	6.70	5.26	−0.18
Manure Producton		*(Million tons)*				
Base	38.74	59.05	73.31	65.20	65.72	23.28
New Level	39.48	58.77	73.32	64.89	66.27	23.61
Change	0.74	−0.28	0.01	−0.31	0.55	0.33
% Change	1.91	−0.47	0.01	−0.48	0.84	1.421
Manure Nitrogen		*(Million lbs)*				
Base	231.40	264.01	346.29	266.48	348.10	259.02
New Level	235.67	263.23	347.63	265.37	352.50	262.96
Change	4.27	−0.78	1.34	−1.11	4.40	3.94
% Change	1.85	−0.30	0.39	−0.42	1.26	1.52
Manure Phosphorus		*(Million lbs)*				
Base	102.22	136.02	229.26	187.09	227.21	111.28
New Level	103.99	135.95	230.26	186.41	229.19	112.95
Change	1.77	−0.07	1.00	−0.68	1.98	1.67
% Change	1.73	−0.05	0.44	−0.36	0.87	1.50

Continued—

Table 3.3b Simulated environmental changes without associated quantification of monetary values under the agricultural trade liberalization scenario[1]—Continued

Region[2]	SP	DL	MN	PA	US
Phosphorus Lost to Water		*(Million tons)*			
from Crop Production					
Base	0.05	0.06	0.02	0.00	0.62
New Level	0.05	0.06	0.02	0.00	0.62
Change	0.00	0.00	0.00	0.00	0.00
% Change	–0.64	0.17	–0.12	–0.05	0.37
Pesticides Lost to Water		*(Million tons)*			
from Crop Production					
Base	50.27	18.62	9.79	8.33	378.02
New Level	50.16	18.70	9.85	8.32	384.75
Change	–0.11	0.07	0.06	–0.01	6.72
% Change	–0.22	0.40	0.56	–0.13	0.02
Manure Producton		*(Million tons)*			
Base	18.66	46.24	32.65	39.65	462.50
New Level	18.91	46.54	33.32	37.91	463.01
Change	0.25	0.30	0.67	–1.74	0.51
% Change	1.34	0.65	2.05	–4.39	0.11
Manure Nitrogen		*(Million lbs)*			
Base	198.87	243.44	140.43	219.00	2517.03
New Level	201.88	245.43	143.41	212.33	2530.41
Change	3.01	1.99	2.98	–6.67	13.38
% Change	1.51	0.82	2.12	–3.05	0.53
Manure Phosphorus		*(Million lbs)*			
Base	89.19	141.36	78.36	101.28	1403.25
New Level	90.50	141.93	79.49	98.86	1409.54
Change	1.31	0.57	1.13	–2.42	6.29
% Change	1.47	0.40	1.44	–2.39	0.45

[1] Estimates of erosion, nutrient and pesticide losses are aggregate values to the edge-of-field simulated for predominant cropping practices over 67 years using the Environmental Policy Integrated Climate (EPIC) model. Manure values are estimated using Census of Agriculture (USDA/NASS, 1997) data for regional shares and nutrient availability coefficients from Kellogg *et al.* (2000).

[2] Region definitions: NT = North East; LA = Lake States; CB = Corn Belt; NP = Northern Plains; AP = Appalachia; SE = South East; SP = Southern Plains; DL = Delta States; MN = Mountain; PA = Pacific; US = United States.

For the change in environmental effects, a minus sign indicates a decrease in damage and a positive sign an increase.

Figure 3.3 Change in monetary value of selected environmental indicators

Change ($ million US)

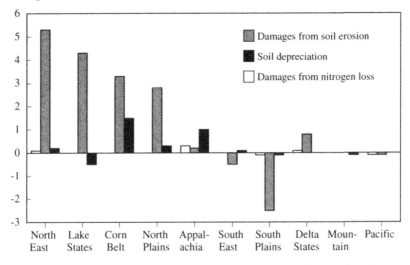

Note: Increasing the value of an indicator represents a decrease in environmental quality.
For keys to regions, please see note to Table 3.2.

decreasing in the Southern Plains (-0.8 per cent), Southeast (-0.2 per cent), and Pacific (-0.1 per cent) regions. In another example, nitrogen loss to water from crop production is likely to increase in the Northern Plains (1.7 per cent), Southeast (0.1 per cent), and Northeast (0.5 per cent) regions, while decreasing in the Southern Plains (-0.5 per cent) and the Pacific (-0.1 per cent) regions.

While our modeling framework does contain some of the important agri-environmental indicators, the set is by no means complete. Not included in this analysis are the damages due to greenhouse gas emissions, pesticide losses, manure nutrient and bacterial discharges, among others. One specific example of an omitted indicator is emissions of pollutants associated with fuel usage. Expanding agricultural trade leads to increasing international commerce, and the associated increases in transportation and fuel usage may contribute to increased emissions of pollutants. Increased ground transportation is often concentrated in a few border corridors, resulting in hotspots of localized environmental stress, such as the high traffic areas in and around Laredo, Texas, and Detroit, Michigan (Sierra Club and Holbrook-White, 2000). A recent study of the border corridors of Vancouver-Seattle, Winnipeg-Fargo, Toronto-Detroit, San Antonio-Monterrey, and Tucson-Hermosillo concludes that

NAFTA trade "contributes significantly to air pollution" in all five corridors (ICF Consulting, 2001). In addition, USMP cannot estimate environmental impacts associated with commodities not in the model, such as sugar and fruit and vegetables. Finally, USMP cannot estimate the value of changes in the level of environmental amenities (for example, open space and scenic views) generated by agricultural activities. The amenities may not be highly correlated with agricultural production and may be quite site-specific as well (Chapters 2 and 7).

In addition to the types of impacts modeled in our quantitative analysis, technological modernization, transboundary issues such as the importation of harmful, nonindigenous species (HNIS), environmental consequences of increased use of transportation, the creation of "pollution havens," and the development of environmentally friendly products are other examples under which expanded agricultural trade could have positive or negative effects on the environment.

Although this chapter focuses on impacts in the US, the environmental impacts of trade liberalization, and the assessments thereof, are of global interest. For instance, paragraphs 6 and 31–3 of the ministerial declaration of the Fourth WTO Ministerial Conference held in Doha, Qatar in November 2001 address trade and environment issues. These include "the efforts by members to conduct national environmental assessments of trade policies on a voluntary basis."[11] Chapter 4 examines the prospects for assessing the global environmental impacts of agricultural trade liberalization, albeit using more general environmental measures than are utilized by the model presented in this chapter.

NOTES

1. The views presented herein are those of the authors, and do not necessarily represent the views or policies of the Economic Research Service or the United States Department of Agriculture.

2. A draft of this review is available online at *www.ustr.gov/environment/ environmental.shtml*.

3. See *www.wto.org/english/thewto_e/minist_e/min01_e/mindecl_e.htm* for text of the declaration.

4. The Commission on Environmental Cooperation (CEC) recently held a conference on this topic, "Assessing the Environmental Effects of Trade Liberalization: Lessons Learned and Future Challenges" (see available papers at *www.cec.org/programs_projects/trade_environ_econ/*).

5. Preliminary documentation of the model can be found at *http://trade.aers.psu.edu/documentation.cfm*. See Appendix 3 to this book for a brief overview of the model.

6. The choice of yearly change in production as the standard for comparison is admittedly an arbitrary one, but little guidance exists to drive the choice of a standard for comparison.

7. See Appendix 3 for a brief overview of USMP.

8. The crop production enterprises in USMP have been simulated using EPIC, the Environmental Policy Integrated Climate Model (USDA Agricultural Research Service, 1990; Mitchell *et al.*, 1998), which includes weather, hydrology, soil temperature, erosion-sedimentation, nutrient cycling, tillage, crop management and growth, and pesticide and nutrient movements with water and sediment. Please see Appendix 3 for more information.

9. See Chapter 7 for additional discussion of issues in developing indicators for environmental quality.

10. The interested reader can obtain the dollar per ton figures for off-site erosion and nitrogen loss to water for each region by dividing the base levels of the dollar values by the base levels of the physical values in Table 3.3a.

11. See *http://www.wto.org/english/thewto_e/minist_e/min01_e/mindecl_e.htm* for text of the declaration.

4. Global environmental effects of agricultural adjustments under liberalized trade

John Sullivan and Kevin Ingram[1]

I. INTRODUCTION

The previous chapter examined the US environmental impacts of world agricultural trade liberalization. This chapter illustrates a process for estimating the global environmental impacts of world agricultural trade liberalization. Results reported in this chapter are based on the ERS' Future Agricultural Resources Model (FARM). There are at least three reasons why the FARM model is useful for analyzing trade liberalization scenarios. First of all, it is one of few trade models available for use in the estimation of environmental effects. Secondly, this exercise can help to clarify what can be feasibly accomplished in the near future in terms of global environmental analysis. In particular, it is not practical to achieve the levels of disaggregation in a global model as it is in a single country model, such as the USMP model in Chapter 3. FARM cannot provide changes in sheet and rill erosion, for example. Instead, environmental impacts must be presented in a more aggregated fashion. Thirdly, as the literature review in the previous chapter suggests, when taken as a whole, the myriad of existing environmental assessment studies fail to suggest a consistent overall theme. In contrast, the FARM model can produce a set of results that are derived with a consistent methodology across countries.

Furthermore, policy motivations for analyzing domestic and global effects differ as well. Executive Order 13141 does not mandate that a review of global environmental impacts be undertaken. Instead, Section 5(b) of the Order provides "that, as a general matter, the focus of reviews will be on impacts in the United States; however, reviews may also examine global and transboundary impacts as appropriate and prudent," that is, essentially those global impacts that directly affect the US.[2] In addition, results from a global model can potentially be used to construct indicators for inter-regional comparisons that may be useful to operate some future multilateral environmental agreement (MEA) or environmental side agreement to a trade agreement, as with the NAFTA agreement.

The rest of the chapter is organized as follows. First, a description of the modeling framework and database is presented. Next, a numerical illustration of the global environmental impacts of agricultural trade liberalization is provided. This is an analysis of one of many possible outcomes of negotiations over trade liberalization, and can serve as a concrete representation of the estimation process that might be used in the future for actual policy analysis. The final section discusses limitations of the current analysis and directions for future research.

II.   FARM AND GTAP MODELING FRAMEWORKS

FARM's economic framework consists of a multiregion, multisector, economic simulation model (see Appendix 3 for more information). This simulation model explicitly accounts for all domestic and international money flows for 1990. Households are assumed to own the four primary factors of production—land, water, labor and capital. They use the revenues from the sale of these factors to purchase consumer goods and services from the producing sectors in domestic and international markets. Accounting for this circular flow enables the model to provide comprehensive measures of economic activity.

FARM's economic simulation model is an aggregation and an extension of the GTAP model. The Global Trade Analysis Project (GTAP) modeling framework was established in 1992. It is an international collaborative effort to assist researchers conducting quantitative analyses of international economic issues in an economy-wide, general equilibrium framework. It has been widely used for trade liberalization and other analyses due to three major features. These are: a fully documented global database; a standard modeling framework; and software for manipulating the data and implementing the standard model. In addition, a group of national and international agencies provide ongoing support for GTAP development, revisions and updates. The FARM model provides three major extensions to GTAP. These are: the inclusion of land as a primary input in all producing sectors; the introduction of water as a primary input in the crops, livestock and service sectors; and the modeling of crop production as a multi-output sector. The inclusion of land is particularly important because it allows the model to simulate land use changes.

FARM is composed of a geographic information system (GIS) as well as an economic simulation model. The GIS links climate variables with land and water resources in FARM's environmental framework. FARM's GIS can be described as a grid overlaid on a map of the world. Grid cells generally have a spatial resolution of 0.5 degrees by 0.5 degrees and contain information from

several global databases relating to the associated area's climate, natural vege-
tation, and current land use. FARM's environmental framework is dominated
by climate. Broad differences in land productivity are obtained by associating
each grid with one of six globally defined land classes based on length of
growing season, a measure that is highly correlated with primary production,
and then aggregating grids into regions (see Table 4.1). Length of a growing
season is defined as the longest continuous period of time in a year that soil
temperature and moisture conditions support plant growth. Growing season
lengths were computed from monthly temperature and precipitation data.

Table 4.1 Land class boundaries in FARM

Land class	Length of growing season	Time soil temperature above 5*C	Principal crops and cropping patterns	Sample regions
		--Days--		
1	0–100	<125	Sparse forage for rough grazing	US: northern Alaska World: Greenland
2	0–100	>125	Millets, pulses, sparse forage for rough grazing	US: Mojave Desert World: Sahara Desert
3	101–165	>125	Short-season grains; forage: one crop per year	US: Palouse River area, western Nebraska World: southern Manitoba
4	166–250	>125	Maize: some double-cropping Possible	US: Corn Belt World: northern European Community
5	251–300	>125	Cotton and rice: double-cropping common	US: Tennessee World: Zambia, nonpeninsular Thailand
6	301–365	>125	Rubber and sugarcane: double-cropping common	US: Florida, southeast coast World: Indonesia

Source: Darwin *et al.* (1995).

III. LAND CLASS DEFINITIONS

Land classes (LCs) 1 and 2 have growing seasons of 100 days or less. LC 1 occurs where cold temperatures limit growing seasons, which is mainly the polar and alpine areas. High latitude regions such as Canada and the former Soviet Union contain 79.3 per cent of the world's stock of LC 1. LC 2 occurs where growing seasons are limited by low precipitation levels. Africa and Asia contain 56.6 per cent of the world's stock of LC 2. Australia and the former Soviet Union contain another 27.2 per cent of LC 2. LC 3 has growing seasons of 101–165 days. About half of this land, which is 13 per cent of all land, is located in Canada and the former Soviet Union. Growing seasons on LC 4 range from 166 to 250 days, and LC 4 accounts for 10.2 per cent of all land. Of this Africa contains 28.9 per cent, and the United States and Europe together have 27.6 per cent. LC 5 is only 7.7 per cent of all land, and has growing seasons of 251–300 days. Over 78 per cent is located in Africa, Latin America, and Asia. Year-round growing seasons of longer than 300 days characterize LC 6. LC 6 accounts for 20 per cent of all land. Some 87.2 per cent of LC 6 land is located in tropical areas of Africa, Asia, and Latin America. See Darwin *et al.* (1995) for a geographic map of land classes under current climate conditions.

The analysis contained in this chapter is based on the GTAP model, which has been extended by linkages to the FARM model. It contains 8 regions and 13 sectors, so the analysis can only provide a general overview of possible global movements in production between regions and sectors.[3]

FARM's results differ from GTAP's results because the structure of production varies by agri-ecological zone (AEZ). In the crop sectors, variation is due both to the mix of outputs and inputs, particularly primary factors. In the livestock sectors, variation is due to the mix of outputs and the mix of both primary and intermediate inputs. In the forestry sectors, variation is captured by differences in output prices, which are due in turn to differences in the mix of forestry outputs across AEZs.

IV. LAND AND WATER RESOURCES DATABASE

The FARM model has a land and water resources database that is compatible with the GTAP database. This database has six major components—a political unit component, a production component, a land use component, an agro-ecological zone (AEZ) component, a regression (that is, statistical functions) component, and a GTAP allocation component. The political unit component organizes data by administrative area. The production component organizes data on prices and quantities of inputs and outputs at country and subcountry levels. It provides information with which to calculate the revenues and costs associated with the production of various commodities. The land use component organizes data on land cover characteristics and population data at sub-country levels. It provides the mechanism whereby commodity-specific revenues and costs are distributed across the AEZs within a given country. The AEZ component organizes meteorological, geological, hydrological, and pedological (soil moisture and temperature) data on the 0.5 degrees latitude and longitude grid. It defines the AEZs to which the land covers within the 0.5 degree grids belong. The regression component provides coefficients for distributing production inputs and outputs to the AEZs. The GTAP allocation component provides value share coefficients used to distribute GTAP values to the AEZs plus the final FARM database.

Because FARM calibrates crop, livestock, and forestry production by land class and water use by sector, the GTAP data on regional revenues and expenditures for sectors and consumers needs to be disaggregated. Several global databases were used in conjunction with FARM's geographic information system to do this. All acreage in each region is allocated to one of four land use types—cropland, permanent pasture, forest, and other—using estimates from the Food and Agricultural Organization of the United Nations (FAO). Regional land use acreage is allocated to land classes by combining land use and cover data with the land class data set pertaining to current climatic conditions. These regional land class distributions of cropland, permanent pasture, and forestland are used to allocate the GTAP input and output values associated with the crop, livestock and forestry sectors.

Regional water supply estimates are derived from water withdrawal data, which give water withdrawals for agriculture and nonagriculture by country. In each region, irrigated acreage is distributed to the land classes based on irrigated land data, crops and settlements data, and length of growing season data. Various allocation methods also distribute values for outputs, inputs, water, irrigation capital, and livestock feed and pasture.

Table 4.2 contains the base data for land class endowments and agricultural water use, for the four model regions that will be highlighted in the illustrative modeling exercise. These data are used to help evaluate the significance of the percentage changes generated by the modeling scenario. Table 4.3 contains the base data for per hectare production of crops, livestock and forest products, by region and land class. These data highlight the initial levels of intensity of land use, and are used to evaluate the changes in intensity of land use implied by the modeling results. Columns 2 through 5 of Tables 4.4 and 4.5 contain the base data for the distribution of crop, livestock, and forest products, by region and land class. Again, these data are used to put modeling results into perspective.

For comparison to this base data, impacts are estimated for the United States, the European Community, Southeast Asia and Rest of World regions (see Tables 4.4, 4.5 and 4.6). Southeast Asia consists of Thailand, Indonesia,

Table 4.2 Current land class endowments, by region

Land class	Region			
	US	EC	SEA	ROW
Current land class endowments	*Million hectares*			
1	120.45	3.1	0	1,413.1
2	300.97	7.07	0	2,985.81
3	116.21	33.27	1.34	1,014.91
4	198.8	117.63	4.36	785.08
5	68.96	45.07	39.8	748.14
6	111.26	16.69	249.48	2,003.79
Total	916.66	222.82	294.98	8,950.83
Current agricultural water use	*km3*			
1	0	0	0	2
2	149	46	0	971
3	14	19	0	96
4	19	26	0	85
5	4	0	23	182
6	10	0	41	60
Total	196	91	64	1,396

Phillipines, Malaysia, and Singapore. The Rest of World region is a large composite of Latin America, Africa, West Asia, much of South Asia, the former Soviet Union plus Mongolia, and countries in Europe outside the EC (circa 1990). Despite its great geographic size, the Rest of World region is about the same economic size as the EC or United States, so it should not distort the economic results. It does limit, however, what can be said about where the economic effects of the global changes might occur in the Rest of World region.

V.   MODELING SCENARIO

FARM's economic simulation model used for this analysis represents equilibrium conditions in 1990. Global changes were simulated by exogenously changing model parameters. Changes in trade policies are translated into price changes. The model then calculates an alternative set of equilibrium conditions that reflect policy changes.

Changes in global trade policies are simulated by adjusting the wedges between producer and market prices (subsidies) and between domestic and foreign prices (duties and tariffs) of wheat, other grains, nongrain and livestock

Table 4.3 Per hectare production, by region and land class

	Region			
Land class	US	EC	SEA	ROW
Crops	*Metric tons*			
1	0.71	1.27	0	1.27
2	1.56	2.07	0	2.83
3	1.09	3.76	0.66	2.13
4	3.21	5.88	0.87	2.95
5	2.89	4.91	3.03	3.84
6	3.87	2.06	5.78	4.05
Total	2.66	4.95	5.1	3.14
Livestock	*Head*			
1	0.04	0	0	0.26
2	0.28	1.46	0	0.92
3	0.93	3.03	2.11	1.64
4	2	7.22	3.19	1.79
5	1.22	3.57	5.59	1.57
6	1.02	3.35	5.6	1.29
Total	0.71	5.36	5.35	1.17
Forest Products	*Cubic meters*			
1	0.47	1.07	0	0.39
2	0.63	1.62	0	0.23
3	1.1	2.53	0.67	0.7
4	1.59	3.13	1.44	0.72
5	2.45	3.14	1.51	0.74
6	3.4	4.47	1.67	0.79
Total	1.69	3.14	1.65	0.65

commodities. A 30 per cent across-the-board cut in agricultural subsidies, duties, and tariffs is applied to all regions. This is meant to serve as an approximation of a possible trade liberalization agreement. It is not meant to be an exact analysis of specific agreements, which tend to be quite complex in their details and specifics. Trade policy analysis is limited to the agricultural sectors because that is the focus of our environmental analysis, and FARM's economic simulation model contains the necessary price support and other protection data for agricultural products in all regions to carry out that analysis.

Table 4.4 Production impacts of liberalizing agricultural trade, by commodity, region and land class

Land Class	Region			
	US	EC	SEA	ROW
Base production				
Crops		*Million metric tons*		
1	0	1	0	19
2	58	5	0	566
3	25	44	0	380
4	276	243	1	500
5	69	82	33	411
6	78	11	255	1007
Total	506	385	289	2884
Livestock		*Million head*		
1	1	0	0	54
2	38	3	0	826
3	17	28	1	395
4	79	215	3	473
5	17	39	13	338
6	20	9	57	520
Total	171	295	74	2606
Forest Products		*Million cubic meters*		
1	17	1	0	254
2	31	2	0	27
3	62	19	0	304
4	93	91	1	147
5	66	30	23	251
6	230	28	237	902
Total	498	171	261	1884

Continued—

VI. RESULTS FROM SHIFTS IN PRODUCTION AND TRADE

When a scenario of 30 per cent agricultural trade distortion reductions is adopted, lower producer subsidies in the US and EC (circa 1990) reduce the supply of some agricultural products from these regions (Table 4.4 and Figure 4.1). Hence one would expect supply and demand from other regions to increase. For the US, there is an aggregate crop supply increase of roughly 10 million metric tons, while livestock gains in land classes 1 and 2 are outweighed by slight losses in the other

Table 4.4 Production impacts of liberalizing agricultural trade, by commodity, region and land class—Continued

Land class	Region			
	US	EC	SEA	ROW
Impacts of liberalizing agricultural trade				
Percent change				
Crops				
1	−1.78	−0.28	0	−0.33
2	2.14	−12.94	0	1.02
3	1.59	−20.89	10.88	0.47
4	1.32	−17.21	11.53	0.37
5	1.69	−10.48	0.93	1.62
6	4.43	−3.38	1.89	2.12
Total	1.96	−15.75	1.81	1.29
Livestock				
1	3.55	1.4	0	0.16
2	2.77	−1.48	0	0.07
3	−1.48	−1.53	0.35	1.31
4	1.65	−0.84	0.08	1.29
5	1.77	−2.22	0.75	0.75
6	−2.83	−3.65	0.13	0.44
Total	−0.78	−1.18	0.24	0.64
Forest Products				
1	0.48	−2.39	0	0.48
2	0.24	−1.69	0	0.34
3	0.73	0.35	−0.52	0.42
4	0.52	1.02	−0.79	0.41
5	0.4	−0.39	−0.04	−0.15
6	−0.67	−1.84	−0.7	−0.43
Total	−0.04	0.18	−0.64	−0.06

Continued—

land classes for a net loss of just over 1 million metric tons. This reflects the lower initial level of subsidies in the US relative to the EC, which allows for some overall expansion of the US crop sector. For the EC, there are also declines of over 3 million tons in livestock supply, but here there are also large crop reductions of 60 million metric tons. Lower tariffs in the United States, European Community and Japan simultaneously increase the quantity demanded in these regions for other regions' agricultural products. This induces greater crop and livestock production in Southeast Asia and other tropical areas. As more land is converted to agricul-

Table 4.4 Production impacts of liberalizing agricultural trade, by commodity, region and land class—Continued

Land Class	Region			
	US	EC	SEA	ROW
Impacts of liberalizing agricultural trade				
Quantity change				
Crops		*Million metric tons*		
1	0	−0.003	0	−0.063
2	1.241	−0.647	0	5.773
3	0.398	−9.192	0	1.786
4	3.643	−41.82	0.115	1.85
5	1.166	−8.594	0.307	6.658
6	3.455	−0.372	4.819	21.348
Total	9.90	−60.628	5.241	37.352
Livestock		*Million head*		
1	0.036	0	0	0.086
2	1.053	−0.044	0	0.578
3	−0.252	−0.428	0.004	5.175
4	−1.304	−1.806	0.002	6.102
5	−0.301	−0.866	0.098	2.535
6	−0.566	−0.329	0.074	2.288
Total	−1.33	−3.473	0.178	16.764
Forest products		*Million cubic meters*		
1	0.082	−0.024	0	1.219
2	0.074	−0.034	0	0.092
3	0.453	0.067	0	1.277
4	0.484	0.928	−0.008	0.603
5	0.264	−0.117	−0.009	−0.377
6	−1.541	−0.515	−1.659	−3.879
Total	−0.18	0.305	−1.676	−1.065

tural purposes, forestland in moist tropical regions declines slightly, while there is a slight increase in timber harvest rates.

VII. ENVIRONMENTAL IMPLICATIONS

We draw the environmental implications of trade liberalization by inferences based on the changes FARM predicts for inputs such as irrigation water and land

Table 4.5 Land use impacts of liberalizing agricultural trade, by land area, region and land class

Land Class	Region			
	US	EC	SEA	ROW
Base area	*Million hectares*			
Cropland				
1	0.06	0.54	0	15.36
2	37.01	2.38	0	200.08
3	22.68	11.72	0.4	178.54
4	85.93	41.24	1.32	169.43
5	23.97	16.7	10.92	107.09
6	20.27	5.25	44.03	248.63
Total	189.92	77.84	56.68	919.14
Pasture				
1	13.49	0	0	210.01
2	137.11	2.23	0	896.82
3	18.18	9.38	0.36	241.59
4	39.71	29.86	0.91	264.79
5	13.71	10.88	2.41	214.53
6	19.26	2.72	10.16	404.35
Total	241.47	55.07	13.84	2232.1
Forest				
1	36.07	0.59	0	658.38
2	48.76	1.45	0	115.9
3	56.2	7.4	0.17	436.4
4	58.48	29.14	0.6	204.2
5	26.77	9.5	14.99	340.89
6	67.62	6.33	142.22	1143.22
Total	293.9	54.41	157.98	2898.99
Cropland + Pasture + Forest				
1	49.62	1.13	0	883.75
2	222.88	6.06	0	1212.8
3	97.06	28.5	0.93	856.53
4	184.12	100.24	2.83	638.42
5	64.45	37.08	28.32	662.51
6	107.15	14.3	196.41	1796.2
Total	725.29	187.32	228.5	6050.23

Continued—

Table 4.5 Land use impacts of liberalizing agricultural trade, by land area, region and land class—Continued

	Region			
Land Class	US	EC	SEA	ROW
Impacts of liberalizing agricultural trade				
Percent change				
Cropland				
1	−1.42	−0.01	0	−0.37
2	0.29	−0.16	0	0.06
3	0.08	−1.25	0.73	0.02
4	0.07	−8.69	5.61	0.02
5	0.07	−0.64	0.52	0.88
6	0.33	−0.07	1.09	1.13
Pasture				
1	1.03	0.82	0	0.02
2	1.04	−0.02	0	0
3	−1.34	−0.02	0	0.07
4	−1.46	3.88	−2.13	0.08
5	−1.39	−0.08	0.33	0.29
6	−1.94	−0.07	−0.07	−0.01
Forest				
1	0.08	−0.08	0.0	0.19
2	−1.0	−0.02	0.0	0.14
3	0.21	0.96	−0.53	0.02
4	0.07	5.06	−2.67	0.02
5	0.09	0.21	−0.16	−0.34
6	−0.41	−0.04	−0.25	−0.02
Cropland + Pasture + Forest				
1	0.34	−0.09	0	0.14
2	0.47	−0.09	0	0.02
3	−0.11	−0.27	0.22	0.03
4	−0.26	−0.95	1.38	0.05
5	−0.23	−0.26	0.14	0.06
6	−0.55	−0.06	0.06	0.14
Total	−0.02	−0.61	0.09	0.08

Continued—

Table 4.5 Land use impacts of liberalizing agricultural trade, by land area, region and land class—Continued

Land Class	Region			
	US	EC	SEA	ROW
Impacts of liberalizing agricultural trade				
Quantity change		*Million hectares*		
Cropland				
1	–0.001	0	0	–0.057
2	0.107	–0.004	0	0.12
3	0.018	–0.147	0.003	0.036
4	0.06	–3.584	0.074	0.034
5	0.017	–0.107	0.057	0.942
6	0.067	–0.004	0.479	2.809
Total	0.268	–3.846	0.613	3.884
Pasture				
1	0.139	0	0	0.042
2	1.426	–0.001	0	0
3	–0.244	–0.002	0	0.169
4	–0.579	1.159	–0.019	0.212
5	–0.191	–0.009	0.008	0.622
6	–0.374	–0.002	–0.007	–0.041
Total	0.177	1.145	–0.018	1.004
Forest				
1	0.029	–0.001	0	1.251
2	–0.488	–0.001	0	0.162
3	0.118	0.071	–0.001	0.087
4	0.041	1.474	–0.016	0.041
5	0.024	0.02	–0.024	–1.159
6	–0.277	–0.003	–0.356	–0.229
Total	–0.553	1.56	–0.397	0.153
Cropland + Pasture + Forest				
1	0.167	–0.001	0	1.236
2	1.045	–0.006	0	0.282
3	–0.108	–0.078	0.002	0.292
3	–0.478	–0.951	0.039	0.287
5	–0.15	–0.096	0.041	0.405
6	–0.584	–0.009	0.116	2.539
Total	–0.108	–1.141	0.198	5.041

Table 4.6 Impacts of liberalizing agricultural trade on total primary factors

Primary Factor	Region			
	US	EC	SEA	ROW
	Percent change			
Water	1.81	−13.29	0.81	0.61
Labor	1.61	−8.63	1.82	1.32
Capital	2.1	−8.38	1.8	1.33
Cropland	0.91	−4.94	1.09	0.54
Pasture Land	0.07	2.08	−0.13	0.04
Forest Land	−0.19	2.87	−0.25	−0.07
Other Land	−0.71	3.2	−0.29	−0.14

Figure 4.1 Impacts of liberalizing agricultural trade on crops

Percent change

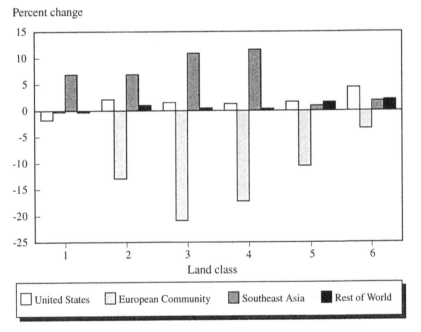

Land class

United States   European Community   Southeast Asia   Rest of World

use. Aggregate impacts of liberalizing agricultural trade noted above are discussed in more detail in this section for crops and cropland, livestock and pasture, irrigation water, timber and forestland, and other land. A brief description is also provided of possible impacts on total primary factors. These results are broadly consistent with the work reported by Diao, Somwaru and Roe (2001).[4] Two main areas of consensus emerge from the literature, as well as this analysis. The first is that subsidies are persistently highest in Europe over time, so liberalization scenarios will always show the greatest effects there. The other area of agreement is that the removal of the generally higher subsidies in developed countries can be associated with shifts in some crop and livestock production to less developed countries (for example, Table 1.5 in Diao, Somwaru and Roe, 2001).

VIII. IMPLICATIONS FOR INTENSIVE AND EXTENSIVE CHANGES IN CROPLAND USE

Under the trade liberalization scenario, for US crops and cropland, crop production and cropland increase on all land classes except LC 1, which accounts for only a very small portion of US land (see Figures 4.1 and 4.2 and Tables 4.4 and 4.5). Land class 4, which includes the Corn Belt, shows a 1.32 per cent increase in crops and 0.7 per cent increase in cropland. This implies that pollution associated with crop production will increase, a result that is generally consistent with that in Chapter 3. Since the percentage increase in crop production is greater than the percentage increase in cropland in all areas except LC 1, this indicates a more intensive use of cropland. This also implies that water-borne pollutants from cropland are likely to become more concentrated.

For EC crops and cropland, crop production and cropland decrease for all land classes. This reflects the reduction of subsidies which are larger in the EC, compared to the US Land class 4, which comprises just over half of EC land, shows a 17.21 per cent decrease in crops and an 8.69 per cent decrease in cropland. In all land classes, the percentage reduction in crop production is much larger than the percentage decrease in cropland. This indicates a doubly beneficial impact on the environment, since the reduction in pollution associated with production is accompanied by a less intensive use of remaining cropland.

For crops and cropland in Southeast Asia, there is no land in LC 1 and LC 2 (small numbers are used as placeholders for model calibration purposes). For the other four land classes, all show increases in crop production and cropland. Land class 6, which accounts for 80 per cent of land in the region, has a 1.89 per cent increase in crop production and a 1.09 per cent increase in cropland. In each case, the percentage increase in crop production is roughly double the percentage increase in cropland. This would signal a potential area for concern,

Figure 4.2 Impacts of liberalizing agricultural trade on cropland

Percent change

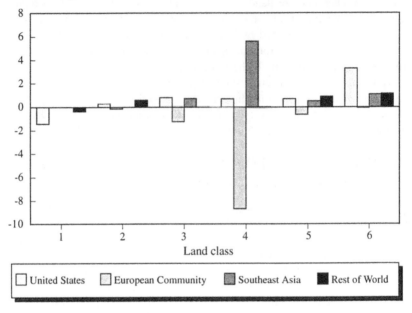

in that pollution impacts are associated with increased production and with more intensive use of cropland.

For Rest of World, crop production and cropland increase for all land classes except LC 1, of which there is very little land to start with. All the increases are relatively small, however, given that very few subsidies existed for removal. Land class 2 comprises about a third of the land in this region, and shows a 1.02 per cent increase in crops and a 0.6 per cent increase in cropland. There could be some adverse environmental impacts associated with the increased intensity of use of LC 5 and LC 6, but given the number of countries in the Rest of World region, it would be hard to be more specific.

IX.   IMPLICATIONS FOR LIVESTOCK AND PASTURE

For US livestock and pasture, livestock production and pasture increase on LC 1 and LC 2, and decrease on LC 3 through LC 6. Intensity, as measured by head per acre, also increases on LC 1 and LC 2, and decreases on LC 3 through LC 6. This indicates that, although some grassland habitats increase in the West, grazing pressure on these habitats increases as well. For land class 2, which includes forage for rough grazing, livestock increases 2.77 percent, while pasture increases by 1.04 per cent. Other grassland habitats decrease, but grazing pressure decreases as well.[5]

For EC livestock and pasture, livestock production decreases on all land classes except LC 1. For pasture, however, increases are shown for LC 1 and LC 4, with slight decreases in all other classes. Apart from the small amount of land in LC 1, all other results indicate reduced stress on the environment from livestock production and use of pasture. The relatively large increase in pasture in LC 4 (despite a decrease in production) is particularly interesting, with livestock decreasing 0.84 per cent while pasture increases 3.88 per cent. This is because there was also a relatively large decrease in use of LC 4 for cropland given the reduction in subsidies for crops.

For Southeast Asia livestock and pasture, there is hardly any land in LC 1 and LC 2, and little in either LC 3 or LC 4. Thus the slight increase in production and larger decrease in pasture in LC 4 presents little reason for environmental concern. For LC 5, there is a larger percentage increase in production than pasture, so there could be a problem that is associated with more intensive use, since livestock increases 0.75 per cent as pasture increases 0.33 percent. There is a small percentage increase in production and a smaller decrease in pasture in LC 6, but this could still represent an environmental problem in some areas, given that over 80 per cent of Southeast Asian land is in LC 6.

For Rest of World livestock and pasture, livestock production increases on all land classes. As for pasture, there is no change in LC 2 and a slight decrease in LC 6, and relatively small increases on all other land classes. These results indicate potential environmental problems for all land classes, since greater percentage increases in production than pasture indicate greater intensity of use of resources. The largest increase in livestock is in land class 3, where it increases 1.31 per cent relative to a 0.07 per cent increase in pasture.

X.   IMPLICATIONS FOR IRRIGATION

For the US, the use of water for irrigation increases on all land classes except LC 1, for which there is no irrigation (see Figure 4.3). Irrigated land on LC 2 through LC 5 is located primarily in the West. LC 6 irrigated land is located primarily in the Southeast, and shows the largest increase at 3.83 per cent. Water values are used as weights to combine irrigation water changes on cropland and pasture. As global data on water prices is limited, a price of $2.55 million dollars per cubic kilometer is used in all regions, based on US data (US Department of Commerce, Bureau of the Census, 1990). On LC 2, irrigation water increases by 1.8 and 3.0 per cent, while cropland and pasture increase by only 0.3 and 1.0 per cent. This indicates that most new cropland and some new

Figure 4.3 Impacts of liberalizing agricultural trade on irrigation water

Percent change

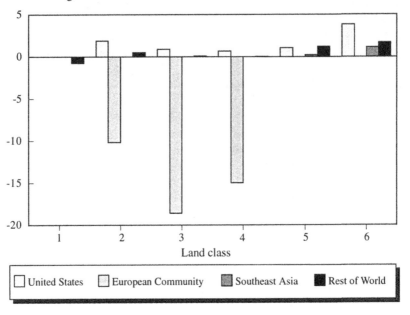

Land class

□ United States □ European Community ▨ Southeast Asia ■ Rest of World

pasture will be irrigated. It should be noted that while the model simulates irrigation capital, potential problems may occur if irrigation supply infrastructure is not located in proximity to the location with the new demand for irrigated agriculture. Results show that trade liberalization could increase competition for water in the Arid West. Using data from Tables 4.2 and 4.6, 76 per cent (149 km³) of agricultural water use in the US is in land class 2, so a 1.81 per cent increase is equal to a 2.7 km³ increase in use of water for agriculture.

For the EC, irrigation is confined to land classes 2, 3 and 4. The large decreases in irrigation for these three classes reflect the large decreases in cropland and slight increase in pasture. For LC 4, irrigation water decreases 16.8 per cent for cropland, while increasing 1.7 per cent for pasture. This is associated with an 8.7 per cent decrease for cropland, and a 3.9 per cent increase for pasture. Both results indicate reduced stress on the environment from reductions in irrigation intensity.

For Southeast Asia, irrigation (and almost all land) is confined to LC 5 and LC 6. In this region, increases in irrigation result from cropland increases and pasture reductions. For LC 6, irrigation water increases 1.4 per cent for cropland, and decreases 0.7 per cent for pasture. Comparing this to a 1.1 per cent increase in cropland and 0.1 per cent decrease in pasture, there could be increased environmental stress associated with more intensive use of cropland.

For the Rest of World region, irrigation decreases on LC 1, and increases on all other land classes. The largest increase is for LC 6, which comes from a 1.9 per cent irrigation water increase for cropland, and a 0.1 per cent increase for pasture. Given that LC 6 cropland increases by 1.1 per cent, this indicates increased intensity of use of irrigation.

These results assume that water supplies are sufficient to accommodate increased use. Also, as data on the price of water around the world is currently limited, the relative valuation of water in the different regions may be subject to change with improved information.

XI. IMPLICATIONS FOR TIMBER AND FORESTLAND

For US timber and forestland, timber production increases on all land classes except LC 6. In terms of quantity of timber (thousand cubic meters), production increases are ranked from high to low as LC 4, LC 3, LC 5, LC 1, LC 2, and LC 6. Forestland increases on all land classes except LC 2 and LC 6. Intensity, measured in cubic meters per acre, also increases on all land classes except LC 6. This indicates that, although forestland habitats would increase in many areas, they would also face pressure from higher harvest rates. It should be noted that while any conversion of crop or pasture to forest may occur relatively quickly, its harvest may not occur for 20 to 40 years after conversion. Given that our model focuses on a shorter time frame, the implications of this longer term harvest are potentially significant, but beyond the scope of this analysis.

For the EC, timber production decreases on all land classes except LC 3 and LC 4, which experience slight increases. Forestland decreases slightly for LC 1, LC 2 and LC 6, and increases for the other three land classes. The largest increases are for LC 4, where 1 per cent more timber is harvested from 5 per cent more forestland. This would seem to indicate little or no stress additional stress on the environment as a result of these changes.

For Southeast Asia, there is little land in LC 1 and LC 2. For the other four land classes, both timber production and forestland experience small declines. The largest decline is for LC 4, where forestland declines 2.67 per cent but timber production declines only 0.79 percent. This could increase environmental stress, but less than 15 per cent of all Southeast Asian land is in LC 4. The bulk of land is in LC 6, where timber production declines at three times the rate of forestland, with a 0.7 per cent decrease in timber associated with a 0.25 per cent decrease in forestland. This decline in harvest intensity could indicate positive environmental benefits. Note that deforestation as modeled here describes economic opportunity.

For the Rest of World region, timber production and forestland increase for LC 1 through LC 4, and decline for LC 5 and LC 6. The biggest increase is in land class 1, where timber increases 0.48 per cent and forestland increases 0.19 percent. For LC 1 through LC 4, while the increases are small, timber production percentage increases are at several times the rate of increase in forestland. These results indicate the potential for increased environmental stress in LC 1 through LC 5. The greater percentage decline of forestland over timber production in LC 5 could also be a problem. Only in LC 6, where timber production declines at double the rate of decline in forestland, do positive environmental benefits seem possible, with timber declining 0.43 per cent while forestland declines 0.2 per cent.

XII.   IMPLICATIONS FOR OTHER LAND

In the US, land that is not used for agriculture or forestry decreases in all land classes. For LC 1, this is other land converted to pasture. For LC 2, this is other land and woodland converted to cropland and pasture. For LC 3, this is other land and pasture converted to cropland and forestland. For LC 4 and LC 5, this is other land and pasture converted primarily to cropland. For LC 6, this is other land, pasture, and forestland converted to cropland. Natural habitats on other land include ice, tundra and wetlands for LC 1, desert for LC 2, and wetlands for LC 3 through LC 6. The largest decline for the US is 1.34 per cent for LC 2, while all the other declines are quite small. Since these different types of land differ in their vulnerability to environmental stress, on which land class cropland use is changing makes a difference in terms of environmental impacts,.

For other land in the EC, small increases are shown for all land classes, with the largest increase of 5.46 per cent for LC 4. This largely reflects the decrease in cropland and increase in pastureland associated with this trade liberalization scenario. For other land in Southeast Asia, there are small decreases for LC 3 through LC 6. The largest decrease is 2.53 per cent for LC 4, but total LC 4 land for all uses in Southeast Asia only account for about 1 per cent of all land. For other land in the Rest of World region, small percentage declines are shown in all land classes.

XIII.   IMPLICATIONS FOR PRIMARY FACTORS

Possible effects of trade liberalization on total primary factors are consistent with the changes in resources described above (see Table 4.6). In the US, results suggest slight increases in the use of water, labor, capital, cropland and pasture, and slight decreases in forestland and other land. This reflects the lower initial level of subsidies to reduce relative to the EC, which allows for some expansion of the US crop sector. Conversely, the EC experiences relatively large reductions in the use of water, labor, capital and cropland, and slight increases in pasture land, forestland and other land. This reflects the larger reduction in the EC crop sector. As for Southeast Asia, all changes are small, with increases in water, labor, capital and cropland, and decreases in pasture land, forestland, and other land. As noted above, the reduction in forestland may indicate the potential negative environmental effects. Finally, for the Rest of World region, results indicate small increases in the use of water, labor, capital and cropland, and pasture land, and slight decreases in forestland and other land. Given the size of the region, it is difficult to say whether this is indicative of potential environmental problems within the region.

XV. CONCLUSION AND SUGGESTIONS FOR FURTHER RESEARCH

The analysis presented in this chapter suggests that trade liberalization can have both positive and negative environmental effects in agricultural production regions worldwide. As production shifts around the world in response to reductions in government support, changes in the intensity of use of cropland, pastureland, forestland and other land are predicted. Whether this more or less intensive use of land is harmful to the environment depends on the relative absorptive capacity of the different land classes to the various pollutants that are associated with agricultural activity. Similarly, whether the environmental gains (losses) a country might experience outweigh possible economic losses (gains) from reduced (increased) production is a judgement outside the scope of this modeling exercise.

Current work underway will significantly update and revise our modeling capability. The latest version of GTAP has a 1997 base period with 66 regions and 57 sectors, and a revised FARM model is currently being constructed to complement and extend that version of GTAP. In particular, the new land and water resources database being developed for the FARM modeling effort will provide more capability for economic and ecological analysis than other major models in use today. The plan is to increase the scope, precision, and geographic resolution of the estimated environmental effects generated during FARM's simulations of trade liberalization and other global changes. Efforts will also be made to make methods more accessible to departments and agencies within the US government through the GTAP consortium based at Purdue University. The goal of this exercise is to inform the debate on coordinating trade and environmental policies to address domestic and global environmental concerns.

NOTES

1. Acknowledgements are due to Marinos Tsigas and Roy Darwin for extensive contributions to model development and scenario construction. The views presented herein are those of the authors, and do not necessarily represent the views or policies of the Economic Research Service or the United States Department of Agriculture.

2. "Transboundary and global impacts may include those on: 1. Places not subject to national jurisdiction or places subject to shared jurisdiction, such as Antarctica, atmosphere (including ozone and climate change features), outer space, and the high seas; 2. Migratory species, including straddling and highly migratory fish stocks and whale; 3. Impacts relating to other environmental problems identified by the international community as having a global dimension and warranting a global response; 4. Transboundary impacts involving the boundaries of the United States" (USTR, 2000a).

3. The current GTAP and FARM models under construction will provide much more detail when they are properly linked. The GTAP Version 5 database now has 66 regions and 57 sectors, and a linked extension into the revised FARM framework will provide significantly more analysis at the subpolitical unit level.

4. These results are not directly comparable with the other modeling results in this report (for example, Chapter 3), given that they reflect different base years and different commodity and regional aggregations.

5. One caveat to note is that FARM models an aggregate livestock of cattle and hogs, so the mix of hogs and cattle, or vice versa, can vary over land class.

PART II

Trade Impacts of
Agri-Environmental Programs

5. Domestic agri-environmental policies in a trade perspective

Mark Peters and Mark Smith[1]

I. INTRODUCTION

Among the topics covered in Chapter 2 is a general discussion of agri-environmental policy design and the targeting of policy to specific environmental issues. This chapter and the next empirically address some of the possible environmental and economic impacts of agri-environmental policy instruments and environmental instruments. A variety of policy instruments, ranging from taxes on inputs to agri-environmental payments, are available to help achieve the desired environmental goals (Heimlich and Claassen, 1998; Appendix 2). While it is theoretically possible for a number of different instruments to achieve the same environmental goal, one would not expect them to accomplish a specific goal with the same economic effects. This is especially pertinent when domestic environmental policies are considered in a global perspective. For example, under the Uruguay Round Agreement on Agriculture, permissible environmental policies are those that have "minimal" production and trade effects (USDA, FAS 2000; Vasavada and Warmerdam, 1998). This raises the prospect that the most cost-effective policies for achieving an environmental goal will conflict with trade policy goals.

With respect to agriculture, one line of research shows that environmental regulations have little effect on agricultural trade. Work by Tobey (1991) implies that domestic environmental policies have relatively small agricultural trade effects. Bohman and Lindsey (1997b) simulated harmonization of environmental regulations for chicken production in the NAFTA market, and found relatively little trade effect of regulations. Valluru and Peterson (1997) examined the impact of environmental regulation on grain trade, and also found little impact. Since environmental regulation was broadly proxied in the latter study by variables, such as the proportion of arable land area in parks, or the proportion of known bird and mammal species that are endangered, or similar variables, it is not surprising that no significant relationship was found.

However, other research shows that environmental policies may significantly affect agricultural trade. Restrictions on agricultural chemical use have been shown to significantly alter trade. Abler and Shortle (1992) found that chemical use restrictions in the United States and the European Union (EU) may have significant trade effects. Likewise, for specific vegetables, significant production shifts from the United States to Mexico may result from a ban on methyl bromide use in the United States (Van Sickle, Brewster and Spreen 1999). Leuck *et al.* (1995) examined the trade and environmental implications of the EU's Nitrate Directive (which limits the net delivery of nitrogen to the soil). Large effects from an assumed implementation of the Directive were found in EU net trade of livestock, livestock products, and grains and oilseeds. Bohman and Lindsey (1997a) show that policy effects depend upon the relative size of trading partners and whether policies are imposed unilaterally or bilaterally.

Research on how agricultural conservation policies affect trade flows is relatively sparse. Among US conservation policies, research has centered on the Conservation Reserve Program (CRP). Young and Osborn (1990) assessed a potential 45 million acre program and estimated that US wheat exports would have fallen by almost 20 per cent by the mid-1990s, assuming no expansion in set-asides. Leetmaa and Smith (1996) estimated that if CRP acreage were reduced by about half in the early 1990s, the volume of US grain exports would have increased between 5 and 10 per cent, chiefly at the expense of Canadian exporters. Neither study attempted to estimate environmental effects.

All the above studies lack an evaluation of the environmental effects of the studied policies. Also missing from this research is an evaluation of how different policy instruments could be used to achieve the same environmental goal or how the different policy instruments would affect trade. Consequently, little is known about the economic effects of agri-environmental policies across environmental goals. Does the ranking of policy instruments with respect to economic efficiency change across environmental goals? Do policies with similar outcomes with respect to economic efficiency have significantly different trade effects? Does the magnitude of differences in trade effects of policy instruments vary greatly across targets?[2] To better understand the economic issues (tradeoffs) associated with stricter environmental policies, we examine the relative effects of alternative agri-environmental policies designed to achieve a set objective. Since the specific features of future programs cannot be known and we are looking ahead rather than looking back, generic representations of policies are examined rather than actual programs. Our empirical model considers not only economic aspects of alternative policies, but their environmental impact as well. It allows producers to alter their scale of operation (acreage planted), product mix chosen (crops grown) and the production technology employed (rotations, tillage practices and fertilizer application rates) in response to the incentives created by the policies. This chapter is organized as follows. The next section describes our estimation process. Results in terms of market impacts, welfare measures, and environmental indicators are then discussed. Finally, we draw some conclusions from this analysis, with a focus on the variety of tradeoffs inherent in the intersection of environmental and trade concerns.

II. METHODOLOGY FOR EMPIRICAL ANALYSIS

A wide variety of agri-environmental policies are available for dealing with pollution resulting from agricultural production. These policies can be placed into several broad or generic categories: education and technical assistance, government labeling standards for private goods, incentive payment policies, land retirement programs, environmental taxes, and regulatory requirements. Of these incentive payment policies, land retirement programs, environmental taxes and regulatory requirements influence producer decisions regarding management practices most directly. Over the past two decades, US agri-environmental policy has relied primarily on land retirement programs, such as the Conservation Reserve Program and Swampbuster, to achieve its agri-environmental goals. It has been recognized that land retirement programs may be poor mechanisms for addressing water quality problems (Claassen *et al.*, 2001). There is also some concern that because they take productive land out of production, land retirement programs may achieve their goals at a considerable cost to society (for example, higher commodity prices, economic costs to rural communities). Consequently, there is considerable interest in using instruments, such as agri-environmental payments, input taxes and regulatory requirements that can achieve the desired agri-environmental goals, while permitting productive land to be fully utilized. See Appendix 2 for a general discussion of the different types of agri-environmental instruments and Appendix 6 for an overview of key US agri-environmental programs.

To consider the effects of alternative environmental policies on traded volumes, market prices and agriculture's environmental performance, we employ USMP, which is a regional model of the US agricultural sector that also includes major government ‚agricultural programs, chiefly the Flexibility Contract Program (FCP), the Conservation Reserve Program (CRP), and conservation compliance. The most important of these for our analysis is conservation compliance, which limits expansion of production onto highly erodible land (HEL) by requiring producers to forego FCP and CRP payments when bringing new HEL into production. USMP is a comparative-static, spatial and market equilibrium model and is described in Appendix 3, and a visual schematic of the model is provided in Chapter 2, Section I.

A plethora of environmental goals could be identified for our study. However, we focus on two such goals. The first of these is a reduction in nitrogen losses from the agricultural sector. Nutrient runoff from agricultural production has been identified by the EPA as a key source of US surface water quality problems. Nitrogen emissions into the Gulf of Mexico are believed to be the cause of hypoxia which, where it occurs, creates large areas devoid of marine life in the Gulf of Mexico (Claassen *et al.*, 2001). In addition, nitrogen emissions from livestock farms are believed to be responsible for outbreaks of water-borne pathogens in coastal estuaries. Finally, because problems associated with nutrient runoff are worldwide, the OECD (1998) has recommended that measures of nutrient losses be developed to assist in multinational comparisons of agri-environmental policies. For this study, we examine a 10 per cent reduction in nitrogen losses.[3]

To achieve this nitrogen loss reduction goal, four alternative policies are evaluated: a tax on nitrogen fertilizer use, a regulation requiring uniform reductions in nitrogen fertilizer application rates, a voluntary land retirement (riparian buffers) program targeted to intercept field runoff, and an agri-environmental payment policy where a payment per unit of reduced fertilizer use is provided to offset producers' cost of reducing the fertilizer use.[4] The fertilizer tax was applied to each unit of nitrogen applied, while the agri-environmental payment was paid for each unit of nitrogen fertilizer reduction below each system's base application rate. The regulatory scenario was implemented by cutting nitrogen application rates by the same percentage across all systems. For the land retirement (buffer) scenario, buffers were allocated regionally in proportion to a region's average annual rainfall relative to national average annual rainfall. The payment to producers included the opportunity cost of cropland plus the costs involved to establish a buffer. In setting the payment, it was assumed that one acre of cropland was retired for every three acres put into buffers. The amount of nitrogen filtered from edge of field losses was obtained by multiplying acres of riparian buffer by an assumed filtering capacity of 360 pounds per acre (Mitsch *et al.*, 1999). In the scenarios, producers had to be paid to retire about 21 million acres in order to achieve the goal of reducing nitrogen loss by 10 per cent.

The second goal we simulate is a reduction in soil erosion, which has been a goal of many USDA (US Department of Agriculture) conservation programs. Prior to 1990, USDA soil erosion policies focused on soil productivity impacts. Since 1990, the USDA has expanded its concerns for soil erosion to include the problems it causes for water and air quality. In addition, the OECD (1998) also recommends that measures of erosion be developed to assist multinational comparisons of agri-environmental policies. As in the analysis of nitrogen reduction, we choose as a policy target a 10 per cent reduction in erosion.

To achieve a 10 per cent reduction in soil erosion, three alternative policy scenarios are evaluated: a green payment plan in which a payment is provided to offset the producers' opportunity cost of reducing conventional tillage on HEL; a regulation requiring adoption of conservation on a specified share of HEL; and a land retirement policy focusing on HEL. The green payment to a producer is based on the difference in erosion between the employed tillage (ridge-till, mulch-till, and no-till) and erosion that could result from conventional tillage in the same operation. Under this scenario, a payment rate of $1.60 per ton of erosion reduction was required to reach the target. For the regulatory scenario, a constraint was applied in the simulation model to shift conventional tillage practices to conservation tillage practices sufficient to meet the policy goal. To meet the 10 per cent reduction in erosion under the regulatory scenario, it was necessary to require a 50 per cent reduction in conventional tillage practices on HEL. For the land retirement scenario, producers were paid to retire sufficient HEL—24 million acres in this simulation—to meet the policy goal.

Since no specific input increases erosion and since a tax on erosion has received little, if any, attention within policymaking circles in the US and the EU, we chose not to examine a tax policy for erosion reduction. However, the regulatory policy that we examine can be interpreted as a tax on conventional tillage practices. The only difference between the outcomes for the two scenarios considered would be on the distribution of costs between producers and government. Under the regulatory policy, farmers would only have to pay for the costs of switching tillage practices, whereas under a tax farmers' income would fall by the cost of switching tillage systems and the amount of tax that they pay. Because government revenues would increase by the amount of tax paid by producers, the change in net social cost under the two policies would be approximately the same.[5]

III. EMPIRICAL RESULTS FOR THE NITROGEN REDUCTION ANALYSIS

In order to achieve the goal of reducing nitrogen loss nationally by 10 per cent, nitrogen use is reduced by 18 and 19 per cent under the tax and agri-environmental payment approaches, respectively. Under the regulatory approach however, nitrogen use needs to be reduced by only 14 per cent in order to meet the nitrogen loss goal. The necessary reduction in nitrogen use is smaller than under the tax and payments approaches because the regulatory approach forces greater reductions in application rates in cropping systems with high rates of nitrogen loss per acre than does either the tax or payments approaches. The tax and agri-environmental payments approaches reduce nitrogen fertilizer application rates based on their impact on net returns to producers. It turns out that those systems with the highest nitrogen fertilizer application rates are generally systems where it is least economical to reduce application rates. High nitrogen losses per acre are generally associated with higher nitrogen fertilizer application rates. Hence, cropping systems for which it is least economical to reduce rates tend to have higher rates of nitrogen loss than systems under which it is most economical to reduce application rates. This means that the reduction in nitrogen loss per acre under the regulatory approach will be greater than the reduction in nitrogen loss per acre that occurs under either the tax or payments approaches. As a result, the reduction in nitrogen use needed to meet the nitrogen loss goal will be less than the reduction in use that occurs under the other two approaches.

As noted earlier, to reduce national nitrogen losses by 10 per cent under the land retirement (buffer) approach, producers retired about 21 million acres, causing nitrogen use nationally to decline 3 per cent. This decline is significantly less than the decline in nitrogen use that occurs under the other policies. The relatively small decline in nitrogen use is to be expected as the primary goal of creating buffers is to filter the nitrogen out of the water after it has been applied, and not to reduce fertilizer application rates. As a result, one should not expect reductions in nitrogen use under this scenario to be as great as that which occurs under policies that directly target nitrogen application rates.

An agri-environmental payment rate of four times the price of nitrogen fertilizer was needed to reduce nitrogen loss by the targeted amount. This increase contrasts with the tripling of the nitrogen fertilizer price needed to achieve the targeted reduction in nitrogen loss with the fertilizer tax. The payment rate needed to achieve the nitrogen loss goal was larger than the tax rate primarily because crop production falls less under the agri-environmental payment program than under the tax program. Because production falls less, reductions in nitrogen fertilizer application rates have to be greater and, as a consequence, incentives to producers need to be higher.

The difference between the fertilizer tax and the agri-environmental payment rate needed to reduce nitrogen loss to the targeted amount highlights the difficulty in achieving environmental goals through agri-environmental payments programs focusing on reduced input use. While it is true that, for any particular field or acre of land, the payment or subsidy needed to get a producer to reduce the nitrogen fertilizer application rate to a particular level will be the same as the tax needed to accomplish the same reduction in application rates, this equivalence will not be the case when land is allowed to be brought into or out of production. This is because an agri-environmental payment and a tax—while having the same impact on the producer's cost of applying an additional pound of fertilizer to the field—will have opposite effects on the producer's average cost per of production for that field. While the tax increases the average cost of production, the agri-environmental payment reduces it. The increase in the average cost of production resulting from the nitrogen tax will cause producers to reduce the amount of land they put into production while the reduction in average cost resulting from the agri-environmental payment will cause producers to increase the amount of land they put into production. Because the incentive for producers to expand production increases as the payment rate increases, it is possible for nitrogen use and nitrogen losses to increase under an agri-environmental payment program even though it achieves significant reductions in nitrogen fertilizer application rates. Indeed, the greater the reduction in fertilizer application rates achieved, the more likely it is that total nitrogen loss will actually increase.

The incentive for expanding land use created by the payments approach is separate from the incentive created for expanding land use caused by increases in market price resulting from declining production. The incentive for expanding land use created by the effect of declining production on prices exists under all approaches. Under none of the approaches considered are the incentives for changing land use caused by the increase in commodity prices greater than the incentives for changing land use created by the effect the payments and tax programs have on average costs.

Table 5.1 shows changes in commodity markets (production, consumption, US trade, and market price) and economic impacts on domestic and Rest of World (ROW), consumers, and producers from alternative policies to meet the nitrogen-loss reduction goal. In addition, consideration of soil erosion (including erosion damages as discussed in Appendix 3) is shown. Summed production, consumption, and trade is shown for barley, corn, cotton, hay, oats, rice, silage, sorghum, soybeans, and wheat, as is a weighted average of world prices for those commodities. Economic costs reflect sector-wide effects and environmental impacts reflect national changes.

The agri-environmental payment to encourage producers to reduce nitrogen use has smaller market effects than all other policies considered in our study. Acreage planted expands for two reasons. First, acreage planted expands in response to the increase in prices brought about by the decline in yields associated with lower fertilizer application rates. Second, as discussed above, acreage expands because the agri-environmental payment reduces producers' average production costs, causing them to bring more land into production. The first effect will be observed under all the approaches, but the second effect only occurs with an agri-environmental payments approach. As the agri-environmental payment encourages planted acreage to expand, it partially offsets the production-depressing effects of reduced fertilizer use. Hence, production declines less with agri-environmental payments than it does with the other

Table 5.1 Relative effects of environmental policies designed to reduce agricultural nitrogen losses

Indicator/Goal	Base	Nitrogen reduction goal achieved through			
		Agri-environmental Payment	Regulation	Taxation	Land Retirement
Commodity market impacts (selected crops)		*Per cent change from base*			
Production (MMT)	705.5	–0.5	–1.1	–2.7	–3.6
Consumption (MMT)	556.1	–0.3	–0.6	–1.5	–3.0
Trade vol. (MMT)	156.9	–1.1	–2.7	–6.3	–5.4
Trade value ($Billion)	27.5	0.4	–0.1	–0.4	0.4
Market price (Weighted Index $/MT)	128.6	1.6	2.4	5.8	6.5
Economic benefits ($Billion)					
US consumer surplus	619.4	–0.1	–0.2	–0.5	–0.6
US producer surplus	95.7	3.2	0.8	–2.3	3.4
Consumers of US exports	28.9	–1.2	–2.3	–5.5	–7.1
Producers of US imports	7.9	0.3	0.5	1.3	1.4
Environmental effects					
Total erosion (MMT)	1.8	2.4	0.4	–3.2	–2.8
Erosion damages ($B)	3.7	2.6	–0.9	–2.7	–4.1
Nitrogen damages($B)	0.17	–11.3	–9.7	–11.2	–15.1

Note: For the change in environmental effects, a minus sign indicates a decrease in damage and a positive sign an increase.

policies. This in turn causes consumption, price, and trade effects under this policy to be relatively modest.

The market effects associated with the regulatory policy are greater than those associated with the agri-environmental payments policy, but the difference between the two is negligible. Cultivated acreage increases slightly under the regulatory policy, countering some of the contraction from reduced per acre fertilizer use, though not as much as when an agri-environmental payment is provided. Acreage planted expands in this case as producers bring more land into production in response to the increase in prices brought about by the decline in yields that are associated with lower fertilizer application rates. Under the regulatory approach, because the producers do not benefit from the reduction in average costs associated with the agri-environmental payments, the expansion of acres is less than that which occurs with the agri-environmental payments approach.

Under a nitrogen tax, cultivated acreage declines as the costs of the tax to producers are greater than the increase in revenues they receive from increased prices. Because the nitrogen tax increases average costs of production, it causes producers to move land out of production and acreage declines. By increasing average costs, the tax provides producers with an incentive to reduce the amount of land they have in production. This is the opposite of the incentive provided to producers for changing land use by the agri-environmental payment program. The decline in acreage reinforces the production-depressing effect of reduced nitrogen fertilizer use and, as a result, the nitrogen tax policy has more than twice the impact on agricultural markets than does the regulatory policy.

The land retirement policy has the greatest market effects as it leads to the largest declines in production and consequently changes in consumption, and prices. Production declines more under this approach than the others because a substantial amount of land, nearly 21 million acres, needs to be put into buffers to achieve the 10 per cent reduction in nitrogen losses. The land retirement policy has slightly less of an effect on trade than the tax policy, which cuts production by less, because of differences between the two policies in the mix of crops used to reduce production.

The distribution of changes in benefits and costs across consumers and producers follows from market effects and the distribution of taxes and subsidies. US consumer surplus declines under all policies, but significantly less with agri-environmental payments because it has the smallest impact on production.[6] Gains to producers increase the most under the land retirement policy due to higher market prices from its impact on production and government payments for retiring land from production. The agri-environmental payments policy also causes a significant increase in producer net returns, nearly equaling the increase to producers under the land retirement policy. Even under the regulatory policy, producers would see a slight increase in net returns. This reflects the gains producers receive from higher commodity prices as well as the gains they receive from reducing fertilizer application rates closer to the point where expected net returns are maximized. Producers receive this gain because the regulatory requirements force producers to ignore the risk they associate with applying less fertilizer. This perception of risk, absent the regulation mandating that they reduce their fertilizer application rates, causes producers to apply more fertilizer than needed to maximize expected returns in order to avoid the losses to yields associated with not having sufficient fertilizer available to meet plant needs under likely growing conditions (Babcock, 1992). Abroad, RoW consumers of US exports fare the worst under all policy instruments and in percentage terms bear most of the cost of achieving a reduction in US nitrogen losses. RoW suppliers to US markets benefit under all policies as the reduction in US production causes the US demand for imports to increase. RoW suppliers' gains are greatest under a land retirement policy. In terms of US taxpayer costs, the agri-environmental payment policy increases government expenditures (approximately $2.9 billion), which are nearly double those for the land retirement policy ($1.7 billion).

In terms of nitrogen losses, the policies vary considerably with respect to their effectiveness in reducing offsite damages (see Appendix 3 for a discussion of the offsite damages that are addressed in the model). The riparian buffer policy reduces nitrogen damages the most followed in order of magnitude by the agri-environmental payments policy, the nitrogen tax policy and the regulatory policy. That the agri-environmental payments policy reduces nitrogen damages slightly more than the nitrogen tax policy is somewhat surprising, given that agri-environmental payments led to a much smaller decline in production than a nitrogen tax. The definition of estuaries and the location of land contraction and expansion under the tax and agri-environmental payment policies can explain most of the difference. Our estimates of the damages caused by nitrogen loss are based on decreased recreational benefits associated with this loss. Our measure of damages from nitrogen loss does not include nitrogen emissions flowing into the Gulf of Mexico as, by definition, the Gulf of Mexico is not an estuary, and consequently, we do not have damage estimates for it. As a result, reductions in nitrogen emissions that occur in the Mississippi Basin will have less of an impact on reducing damages from nitrogen loss than reductions in nitrogen emissions flowing into estuaries that are accounted for in our index. Also, note that no benefit estimates exist for the decrease in hypoxia that is associated with decreased nitrogen loss. At the same time, differences between the two policies in terms of changes in cropped land are concentrated in the Mississippi River Basin that flows into the Gulf of Mexico. Consequently, the primary source of the differences between the two scenarios in terms of changes in nitrogen emissions is excluded in the measure of nitrogen damages.

Ancillary environmental benefits also vary significantly across the policy instruments. Those policies, such as agri-environmental payments and the uniform reduction in nitrogen fertilizer rates that lead to increases in planted acreage, have far less ancillary benefits—and even some costs in the case of agri-environmental payments—than those policies that lead to reductions in acreage planted. The nitrogen tax leads to greater reductions in erosion than do any of the other policies—even land retirement. In terms of the reducing offsite damages from nitrogen loss and erosion, however, the land retirement policy has the greatest impact. This occurs because the nitrogen tax leads to reductions in production in areas where fertilizer use is highest—such as the Corn

Belt, but not necessarily in the areas where offsite damages in erosion are the greatest—such as the Northeast. The land retirement policy, by focusing on buffering of emissions into waterways targets, causes land retirement to be targeted to those areas with the highest concentrations of waterways and thus does a better job of targeting locations where offsite damages are the greatest. Note that policies designed to address a particular environmental problem may simultaneously increase or decrease the level of other environmental problems. For this analysis, we consider the changes in nitrogen loss due to the soil erosion policies and vice versa.

IV. EMPIRICAL RESULTS FOR THE SOIL EROSION REDUCTION ANALYSIS

Three alternative policies are evaluated for achieving a 10 per cent reduction in soil erosion. These are: an agri-environmental payment where payment is provided to offset the producers' opportunity cost of reducing conventional tillage on HEL; a regulation requiring adoption of conservation on a specified share of HEL; and a land retirement policy focused on HEL. The agri-environmental payment to a producer was based on the difference in erosion from the employed tillage (ridge-till, mulch-till, and no-till) and erosion that could result from conventional tillage in the same operation. A payment rate of $1.60 per ton of erosion reduction was required to reach the 10 per cent reduction target. For the regulatory scenario, a constraint was applied to shift conventional tillage practices to conservation tillage practices sufficient to meet the policy goal. This required a 50 per cent reduction in conventional tillage practices on HEL. For the land retirement scenario, producers were paid to retire sufficient HEL (24 million acres) to meet the goal.

Table 5.2 reports results for the erosion-reduction scenarios. Again, the agri-environmental payments policy, for much the same reasons as discussed for the nitrogen loss scenarios, has smaller market effects than the other policies. Reductions in average costs caused by the payments for reducing conventional tillage motivates an increase in acreage planted that is large enough to almost entirely offset the impact on production from the decline in yields caused by the switch to conservation tillage. As a result, the agri-environmental payments policy causes virtually no market effects. The regulatory policy causes only slightly larger declines in production and consequently also has small impact on prices, consumption and trade. Again, as with the nitrogen policy, the land retirement policy has the greatest market impacts because it causes larger declines in production than the other policies do.

The agri-environmental payments policy, given its limited impact on commodity markets, has little or no effect on US consumers and the RoW. Consumer sur-

Table 5.2 Relative effects of environmental policies designed to reduce soil erosion

Indicator/Goal	Base	Erosion reduction goal achieved through		
		Agri-environmental payment	Regulation	Land retirement
Commodity market impacts (selected crops)		*Per cent change from base*		
Production (MMT)	705.5	–0.1	–0.7	–4.3
Consumption (MMT)	556.1	0	–0.7	–3.9
Trade vol. (MMT)	156.9	–0.2	–0.7	–5.0
Trade value ($M)	27.5	0	–0.2	–0.2
Market price index ($/MT)	128.6	0.1	0.7	6.1
Economic benefits ($Billion)				
US consumers	619.4	0	–0.1	–0.5
US producers	95.7	1.2	0.2	2.7
Consumers of US exports	28.9	0	–0.5	–5.4
Producers of US imports	7.9	0.1	0.2	1.3
Environmental effects				
Erosion damages ($B)	3.7	–6.8	–5.0	–9.7
Nitrogen losses (MMT)	7.0	–2.4	–0.8	–2.7
Nitrogen damages($B)	0.17	–0.1	0	–3.7

Note: For the change in environmental effects, a minus sign indicates a decrease in damage and a positive sign an increase.

plus—both foreign and domestic—remains unchanged and RoW suppliers to US markets see a negligible increase in their net returns. US producers, however, do benefit as their net returns increase as a result of government payments totaling $1.3 billion. A regulatory approach generates slightly greater market impacts and consequently has discernible while still fairly small effects on consumers and producers. Negligible declines in both domestic and foreign consumer surplus and negligible increases in net returns to US and RoW producers are observed. The land retirement approach has a minor impact on US consumers, but reduces the surplus of foreign consumers of US exports significantly. Net returns to producers increase the most under the land retirement policy even though the land retirement policy reduces production substantially more than either of the other two policies. This is in part due to the government payments, totaling $1.7 billion, that producers receive for retiring land, and the increase in revenues caused by the inelastic demand for agricultural commodities.

The land retirement policy to reduce soil erosion generates the greatest increase in ancillary environmental benefits. While all scenarios achieve the same reduction in soil erosion at the national level, sheet and rill erosion reduction accounts for a larger share of erosion reductions with land retirement than under the agri-environmental payment and regulatory scenarios. Hence, reductions in damages (which are based on sediment in water in USMP) are greater under the land retirement policy than under the regulatory or agri-environmental payment policies. Reductions in offsite damages associated with reductions in soil erosion are greater with the agri-environmental payments policy than they are with regulatory policy. This would seem to indicate that there is a relatively poor correlation between the location of HEL and offsite damages from soil erosion.

Nitrogen losses decline most with the land retirement policy, primarily because it brings about the largest reduction in land under cultivation. Nitrogen losses decline more under the agri-environmental payments policy than with the regulatory policy due to a greater shift in some regions to corn systems with wheat in them, and consequently, lower rates of commercial nitrogen application than under corn-only systems, than occurs under the regulatory policy. Despite slight declines in nitrogen losses, neither the agri-environmental payments policy nor the regulatory policy brings about any significant reduction in damages from these losses. The land retirement policy, on the other hand, brings about a proportionately higher reduction in damages from nitrogen loss than the reduction in nitrogen losses themselves.

V. EVALUATION OF THE ALTERNATIVE ENVIRONMENTAL POLICIES AND CONCLUSION

In Table 5.3, we report the effects of the policy instruments on net social cost and net social benefit. The change in *net social* cost is defined as the change in US consumer surplus plus the change in US producer surplus minus the change in net US government transfers to producers. The change in *net social* benefit is defined as the change in US net social cost plus the change in US environmental benefits. Environmental benefits include reductions in offsite damages from erosion, reductions in nitrogen emissions into estuaries, and increases in wildlife habitat (see Appendix 3). Costs and benefits to foreign producers and consumers resulting from these policies were excluded as this was not seen as a priority of US policymakers. As reported in Table 5.3, positive values for both net social cost and net social benefit represent welfare improvements and negative changes represent welfare reductions.

As the discussion above suggests, the incidence of the costs of all the policies is borne disproportionately by RoW consumers of US exports. Absent any

Table 5.3 Change in US net social costs and benefits

Scenario	Net social cost	Rank	Net social benefit	Rank
	Per cent		*Per cent*	
Nitrogen				
Tax	0.133	1	0.151	1
Regulation	0.068	2	0.076	2
Agri-environmental payment	–0.171	3	–0.183	4
Land retirement	–0.267	4	–0.129	3
Erosion				
Regulation	–0.013	1	0.013	1
Agri-environmental payment	–0.030	2	0.005	2
Land retirement	–0.257	3	–0.120	3

Note: The change in *net social cost* is defined as change in US consumer surplus plus the change in US producer surplus minus the change in net US government transfers to producers. The change in *net social benefit* is defined as change in US net social cost plus change in US environmental benefits. Consequently, positive values for both net social cost and net social benefit represent welfare improvements and negative changes represent welfare reductions.

adjustment for environmental benefits (but noting that ancillary benefits vary across scenarios), this incidence raises the prospect that that US welfare, as represented by a decline in US net social cost, could increase despite the costs to RoW consumers, which occurs across all scenarios.

With respect to net social cost, tax policy is the most efficient policy for achieving the targeted reduction in nitrogen losses, followed by the regulation, agri-environmental payment and land retirement policies. Both the tax and regulatory policies, even without the inclusion of environmental benefits from these policies, are estimated to lead to slight US welfare improvements. The inclusion of environmental benefits does not change the direction of the changes in US welfare, but it does change the ranking of the agri-environmental payment and land retirement policies. When changes in environmental benefits are included, the land retirement policy becomes more efficient than the agri-environmental payment policy. This is because the agri-environmental payment policy causes an increase in offsite damages from erosion, which causes a decline in net social benefit associated with this policy to be greater than the increase in net social cost. At the same time, the land retirement policy benefits from reductions in offsite erosion damages and increases in wildlife habitat.

With respect to achieving the target reduction in erosion, net social cost increases across all policies, with the regulatory policy being the most efficient (least cost) option for achieving the 10 per cent erosion-reduction goal, followed by the agri-environmental payment and then the land retirement policies. The increase in costs associated with the regulation and agri-environmental payment policy are fairly similar, with the increase in costs associated with the land retirement policy being substantially greater than the other two policies. Including changes in ancillary environmental benefits does not change the rankings of these policies in terms of their welfare impacts, but does cause both the regulation and agri-environmental payment policies to lead to slight increases in US welfare. This indicates that the environmental benefits associated with these policies are sufficient to offset the costs of achieving the erosion target.

Finally, we evaluate the agri-environmental policies by ranking them alternatively on the basis of their cost-effectiveness, defined as change in US net social cost, and their impact on US agricultural trade volumes (Table 5.4). The latter is chosen for ranking due to its significance to for WTO's green box (Appendix 4 and Box 2.2 in Chapter 2, Section I). The policies rank similarly across both the nitrogen loss and erosion reduction objectives in terms of their cost effectiveness. With respect to the nitrogen loss analysis, the tax policy as modeled here is most cost-effective followed in order by the regulatory, agri-environmental payments and land retirement policies. For the erosion reduction analyses, the regulatory policy is the most cost-effective, followed in order by agri-environmental payments and land retirement.

Evaluating the policies by their trade effects results in a different ranking than occurs when ranking them according to their economic efficiency, but one that is still consistent across environmental objectives. An agri-environmental payment policy has the least effect on trade, followed by the regulation, tax (in the case of nitrogen reduction), and the land retirement policies. The ranking

Table 5.4 Evaluation of alternative environmental policies

Policy instrument	Policy goal:			
	Nitrogen-reduction rank in terms of:		Erosion-reduction rank in terms of:	
	Cost-effectiveness	Trade impact	Cost-effectiveness	Trade impact
Tax	1	3	n.a.	n.a.
Regulation	2	2	1	2
Agri-environmental payments	3	1	2	1
Land retirement	4	4	3	3

with respect to trade impact is defined by the policy's impact on production. The policy with the least impact on production (that is, agri-environmental payments) has the least impact on trade volume, while the policy with the greatest impact on production has the greatest impact on trade.

Given the rising importance of agri-environmental payments as an agri-environmental policy tool, the next chapter is an in-depth analysis of the effects of agri-environmental payment programs on trade. Instead of examining a set objective as in this chapter, we extend the line of analysis by focusing on payment design issues and conducting a sensitivity analysis of various levels of agri-environmental payments on trade.

NOTES

1. The views presented herein are those of the authors, and do not necessarily represent the views or policies of the Economic Research Service or the United States Department of Agriculture.

2. Utilizing a graphical representation, Appendix 1 provides an overview of the linkages between trade, environment, and environmental policy instruments.

3. Note that in the US, Federal-level agri-environmental policy is not directed to achieving specific environmental goals, but to changes in production practices, with the implicit assumption being that the widespread adoption of these practices will improve the agriculture sector's environmental performance. Because of this a program requiring a large percentage reduction in nitrogen losses or soil erosion does not appear to be realistic. Consequently, we selected a goal (a 10 per cent reduction for the evaluation of both nitrogen loss and soil erosion policies) that would be more likely to fall into a policy relevant range.

4. An agri-environmental payments policy is defined here as a payment to reduce a targeted input use or to employ a management practice appropriate to achieve the policy goal. Such a payment is not a payment to reduce emissions, the reduction of which is difficult to quantify for nonpoint source pollution.

5. Differences in net social cost under the two policies would depend on the social cost of collecting the government revenues.

6. Consumer surplus is the excess of what consumers are willing to pay over what they actually do pay for the total quantity of the good purchased.

6. Effects of agri-environmental payment policies on agricultural trade

Joseph Cooper, Mark Peters and Roger Claassen[1]

I.   INTRODUCTION

Chapter 2, Section I presents an environmental assessment of agricultural trade liberalization. As outlined in that chapter, interest in assessments of this type is strong, with numerous agencies and organizations around the world sponsoring or calling for such activities. However, scant attention has been paid to empirical assessments of the converse issue. Namely, what are the impacts of agri-environmental programs on agricultural trade? The Uruguay Round Agreement on Agriculture (URAA) completed in 1994 under the auspices of GATT, differentiated domestic support policies into various "boxes" according to their effects on production and trade (see Appendix 4 and Box 4.2 in Chapter 2, Section I). "Green Box" policies, or domestic farm programs that meet certain criteria for causing minimal trade distortions, including many agri-environmental programs, were exempted from any expenditure limits.

Agri-environmental payment programs can improve the environmental performance of agriculture and provide an alternative source of farm income (Batie, 1999; Claassen and Horan, 2000; Feather and Cooper, 1995; Lynch and Smith, 1999; Smith, 1992; Chapter 5). Programs that have both environmental and farm income objectives are sometimes referred to as "green payment" programs. The 2002 Farm Bill (formally known as the Farm Security and Rural Investment Act of 2002) creates a new program that can both improve environmental performance and provide some income support to producers. The Conservation Security Program (CSP) can provide payments that exceed the cost-sharing provided by existing programs (for example, the Environmental Quality Incentives Program, or EQIP) for the adoption and/or maintenance of environmentally benign best management practices (BMPs). Beginning in 2003, producers participating in CSP could receive cost sharing in amounts similar to that provided by EQIP for practice adoption, plus cost sharing for the maintenance of previously adopted practices, plus other payments that will depend on the producer's overall level of conservation effort (that is, the number of resource concerns addressed and whether these concerns are addressed on all or only part of the farm). Although many specific implementation decisions that will affect payments are yet to be made, some CSP payments could exceed the producers' cost of adopting the conservation practices.

Unlike commodity program payments, agri-environmental programs meeting the design criteria for the WTO's "green box" would not be subject to the World Trade Organization (WTO) limits on subsidizing production. The CSP is an example of such a program, and is essentially an analog to several types of EU agri-environmental subsidies allowed under their EC Reg. 2078/92.[2] Article 13 ("due restraint"), otherwise known as the "Peace Clause," of the WTO's Agreement on Agriculture protects countries using subsidies that comply with the agreement from being challenged under other WTO agreements. Without this peace clause, under the Subsidies and Countervailing Measures Agreement and related provisions, WTO member countries would have greater freedom to take action against each others' subsidies. However, the peace clause expired at the end of 2003. In the future, an agri-environmental payment program that meets the "basic criteria" and "specific criteria" required for its inclusion in the WTO's "green box" could nonetheless be challenged by WTO member countries on the basis that it does not meet the "fundamental requirement" for inclusion in the green box (see Appendix 4 for the relevant WTO text). Namely, after expiration of the peace clause, even agri-environmental programs that technically satisfy the "criteria" outlined in the green box text could be challenged if some country estimates that the program has more than "minimal" trade-distorting impacts on production.[3] On the other hand, the peace clause could be renewed. In any case, the concept of the green box is an economic concept, and policy instruments that fall into this category are supposed to be minimally trade-distorting (Josling, 2000).

The goal of this chapter is to conduct an *ex ante* analysis of the trade impacts of stylized examples of potential US agri-environmental payment programs. As actual programs of the type we consider here are not yet implemented in the US, we consider several hypothetical programs that are discussed in the next section. To simulate the production and trade impacts of these programs, we use the USMP partial equilibrium model (see Chapter 2, Section I and Appendix 3).

II.   AGRI-ENVIRONMENTAL PROGRAM SCENARIOS

Box 6.1 is a schematic of the links in a chain of impacts that one should factor into a model of the impacts of environmental policy on both environment and trade. To maintain consistency with other ERS research on agri-environmental payments, we consider the trade impacts of the realistic agri-environmental

---

**Box 6.1 Mapping of key factors driving the
economic assessment of the impacts of
agri-enivronmental policy on trade
and the environment**

Change in agri-environmental policy (both domestic and multilateral)
⇓
Changes in domestic production practices, input use and outputs
⇓   ⇓
Changes in physical measures of environmental impacts   ⇓
⇓   ⇓
Changes in economic measures of environmental impacts   Change in world
                                               prices

---

program scenarios in Claassen *et al.* (2001). We examine the impacts of the
programs on exports of the three major grains (corn, wheat, and soybeans) for
three scenarios that cover a range of conservation activities and farm income
support objects. The two bases considered for conservation payments are *good
performance* and *improved performance*. Good performance refers only to the
state of environmental performance, without regard to when that performance
was achieved, while improved performance refers only to actions undertaken
in the context of program enrollment. In these hypothetical scenarios, the environmental objective is to reduce water quality damage due to sediment.
Estimates of sediment damage, including that to freshwater recreation, ditch
maintenance, municipal and industrial water uses, navigation, water storage
capacity, and flooding, are roughly $287 million per year (Feather, Hellerstein
and Hansen, 1999; Ribaudo, 1989). At the farm level, soil conservation or erosion reduction is the focus of the program alternatives.

Our stylized scenarios do not precisely match any existing or pending program. We analyze some program designs that are relatively inefficient in terms
of targeting, and as such, can be expected to have relatively large market
impacts (see Chapter 2 for a discussion of targeting).[4] Payments are based on
erosion rates or erosion reductions and are not crop- specific. While different
crops do have different erosion consequences, payments do not depend directly on crop choice. For each of our three scenarios, we look at a range of payment rates that result in programs that spend as much as $3 billion in agri-
environmental payments to producers. The upper end of this range is as much,
or more than, anticipated expenditures for the new Conservation Security
Program (CSP), for which the Congressional Budget Office (CBO) estimates

expenditures of $2 billion over ten years. Moreover, the estimated potential to increase production, and decrease world prices, would most likely be larger for our scenarios than for CSP, given that CSP has stronger acreage limits than any scenario evaluated here.

The *good performance* base requires the farmer to use a "low rainfall erosion" production system, that is, a production system with a rainfall erosion rate below that for a system using a predominant crop rotation in the region in combination with conventional tillage on the same soil and in the same region. Essentially, this example was chosen as being representative of fairly basic environmentally benign production practices that many farmers already use. Payments per acre under our hypothetical program are equal to soil conserved (tons per acre) multiplied by a payment rate per ton of soil conserved. Soil conserved is the difference between: (1) the maximum erosion rate observed for any production system for a given soil in a given region (the reference level); and (2) the estimated rate of erosion for the "low rainfall erosion" system in use on the same soil in the same region. Payment rates used in the analysis range from $1 to $4 per ton of soil erosion reduction.[5]

The *good performance* base is further broken down into two policy scenarios—*sodbuster* and *no sodbuster*—that have potentially different implications for farm income and expansion of commodity production. *Good performance with the sodbuster* scenario is similar to sodbuster provisions of current commodity policy, and farmers in the program who bring previously uncropped highly erodible land (HEL) into production lose other farm program benefits. With the *good performance with no sodbuster* scenario, farmers in the program who bring previously uncropped highly erodible land (HEL) into production do not lose other farm program benefits. Hence, we would expect *a priori* that the *good performance with no sodbuster* program would be more likely to increase production than that with the *sodbuster* provision.

The *improved performance* base requires the farmer to reduce erosion from pre-program levels. Payments are based on actual erosion reduction from pre-program levels rather than erosion relative to the reference level. Payments per acre under our hypothetical program are equal to erosion reduction (tons per acre) *multiplied* by payment rate per ton of erosion reduction. Payment rates used in the analysis range from $4 to $14 per ton of erosion reduction.[6] Payment rates are higher than under the good performance standard because the program budget (up to $3 billion) can support higher payment rates when funds are focused only on erosion reduction.

The simulation results of the *improved performance* base can serve as a useful comparison to those from the *good performance with sodbuster* as the former is reminiscent of the more economically efficient existing USDA programs that provide financial incentives to adopt BMPs only to farmers that do not currently use the BMPs. One would not expect *a priori* that this improved performance base program would lead to expanded crop production. In fact, the higher the payment, the more willing the farmer is to reduce erosion, and subsequently, the more likely production is to fall; the improved performance scenario requires that erosion be reduced throughout the farm, and hence, initiation of crop production on grass/forest land would count against the producer in terms of total erosion. Hence, the meeting of this expectation by the simulations serves as a check on the reliability of the model.

III. RESULTS OF THE ANALYSIS

For analyzing the impacts of the three programs on production and exports, the scenarios are integrated into the USMP model of the US farm sector (see Appendix 3 for an overview of USMP). The domestic impacts of the alternative program designs are measured in three ways: water quality benefits, the change in farm income, and net costs to the economy. Water quality benefits per ton of soil erosion reduction vary spatially as shown in Figure 6.1 (see Appendix 3 for a discussion of the derivation of the estimated dollar value of water quality damage per ton). Net economic cost is the change in total agricultural producer and consumer incomes that result from the subsidy program.

Figure 6.1 Estimated water quality damage from soil erosion

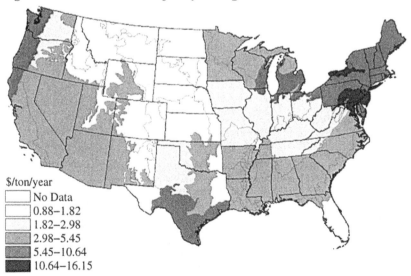

Source: Claassen, et al. (2001)

These costs include the direct cost of changing production management or conservation practices to reduce erosion and indirect costs such as the loss of commodity output if producers shift to less erosive but less productive production
systems.[7] Payments to producers are not a net cost to the economy, but rather
a transfer from taxpayers to agricultural producers.[8]

Water quality benefits are modest relative to net economic costs (Figure 6.2).
The values the public places on reductions in soil erosion have been estimated
for the following environmental amenities: municipal water use, industrial uses,
irrigation ditch maintenance, road ditch maintenance, water storage, flooding,
and soil productivity (Ribaudo *et al.*, 1990; Ribaudo, 1986), freshwater-based

**Figure 6.2 Water quality benefits as a function of payments to
producers and of net economic costs**

Water quality benefits (million dollars)

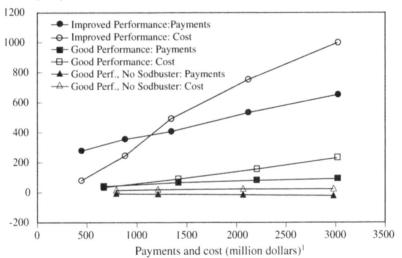

Payments and cost (million dollars)[1]

Notes:
[1] *Producer payments* are the government expenditure for payments to producers, excluding
conservation planning, technical assistance, and enforcement costs. *Measured cost* reflects
the change in total income in the economy required to produce the agri-environmental
gains due to the subsidy program, including the direct cost of changing production
management or conservation practices to achieve environmental gains and indirect costs
such as the loss of commodity output if producers shift to less erosive but less productive
production systems. The *measured costs* reported here *do not include* (1) payments to
producers, (2) government expenditures for program implementation, and (3) economic
costs of raising taxes to fund government program expenditures. Producer payments are
not included because they are transfers of income from taxpayers to agricultural producers
rather that actual costs to the overall economy.

recreation (Feather *et al.*, 1999), and navigation (Hansen *et al.*, 2002). Of course, these represent only a subset of the environmental amenities affected by sediment. Among the amenities not included are increases in waterfowl populations, cleaner coastal and estuarine recreation areas, population survival of endangered species, and quality of commercial fisheries. Therefore, the values used here should be viewed as a minimum estimate of total environmental benefits. Water quality gains as a function of increasing producer payments are greater with the *improved performance* base than with the *good performance with sodbuster* scenario (Figure 6.2). For *good performance without sodbuster*, previously uncropped HEL land is eligible for subsidy payments, so crop production expands significantly onto uncropped HEL, resulting in a net increase in soil erosion and an increase in water quality damage as producer payments increase.

Farm income gains are significant across all policy designs analyzed (Figure 6.3). For the *improved performance* base, farm income gains exceed producer payments because commodity prices rise, albeit modestly. Much of the payment also translates directly into farm income gains because some erosion reduction can be achieved at a cost lower than the payment offered. For example, for a payment of $5 per ton of erosion reduction, producers would take all erosion reduction actions that could be achieved for $5 per ton or *less*. For the *good performance* base, producers mostly collect payment for past conservation actions

Figure 6.3 The relationship between farm income and conservation program payments for the Hypothetical scenarios

Total farm income (million dollars))

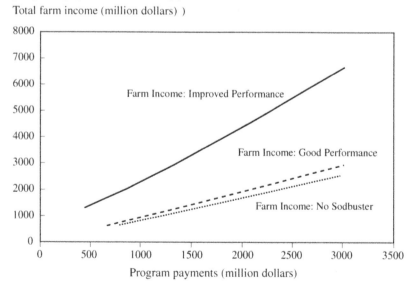

Program payments (million dollars)

and do little to further reduce soil erosion. Commodity prices are largely unaffected. Payments pass through more or less directly to farm income.

Figures 6.4 through 6.6 present the changes in US exports as a function of the agri-environmental stewardship payments by crop. Note, however, that in the analysis, payments are not varied explicitly by commodity. The actual payment system splits the nation into 90 zones (45 USMP regions each with a non-HEL and an HEL soil). For all three commodities, the improved performance program leads to US exports falling as agri-environmental payments increase, with a 7 per cent fall in the case of wheat. Exports increase under the *good performance* with *no sodbuster* provision scenario for all three commodities. Exports are essentially flat, with only slight increases under the *good performance with sodbuster* scenario for all commodities except wheat, which experiences a slight decrease. This decrease is due to some shifting of production from wheat to the other commodities as agri-environmental stewardship payments increase. This switching is likely a consequence of soil conserved varying by commodity, and hence, stewardship payments differing slightly by commodity. If we consider the export increases in percentage terms, the maximum changes for the program with the maximum increase in exports—namely, *good performance without sodbuster provision*—are very small. With increases of

Figure 6.4 Corn exports and stewardship payments

Per cent of current exports

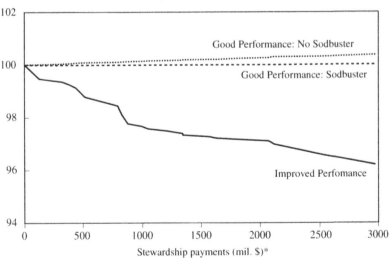

*Total payments to all cereals producers.

Figure 6.5 Wheat exports and stewardship payments

Per cent of current exports

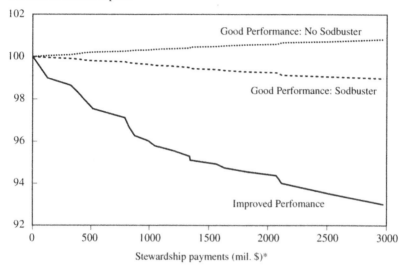

Figure 6.6 Soybeans exports and stewardship payments

Per cent of current exports

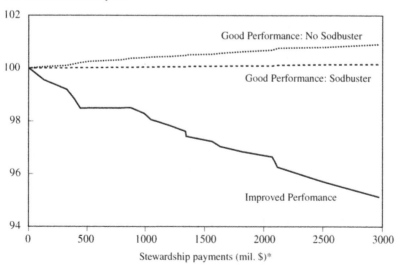

less than 0.5 per cent in the case of corn and approximately 1 per cent for the other two, we do not expect major impacts of the program on the world prices of the commodities, even with this particular program that actually lowers environmental benefits. The 7 per cent fall in wheat exports associated with the *improved performance* scenario is a more notable impact on world trade, but one unlikely to be challenged by other WTO members.

IV. CONCLUSION

As a result of the Uruguay Round in 1995, WTO members agreed that funding for most domestic support policies (through the Aggregate Measure of Support [see glossary for definition]) would have to be reduced. However, an exception was made for agricultural support policies that have a minimal impact on production and trade. Such policies are exempt from funding reductions and are commonly referred to as green box policies.

Given the current interest in the US in expanding agri-environmental payment programs, an important question is whether or not some of these potential programs have more than a "minimal" impact on production and trade. We would expect *a priori* that cost-sharing agreements that simply cover the cost difference per acre of adopting environmentally friendly management practices would have a minimal impact on production and trade. However, addressing the question becomes more complex when the farm stewardship payments have the potential to increase farm income.

The results of our analysis of potential agri-environmental payment programs in the US suggest that they would present minimal trade distortions. While "minimal" in the WTO definition is not defined and is open to interpretation (Nelson, 2002), the maximum increase in predicted exports, at around 1 per cent, is relatively small.[9] In practice, within the WTO trade negotiations context, countries tend not to challenge programs that decrease production, as do some of the scenarios discussed here. As such, inclusion of these programs in the WTO's green box should draw little concern on the basis of their contribution to trade distortion. On the other hand, the three programs considered here may not be considered to meet the specific green box criteria, which state that producers should not be compensated for more than their costs of adopting the practices (see Appendix 4 for the text of the specific criteria, particularly paragraph 12b), and could be challenged on that basis, at least after the Peace Clause expired in 2003. However, more carefully targeted and tailored policies may not be as easily challenged. Note that, as of August 2002, while many of the over 260 disputes brought before the WTO's Dispute Settlement Body since its inception address agricultural issues, none specifically target agri-environmental programs.

A potentially interesting line of research would be to examine the production and trade implications of EU agri-environmental payment programs allowed under regulations EC 2078/92 and 1257/1999. Agri-environmental policy in the EU is in fact now a part of the EU's policy on rural development. Due to this inclusion, it can be difficult to separately identify EU rural development programs (that is, programs that generally address farm income issues) from agri-environmental programs.[10] For example, EU regulation (as embodied in EC 1257/99) allows for compensatory payments to farmers who produce in less favored areas, such as mountainous areas, areas threatened with abandonment, or areas in which "the maintenance of agriculture is necessary to ensure the conservation or improvement of the environment, the management of the landscape, or its tourism value." [11, 12]

A second implication of our analysis applies to potential policy responses to the environmental consequences of agricultural trade liberalization. For instance, it could be possible to respond to regional increases in environmental consequences by targeting those regions with higher levels of agri-environmental payments in order to increase conservation program adoption. Our results demonstrate that the effects of the agri-environmental payments on trade are likely to be small, and hence, bode well for devising a system of harmonization of trade and environmental policy, or perhaps more feasibly in the short run, for developing agri-environmental policy responses to trade-induced environmental consequences (see Appendix 6 for a discussion of the coordination of domestic agri-environmental policies and trade liberalization).

NOTES

1. The views presented herein are those of the authors, and do not necessarily represent the views or policies of the Economic Research Service or the United States Department of Agriculture.

2. EU agri-environmental programs are described in Bernstein, Cooper, and Claassen (2004) and *http://europa.eu.int/comm/agriculture/envir/ programs/evalrep/text_en.pdf.*

3. The peace clause is discussed at *www.wto.org/english/tratop_e/agric_e/negs _bkgrnd10_peace_e.htm.*

4. Programs that are targeted toward farms that are best able to achieve the environmental objectives and in which payments are more carefully tailored to producer costs (even if payments exceed those costs by some modest amount) can be expected to produce greater environmental benefits, at a lower cost to the economy, and with less commodity market impact.

5. For the good performance base, payment to a specific production system is calculated as: S_k $\max(e_k^r - e_{ki}, 0)$ where k indexes regions (a geographic area/soil combination), S_k is the payment rate for region k, e_k^r is the "reference level" for region k, and e_{ki} is the erosion rate for system i in region k. The incentive is fixed so the program size (total government subsidy expenditure) is endogenous.

6. For the *improved performance* base, payment to a specific production system is calculated as: S_k $(e_k^b - e_k)$ where S_k is the payment rate for region k, e_k^b is the erosion pre-program baseline, and e_k is erosion. Essentially each USMP region is treated as a representative farm. Again, the incentive is fixed so the program size (total government subsidy expenditure) is endogenous.

7. Government expenditures for program implementation are a real cost to the economy but could not be included in our modeling framework.

8. Raising government funds through taxation to make these payments imposes real costs on the economy. The economic cost of taxation is the value of economic activity lost due to the tax. Taxes on productive resources will reduce the utilization of those resources. For example, an increase in the tax on labor income may prompt some workers to leave the workforce, reducing production. While the magnitude of these costs is unknown, reasonable estimates range from 20 to 50 cents for each dollar of additional tax revenue (Browning, 1987).

9. In addition, an increase in production and consequent decrease in price as a result of an agri-environmental program could be of domestic policy concern to the extent that it increases the cost of traditional commodity programs such as price supports.

10. See *http://europa.eu.int/comm/agriculture/envir/index_en.htm* for an example of the EU's integration of rural development and conservation.

11. See *http://europa.eu.int/comm/agriculture/envir/programs/evalrep/text_en.pdf* for more detail on EU agri-environmental programs.

12. EC 2078/92 is the forerunner to EC 1257/99.

PART III

Implications for Research and Policy

7. Multilateral environmental agreements and trade

Joseph Cooper and Jonathan Kaplan[1]

I.   INTRODUCTION

Earlier chapters discussed the complications in assessing the relationship between domestic environmental externalities and international trade. Add to this list the complication that arises when environmental issues have an intrinsically transnational or global dimension, in which the actions of one country will affect the welfare of other interested countries. For example, biodiversity in the Amazon rainforest may have implications for US biotechnology or greenhouse gas emissions from any country will affect the atmosphere shared by all countries. However, in the absence of a supranational body, which can issue and enforce directives on environmental policy, the potential gains from policy coordination are limited by the willing participation of diverse and self-interested sovereign countries. The emergence of multilateral environmental agreements (MEAs) as a means to achieving this coordination appears to be growing in the wake of a continuing trend towards globalization of trade and investment. This chapter explores several interrelated themes regarding MEAs, including the economic conditions necessary for MEAs to be successful both in terms of recruiting and retaining parties to the agreements, to contributing to the provision of global public goods, and their relation to trade.

MEAs involve two or more countries entering a mutually beneficial, nonbinding agreement to remediate undesirable environmental impacts, or conserve or enhance desirable environmental goods. One example of the latter is an agreement to conserve genetic diversity in plant genetic resources. These agreements can be complex and their details vary from one agreement to another. However, evidence gathered from existing MEAs reveals several overriding issues. First, membership in an MEA is likely to impose costs on member nations. Second, member nations may not adhere to the language of the agreement. In order to address these compounding issues, an MEA needs to account for compliance and enforcement complications that might arise from the self-interest of nation-states. To achieve this end, MEAs must provide a mechanism for dispute resolution.

Economic incentives embodied in an MEA must motivate participants to accept the provisions of the MEA and must successfully balance the benefits to all participants of signing an MEA with compliance, enforcement, and other costs each participating country may face when administering an MEA. These incentives must provide profitability (that is, benefits exceed costs) for all participants and create a stable environment for all signatories to reap the benefits of participation. If an MEA can create a stable and profitable setting, then the necessary conditions for a self-enforcing MEA exist, thereby increasing the likely success of the MEA. In many situations profitability and stability can be enhanced through transfer payments and issue linkages.

Because costs and benefits may vary among parties, transfer payments can be used to reallocate benefits arising from an MEA to those parties that are adversely affected by the conditions of an MEA. As an alternative, an MEA may link the provision of a global public good with a trade agreement, thereby enhancing the benefits from signing an MEA by providing individual countries with trade-induced benefits as well as any environmental benefits attributable to the MEA. Basically the gains or loss from joining an MEA may require some form of compensation whether it be directly through transfer payments or indirectly through trade agreements.

To date, little formal connection of MEAs with trade agreements exists, with the North American Free Trade Agreement (NAFTA) being the only example of a trade agreement containing an environmental side agreement. There are approximately 200 multilateral environmental agreements in place today. Only 20 of these contain trade provisions (UNEP, 2000). These are the subject of frequent discussion in the WTO's Committee on Trade and Environment (CTE). Linking MEAs to trade agreements may also be an economically efficient method for mitigating potential adverse environmental impacts of trade or minimizing the impacts on trade of environmental agreements.

The compensation of signatory parties to an MEA for any potential losses due to the conditions of the MEA led us to examine potential funding mechanisms for the provision of a global public good when an MEA is created. How will the signatory countries allocate the costs and benefits associated with an operating MEA? Will this allocation be done through transfer payments or through linkages with trade agreements? The low percentage of MEAs linked to trade agreement suggests that transfer payments may be a more likely avenue for increasing the number of countries joining an MEA.

Nonetheless, further investigation into understanding the relationship between MEAs and trade agreements could assist policymakers in reducing adverse environmental consequences that could arise from increased trade. At the same time, because MEAs can restrict the free flow of goods between countries, they can also potentially conflict with trade agreements. With these issues in mind, we begin with an overview of the theoretical literature on the conditions for building a successful MEA. We then move to a review of the relationships between existing MEAs and agricultural trade. Section IV addresses transfer payments and the provision of global public goods through an MEA, using the example of an agricultural MEA. The concluding section discusses the feasibility of devising a meaningful set of agri-environmental indicators for use in an MEA.

II. THE DESIGN OF MULTILATERAL ENVIRONMENTAL AGREEMENTS

This section addresses on a conceptual basis some of the major issues regarding MEAs, including those associated with their voluntary nature, their implicit and explicit linkages to trade, and the potential for conflicts between MEAs and between MEAs and trade agreements. The issue of financing an MEA, that is, how much each party pays, is covered in section IV in the context of an agricultural example.

At the subnational level, both voluntary and involuntary compliance mechanisms are available tools for attaining environmental objectives. However, the essential feature of MEAs is that they cannot be enforced by a third party, that is, they must be self-enforcing for the simple reason that countries cannot be forced to join an MEA.[2] Because of this self-enforcing property, only incentive-based voluntary approaches provide the mechanism for encouraging participation in an MEA. Moreover, once a country has joined an MEA, it can choose to withdraw from the agreement at any time. Hence, an enduring MEA must accomplish two goals. The MEA must appear beneficial to potential signatories and once a nation has joined an MEA, the nation must want to carry out the terms of the agreement.

A substantial body of literature has evolved in the area of self-enforcing MEAs (see, for example, Barrett, 1994b; Batabyal, 2000; Carraro and Sinascalo, 1993). A self-enforcing MEA is one from which no signatory, acting on its own, wishes to withdraw and to which no nonsignatory, acting on its own, wishes to accede. In other words, an MEA is self-enforcing when it is profitable and stable (Carraro, 1997).

Where MEAs exist they are signed by a limited number of countries (Barrett, 1994b; Carraro and Siniscalco, 1993). Why? One explanation given is that signing an environmental agreement may not be profitable for all countries involved in the negotiation process. A second explanation stems from the intrinsic instability of environmental agreements. That is, some countries may receive benefits from the environmental improvement achieved by the signatory countries (because the environmental benefit is not excludable) while not actually signing the environmental agreement because participating in the agreement involves incurring costs (that is, they free ride). Cooperation thus becomes unstable.

Two sets of instruments have been proposed to increase the number of signatories to an environmental agreement when these nonprofitable and free-riding conditions exist. These instruments are issue linkages and transfers. To increase the number of signatories, a negotiation mechanism in which countries negotiate not only on environmental issues but also on an interrelated economic issue (that is, issue linkages) may be necessary to fortify the stability condition. For example, Barrett (1994b) proposes linking environmental negotiations to trade liberalization negotiations. Trade restrictions may also be a useful issue linkage tool. By "linking" two issues, some countries can gain from a given issue and other countries can gain on a second one (Carraro, 1997). NAFTA and its environmental side agreement, the North American Agreement on Environmental Cooperation (NAAEC) rely on this issue linkage approach. In this case, profitability and stability are achieved by linking an MEA and a trade agreement. The NAAEC agreement outlines environmental objectives, such as the promotion of sustainable development, enhancing compliance with and enforcement of environmental laws and regulations, and promoting policies and practices to prevent pollution (Nimon, Cooper and Smith, 2002). NAFTA remains unique in that it is the only trade agreement to address environmental concerns explicitly in an accompanying agreement.

The alternative approach to increasing the number of signatories may require transfer payments to be used for achieving the profitability goal (Carraro, 1997). Transfers can be used to compensate those countries that face economic losses under the provisions of an MEA. A redistribution of benefits from those who gain to those who lose may satisfy the profitability condition necessary for a self-enforcing agreement to exist. Note that transfers need not be explicitly in the form of money. For example, a transfer could be in the form of capacity building or technological assistance, as has been provided by the US to Chile in the 2001–2002 negotiations of the US–Chile FTA (USTR, undated). An important point worth noting here is that incentives such as technology assistance may be useful in encouraging developing countries to join an MEA but may be insufficient to encourage developed countries to join an MEA and comply with it, outside of any benefits they would otherwise receive through membership.

In some sense, there is a likely correspondence between the profitability of a multilateral agreement and the strength of the compliance mechanism. Namely, if the benefit of being a party to an agreement is large and relatively clear-cut, then it may be reasonable to assume that the compliance mechanisms will be relatively more effective than an MEA with benefits that are difficult to quantify. However, the benefits of joining an MEA are often difficult to quantify and thus the motivation to join an MEA is lower than for a trade agreement, and consequently, greater positive incentives for compliance are necessary to encourage universal membership in the MEA.

Although MEAs are a relatively new phenomenon, the institutional arrangements are fairly well established for those with issue linkages. Namely, either an MEA can have a trade provision or a trade agreement can have an MEA component. NAFTA is the only trade agreement to date with an environmental side agreement. Conversely, about 10 per cent of MEAs have trade measure provisions (UNEP, 2000).

Trade-restricting measures can play an enforcement role when linked to an MEA by barring nonparties from trading in restricted goods with parties to the MEA. For instance, if a country is not a party to the Basel Convention, then that country cannot export waste to or import waste from any of the parties. These trade restrictions help ensure the MEA's effectiveness. Without these restrictions "leakage" can occur, where nonparties increase production of the restricted good and export it to the parties that have restricted their own production, possibly in violation of WTO trade rules.

Resolving trade disputes when trade restrictions are used as an enforcement tool may be complicated. Suppose, for example, that a trade dispute arises because a country has taken action on trade (for example, imposed a tax or restricted imports) under an environmental agreement outside the WTO and another country objects. Should the dispute be handled under the WTO or under the other agreement? The WTO's Committee on Trade and Environment says that if a dispute arises over a trade action taken under an environmental agreement, and if both sides to the dispute have signed that agreement, then they should try to use the environmental agreement to settle the dispute. But if one side in the dispute has not signed the environment agreement, then the WTO would provide the only possible forum for settling the dispute. That does not mean environmental issues would be downplayed, as the WTO agreements allow panels examining a dispute to seek expert advice on environmental issues. To add to the complexity, note that MEAs and trade agreements may take different approaches to enforcement and dispute resolution.[3]

III. MULTILATERAL ENVIRONMENTAL AGREEMENTS AND AGRICULTURAL TRADE

Recent history suggests that MEAs can be linked to agricultural trade either formally (albeit rarely), through explicit trade provisions in the MEAs, or indirectly through jurisdictional overlaps. A few examples of each type of MEA and agricultural trade interactions are provided to illustrate the variation of these interactions and the possible implications of each type of interaction.

MEAs with specific trade restrictions are most common and date back to the Convention on International Trade in Endangered Species of Wild Fauna and Flora (CITES) which entered into force in 1975. CITES bans commercial international trade in an agreed list of endangered species. It also regulates (by use of permits, quotas and other restrictive measures) and monitors trade in other species that might become endangered. CITES works by subjecting international trade in specimens of selected species to certain controls. These require that all import, export, re-export and introduction from the list of species covered by the Convention has to be authorized through a licensing system. ('Re-export' means export of a specimen that was imported.)

The USDA's Animal and Plant Health Inspection Service (APHIS) is the US agency responsible for enforcing the provisions of CITES related to plants. In 1999, 19 million of the 694 million plants inspected were regulated as endangered species. Plants protected by CITES that arrive for inspection without appropriate documentation are seized immediately and eventually may be distributed to designated "rescue centers" throughout the United States such as the Smithsonian Institution in Washington, DC.

Another example of an MEA with explicit trade restriction is the Montreal Protocol on Substances that Deplete the Stratospheric Ozone Layer, which became enforceable in 1987. The Montreal Protocol lists certain substances as ozone-depleting, and bans all trade in those substances between parties and nonparties. Similar bans may be implemented against parties as part of the Protocol's noncompliance procedure. In this sense the threat of additional bans may constitute issue linkages as an enforcement tool. The Protocol also contemplates allowing import bans on products made with, but not containing, ozone-depleting substances—a ban based on process and production methods.

In particular, the Montreal Protocol affects international use of methyl bromide that is not only used as a soil fumigant in some high value crops, but has also been used to meet fumigation and quarantine requirements for international trade of agricultural commodities. Most uses of methyl bromide in the US will be phased out under the Montreal Protocol. There are differential restrictions on developed and developing countries, raising the question of whether restrictions will simply cause a "migration" of methyl bromide use to developing countries (Frisvold, 2002).

Yet another example of direct trade restrictions as a provision of an MEA is found in the Basel Convention on the Control of Transboundary Movement of Hazardous Wastes and their Disposal, set into force in 1992. Parties may only export hazardous waste to another party that has not banned its import and that consents to the import in writing. Parties to this agreement may not import hazardous waste from or export hazardous waste to a nonparty. They are also obliged to prevent the import or export of hazardous wastes if they have reason to believe that the wastes will not be treated in an environmentally sound manner at their destination.

The Rotterdam Convention on the Prior Informed Consent Procedure for Certain Hazardous Chemicals and Pesticides in International Trade (PIC), which was completed in 1998 but as yet is not in force, restricts the flow of chemicals and pesticides through trade. Parties to the PIC can decide, from the Convention's agreed list of chemicals and pesticides, which ones they cannot manage safely and, therefore, will not import. When trade in the controlled substances does take place, labeling and information requirements must be followed. Decisions taken by the parties must be trade neutral—if a party decides not to consent to imports of a specific chemical, it must also stop domestic production of the chemical for domestic use, as well as imports from any nonparty. PIC requires exporters trading in a list of hazardous substances to obtain the prior informed consent of importers before proceeding with the trade. PIC also sets an international legal precedent for informed consent and labeling requirements.

Similar to PIC, the Cartagena Protocol on Biosafety, which was completed in 2000 and (as is the case for PIC) is yet to be ratified and put into force, restricts the import of some living genetically modified organisms (GMOs) as part of a carefully specified risk management procedure. Living GMOs that will be intentionally released to the environment are subject to an advance informed agreement procedure, and those destined for use as food, feed or processing must be accompanied by documents identifying them.

We see from the above examples that MEAs may be integrally related to agricultural trade. However, this is just part of the story. MEAs may promote activities that are inconsistent with provisions set out in trade agreements or have jursditional overlap, which leaves open the question of how and where disputes may be resolved. Among the jurisdictional overlaps between MEAs and trade agreements that may be relevant for agriculture are (1): the Cartegna Biosafety Protocol with the WTO's Sanitary and Phytosanitary (SPS) Agreement and the Technical Barriers to Trade (TBT) Agreement; and (2) the International Treaty on Plant Genetic Resources, the Convention on Biological Diversity, and the WTO's Trade-Related Aspects of Intellectual Property Rights (TRIPS) Trips Agreements.

The SPS agreement sets out the basic WTO rules for how governments can apply food safety and animal and plant health measures (sanitary and phytosanitary or SPS measures). The TBT agreement tries to ensure that countries do not use regulations, standards, testing and certification procedures as excuses for trade protectionism. However, the Biosafety Protocol also deals explicitly with potential problems associated with GMOs. Nelson *et al.* (1999) note the potential for duplicative regulation, with the potential consequence for environmental and other nonmarket impacts of GMOs to escape regulation due to the confusion over jurisdiction one can expect from overlapping regulations.

The International Treaty on Plant Genetic Resources establishes a system that facilitates broad access to a list of crops crucial to food security. This includes materials in gene banks, farmers' fields and in the wild. The agreement also provides for the exchange of information and technology between countries, particularly to benefit developing countries and countries in transition. It also calls for "equitable sharing" of the financial benefits resulting from the use of the plant genetic resources covered by the system (this benefit-sharing issue is discussed further in the fourth section). Mandatory payments will be required when commercial benefits are obtained from the use of these resources, but the commercial product derived from these resources is not available for research and plant breeding. Payments will be voluntary, however, when a commercial product derived from these resources is still available for research and plant breeding. These payments will be used for priority activities, particularly in developing countries and countries in transition. However, the agreement does not spell out exactly how the conservation of plant genetic resources for food and agriculture is to be financed multilaterally. The WTO TRIPS council discussions have also addressed the issue of benefit sharing when inventors in one country have rights to creations based on material obtained from another country (WTO, 2002a), which with respect to agriculture could present a source of conflict (for example, possible jurisdictional overlaps) with the International Treaty's treatment of benefit sharing. In addition, the issue of potential conflict between TRIPS and the CBD has been raised in the WTO TRIPS Council (*ibid.*), although specific concerns are not elaborated.

As these examples suggest, MEAs have important implications for agricultural trade. The linkages and jurisdictional overlaps between MEAs and trade agreements suggest that trade will be affected not only through multilateral trade negotiations, but also multilateral environmental negotiations. Hence, interest in agricultural trade policy may require a better understanding of environmental negotiations. Indeed, according to Article 31 of the Doha WTO Ministerial Declaration, trade ministers agreed to launch negotiations on the relationship between existing WTO rules and specific trade obligations set out in multilateral environmental agreements. The negotiations will address how WTO rules are to apply to WTO members that are parties to environmental agreements. The WTO Committee on Trade and Environment is in the process of identifying "special trade concerns" in relevant MEAs and identifying WTO rules relevant to those obligations (for example, WTO, 2001c).

IV. FINANCING THE PROVISION OF GLOBAL PUBLIC GOODS THROUGH MEAS; AN AGRICULTURAL CASE STUDY

How does an MEA finance the provision of a global public good? More specifically, how much will each country "contribute" in terms of financing, pollution abatement, and so on, to allow for the provision of a global environmental good? We now turn to the task of choosing a funding mechanism to make an MEA operational in the case of the conservation of plant genetic resources for food and agriculture. Our goal in doing so is to demonstrate that developing funding mechanisms that serve as valid proxies for the value of environmental benefits and economic costs is not clear-cut.

Agricultural genetic resources are a key input into the development of new crop varieties. Between 1961 and 1999, per capita cereal production increased by 22 per cent while total acreage devoted to cereals increased by only 4.9 per cent.[4] This increase in productivity may be attributable to an increase in fertilizer, pesticide, and water use. However, much of the increase in yields may also be the result of genetic improvements to cultivars made possible through the breeding of new crop varieties. Modern production systems are frequently characterized by their domination by monoculture, the adoption of which can lead to decreased genetic diversity. The concern over the erosion of genetic resources may be linked in part to the increasing globalization of the economy, which has led to the adoption of modern plant varieties around the world and in turn, possible loss of tradition plant varieties. At the same time, some developing countries perceive that major international corporations that are mainly from developed countries are likely to earn much income through the utilization of genetic materials that have been conserved mainly by farmers in developing countries. The desire to maintain national sovereignty over their genetic resources has led to at least a dozen countries establishing controls over access to their genetic resources, and an equal number of nations developing such controls (Convention on Biological Diversity, 2002).[5]

Regardless of the merit of these concerns and actions, enough international concern has developed over the need to conserve agricultural genetic resources that, in April 1999, the 161 member nations of the UN-based Commission on Genetic Resources for Food and Agriculture (CGRFA) agreed that a multilateral system of access and benefit sharing should be established for key crops, with proposals for payment for conservation of agricultural genetic resources in developing countries. This proposal falls under the auspices of the International Undertaking (IU) on Plant Genetic Resources for Food and Agriculture (PGRFA), which is the first comprehensive international agreement dealing with plant genetic resources for food and agriculture. The IU is an evolving international agreement related to the Convention on Biological Diversity, yet a separate agreement in its own right. According to the proposal, financing of the Global Plan of Action for the conservation and sustainable development of plant genetic resources will cost the international community an estimated $155 to $455 million (US) annually (CGRFA, 1999). The "fair and equitable sharing of benefits arising from the use of PGRFA" is expected to be in the "form of transfer of technology, capacity building, the exchange of information, and funding," with the benefits flowing primarily to farmers in developing countries for the conservation of these resources (CGRFA, 2000).[6] In return, the parties agree to facilitate access to PGRFA while at the same time respecting intellectual and other property rights over these resources. In November 2001, the 161 member nations of CGRFA agreed that a multilateral system of access and benefit-sharing should be established for key crops and approved the legally binding International Treaty on Plant Genetic Resources for Food and Agriculture. This treaty will enter into force after ratification by 40 countries.

A subsequent step is to define each party's financial contribution to a benefit-sharing fund. The difficulty with determining each signatory's contribution to a fund comes down to choosing an appropriate metric or indicator that is economically relevant and available for all countries. Agricultural biodiversity "hotspots" tend to be in the developing world, while modern commercial varieties based on PGRFAs tend to be developed and marketed by developed countries. As such, many active promoters of benefit-sharing assert that developed countries are benefiting more from the utilization of PGRFAs from developing countries than do the developing countries themselves, and that these developing countries are not being compensated for use of these resources. On the other hand, while developed countries benefit from new varieties produced using PGRFAs supplied by developing countries, consumers and producers in developing countries may use these new varieties, and hence, benefit from the product development performed in developed countries.

From an economic standpoint, it seems reasonable to tie a country's contribution to the benefit-sharing fund to the benefits it receives. Unfortunately, as noted above, these benefits may be difficult to quantify, except perhaps in limited cases. An alternative can be to appeal to indicators that take equity and development considerations into account in determining contributions given that political considerations dictate that a benefit-sharing fund be created. An indicator is a measurable entity that can serve as a proxy for the costs and benefits attributable to an MEA.

In a world with full information and political cooperation, contributions towards a benefit-sharing arrangement would, from an incentive-compatible perspective, be based on the net economic benefits to each member country, given that the benefit-sharing fund requires contributions from each of the member countries endorsing the international undertaking. Unfortunately, primarily because PGRFAs have the public good characteristics of being nonexcludable, their economic value is not expressed in the market and estimating their benefits to society is difficult at best. The result is an inaccurate measure of the benefits of PGRFA conservation when one of the readily available indicators is used as a proxy. While existing indicators cannot be explicitly based on benefits, the next best option may be to identify existing indicators that are politically acceptable to the parties involved in the negotiations and that appear to have some connection to the benefits associated with the MEA. For example, the following metric can be used to identify each country's contribution to a benefit-sharing fund based upon an agreed upon indicator,

$$C_l = (Total\ Fund\ Value) * \left(Indicator_l \middle/ \sum_l^N Indicator_l \right)$$

where *Indicator$_l$* is the value of the indicator for that country, and $l = 1, ..., N$ countries. Under this formula, every country makes a contribution to the fund. Table 7.1 presents a list of potential country level indicators for benefit sharing. No claim is made that this list is all-inclusive, but it does cover a broad range of indicators. Take Gross Domestic Product (GDP) as an example of an indicator. Using this indicator in the equation above, a country with a larger share of world GDP contributes more to the fund than a country with a lower share.[7]

It is important to note that equity considerations can be important from a policymaking standpoint but allocating costs and benefits based on equity may rely on subjective criteria. On the other hand, economic efficiency uses objective criteria for allocating resources. Under the efficiency criteria, the resources would be allocated such that the marginal benefits of the resources equal their marginal cost. However, an allocation based on the economic efficiency criteria alone may not be particularly relevant at the international level, where equity considerations are a prime concern (Cline, 1992; Hagem and Westskog, 1998; Rose et al., 1998). Unfortunately, no consensus exits on the best definition of equity (Rose and Stevens, 1998). While efficiency–equity tradeoffs receive substantial attention in the mainstream economics literature, equity concerns receive little attention in the resource economics literature. Realistically, however, political realities can require equity concerns to be of important, or even prime, concern. Methodological rules for interactions between efficiency and equity theory have yet to be worked out.

Advantages and Disadvantages of Select Indicators

In this section, we address the merits of each statistic in Table 7.1 as an indicator for benefit sharing. The value of agricultural production (VAP) indicator has several desirable characteristics. First, this indicator is readily available for each country and, among the indicators listed in Table 7.1, is most tied to the value of agricultural activities as it is the value of agriculture production at the farm gate. Second, it is equitable (though perhaps not relative to Gross Domestic Product) in the sense that countries with greater agricultural value pay more, which is analogous to a progressive income tax on agriculture.[8] For instance, if the US payment to the fund were based on its share of total average annual worldwide value of agricultural production, its contribution would represent 12.7 per cent of the total value of the fund. Since most developing countries represent only small shares of the total value of agricultural production, their contribution would be small.

The justification for the use of Gross Domestic Product (GDP), Agricultural Gross Domestic Product (AGDP), and "seed industry profits and/or revenues" indicators are similar to those for VAP. GDP is the value added at each stage of production of all goods and services during one year. A potential benefit of VAP over GDP from a negotiation standpoint is that an indicator based on the former is at least directly tied to agricultural production, if not to the value of PGRFAs. AGDP, which is the value-added only of agricultural goods and services, is more closely tied to agriculture than is GDP but includes the value of services that are not directly related to agricultural production. Its use as an indicator would explicitly acknowledge that consumers and food processors as well as farmers and seed companies benefit from PGRFAs. Therefore, when GDP or AGDP is used as the basis for a funding mechanism, countries which benefit on the consumer side but are without an agricultural production base will contribute to the fund. Similar to VAP, the large size of AGDP relative to any realistic prediction for the total size of the fund suggests that a benefit-sharing payment at the retail level is unlikely to produce significant market effects. In practice, the indicators VAP, GDP, and AGDP are all highly correlated with one another and a country's share of the contributions to the Fund would be similar using any of these as a basis.

As a proportion of total revenues, commercial seed producers are probably the stakeholders most dependent on access to PGRFAs, and therefore, seed industry profits and/or revenues by country could be among the class of measures that may be obtainable, the one most highly correlated with the value of PGRFAs. However, this measure is not currently available for all countries, but with data available for 39 countries, it has better coverage than some other indicators. Given the International Association of Plant Breeders' (ASSINSEL)

Table 7.1 Potential country level indicators for an MEA designed to share the benefits from the utilization of agricultural plant genetic resources

Indicator	Observability[1]	Equity[2]	Correlation[3]
1. Value of agricultural product	+	−	−
2. Gross domestic product	+	+	−
3. Agricultural gross domestic product	+	−	−
4. Seed industry profits and/or revenues	−	+	+
5. The value of agricultural commodities produced using intellectual property rights [IPR] material	−	+	+
6. Value of commodities produced using improved (e.g., "Green Revolution") varieties	−	+	+
7. Royalties earned on agricultural patents	−	+	+
8. Agricultural research and development expenditures by country	−	+	−
9. Plant protection titles issued	−	+	−
10. Number of landraces used in agriculture	−	−	−
11. Domestic-origin patents used in the agricultural and food sectors	−	+	−
12. Matrix of varietal exchange and matrix of parental exchange	−	−	−
13. Diversity measures	−	−	−

Notes: The scale "−" / "+" are used to construct relative ranking within the group of the 13 potentially feasible indicators

[1] Ease in obtaining the data for all countries (and/or crops), where "+"obtainable for all countries and "−"not obtainable for all countries.

[2] In terms of income (re)distribution from developed to less developed countries within the group, "+" = most equitable and "−" = least equitable (assumes that the higher a country's value for an indicator, the more it contributes to the fund).

[3] Subjective ranking of correlation between the true value of PGRFAs and the listed indicator. As this is a relative ranking, no implication is made that any of these indicators are anywhere close to the true value, merely that "+"coded indicators may be closer to the true value than "−" coded indicator.

Source: Cooper (2001).

definition of "commercial seed producer," the value at the world level of the commercial seed industry is $30 billion per year (ASSINSEL, 1998).[9] If industry profits are around 10 per cent, then a $50 million benefit sharing tax levied on the industry represents 1.7 per cent of profits and a $300 million tax represents 10 per cent of profits. While the extent to which this increase in cost would be passed on to downstream stakeholders depends on supply and demand conditions in each stakeholder's market, the relatively large ratio of the tax to total profits (or revenues) suggests that a tax aimed only at commercial seed producers would produce more notable price impacts, at least in the market for seed, than a tax at the farm gate or retail level.

The indicator "value of agricultural commodities produced using intellectual property rights (IPR) material" is more narrow in scope than the previously mentioned indicators. This indicator is available for only a few countries, making it difficult to develop a benefit-sharing mechanism. The indicator "value of agricultural commodities produced using improved varieties" has a slightly broader scope than the IPR indicator, but the term "improved" must be clearly defined. Under many possible definitions, one could expect that all varieties grown in developed countries are improved. If this is the case, this indicator would be the same as the VAP for these countries, but for developing countries the values would be difficult to estimate given the lack of data.

The indicator "royalties earned on agricultural patents," along with the indicator "seed industry profits and/or revenues," focuses on stakeholders who may be the most dependent on PGRFAs relative to other stakeholders. Again the caveat must be noted that the value of the PGRFA contribution cannot be easily separated from the value of the research contribution. At any rate, the royalty data tend to be proprietary, and hence, little of it is available.

The indicator based upon "agricultural research and development expenditures" reflects a country's capacity for upstream use of PGRFAs. It is likely that the higher a country's R&D expenditures are, the greater its relative financial benefits from the use of PGRFAs. This expenditure reflects the R&D industries' expected share of the total value-added in the marketplace resulting from their development of new products, that is, the presumption is that the industries will not spend more than they expect to earn. However, the measure does not include the share of the benefits received by users (both producers and consumers) of the new products. A practical disadvantage is that it is not available for many countries and that private and public expenditures may have to be disentangled.

Unlike the first eight indicators listed in Table 7.1, indicators 9–13 are nonmonetary measures. These nonmonetary measures share the same drawback as the available monetary ones, that is, the connection between them and the value of PGRFAs is unknown. The International Union for the Protection of

New Varieties of Plants (UPOV) charts certificate applications and titles issued for plant variety protection, and has made the data available for 28 member countries (UPOV, 1995).[10] The indicator "number of rice landraces used in agriculture" is available for rice for select countries from the International Rice Research Institute, along with a tabulation by country of own and borrowed rice landraces. Data on "domestic-origin patents used in the agricultural and food sector" are available only for some countries. The indicator "matrix of varietal exchange and matrix of parental exchange" tracks international exchanges of varieties and is available for rice for selected countries.

With nonmonetary measures such as these, one essentially has the problem of comparing apples and oranges. For example, one country could hold 20 plant protection titles, but the sum of their values could be less than one plant protection title held by another country. Most likely, a large proportion of the total value of improved varieties is ascribed to a small percentage of improved varieties. This asymmetry is apparently the case for US university-held patents, in which only a few patents (and universities) account for most of US university royalties on patents (AUTM, 1993). Given the small number of commercially successful varieties relative to the total number of available varieties in genebanks (FAO, 1998), there is reason to believe that this asymmetry is also true for the economic value of PGRFAs. That said, monetary measures as a basis for contributions have the advantage that contributions tend to be equitable (contributors with higher incomes often pay more) and may be rationalized from a development aid standpoint.

The final category in the table (Diversity Measures) covers indicators of PGRFA diversity. Many different measures are available, and no single measure can satisfy all aspects of diversity (see for example, Ferris and Humphrey, 1999). These diversity measures are most useful for tracking changes in diversity over time and for assessing the impact of conservation measures. As with the other indicators, the relationship between this indicator class and the value of the PGRFAs is unclear. Unless the diversity itself is of value (which may be the case for wild species and ecosytems), the degree of crop diversity in a country is somewhat irrelevant as a proxy for the value of PGRFAs. Instead, it is their current or future contribution to agricultural production and to protecting agricultural production (for example, from disease) that are of value, and not the resources themselves (Cooper, 1998). For instance, while two countries may have the same genetic diversity index, there is little reason to assume that their respective contributions to the value of agriculture are equal.

After weighing the advantages and disadvantages of each of the listed indicators, the value of agricultural production (VAP) and agricultural gross domestic product (AGDP) appear to be "superior" in the case of PGRFA conservation. If each country's contribution to a benefit-sharing fund is the ratio of its indicator value to the total world value of the indicator, then application of either of these indicators will be progressive, primarily with respect to equity considerations, but also with respect to efficiency considerations.[11] That is to say that although all countries contribute, those countries with higher VAP and AGDP benefit from PGRFA more than those with lower values and also pay more.

V. DISCUSSION AND CONCLUSIONS

In the second section of this chapter we reviewed the necessary conditions for designing a successful multilateral environmental agreement (MEA)—profitability and stability. When these conditions are not met, economic incentives such as transfers and issue linkage can be used to enhance the ability of the MEA to maintain profitability and stability. To implement transfers, whether monetary or not, a proxy measure of the benefits and costs of an MEA is required, as is a mechanism for reallocating these benefits and costs across participants in the MEA. Linking an MEA with a trade agreement may increase the potential for success of an MEA. However, because MEAs can restrict the free flow of goods between countries, they can also potentially conflict with WTO trade rules. Even so, no country to date has ever challenged a measure purportedly undertaken in pursuance of an MEA before the WTO.

Next, we focused attention on the mechanism for allocating costs and explored the real world example of how to develop a set of indicators for use in funding an MEA that seeks to reduce the potential loss of genetic diversity in agriculture. As the illustration shows, developing indicators that are reasonable proxies for the value of this diversity and can be supplied by both developed and developing countries is difficult. Furthermore, developing countries in general have been voicing concern over the difficulties they experience in fulfilling all of their reporting obligations to multilateral agencies, such as the UN (Seki, 2000).

If an MEA requires member countries to meet specific environmental targets or to fund the provision of a global public good, then environmental indicators become necessary. An environmental indicator measures environmental quality, whether as a measure of the physical quantity itself or of the monetary impact of that quantity. For agriculture, in particular, indicators generally include measures of land use changes between agriculture and other land uses, both on-farm and off-farm impacts of soil erosion, total agricultural water use, nutrient balances, pesticide use, and water quality (OECD, 2002). Obviously some decision on the choice of indicators is necessary if one is to make inter-regional comparisons of the environmental benefits from the MEA.[12]

The OECD has developed a "core set ... of commonly agreed indicators for OECD countries and for international use..." (OECD, 2001a). According to the OECD, the purpose of developing this set of core indicators is to:

- allow countries to track environmental progress;
- ensure integration of environmental concerns into sectoral policies (for example, agriculture);
- ensure integration of environmental concerns into economic policies;
- measure environmental performance;
- determine whether countries are on track towards sustainable development.

Among the criteria for selecting a core set of indicators is that the indicators are policy-relevant, analytically sound, measurable, and easily interpreted (OECD, 2000).

This set of OECD indicators could be used to assess whether or not countries are meeting environmental commitments specified under an MEA. Environmental indicators can also be used to determine a country's funding obligations to an MEA, as well as disbursements from an MEA to member countries, say for conservation efforts. With respect to the agricultural sector, the OECD is seeking to develop 'agri-indicators' to better integrate environmental and economic policies with the goal of sustainable agriculture in mind.[13] While developing such indicators may be a relatively easy task for an MEA seeking to address some fairly concrete externality, such as loss of forest cover, it is not as easy for many of the by-products of agriculture, especially agricultural amenities, which are quite abstract.

The genetic resources example discussed here is not the only multilateral environmental issue in agriculture for which finding relevant indicators is difficult. Another one is the debate between a number of OECD member countries over the "multifunctionality of agriculture," a concept which claims that agriculture produces a number of nonmarketed positive externalities (OECD, 2001b), and is discussed in detail in Chapter 2. In the context of agricultural trade negotiations, some developed countries assert that the impact on the production of these externalities of the lowering of agricultural subsidies and barriers to trade needs to be considered. However, developing indicators for the values of the externalities that can benefit multilateral trade negotiations over "multifunctional" issues is no simple task. For example, the scenic value of an additional acre of agricultural land will vary across regions simply due to the relative differences in supplies of such land and due to differences in preferences and incomes. Moreover, a scenic attribute that is valuable in one location is not necessarily of the same value outside of its original context. Namely, the values of the attributes of a landscape are part of a bundle of landscape attributes that cannot be easily separated from their location (for example, Fry, 1994, p. 51). For instance, the stone wall that looks nice in an agricultural landscape in the South of France may look incongruous placed in the Kansas countryside. That old wood fence that is an attractive part of rural landscapes in Virginia may look inappropriate if placed in the countryside outside of Florence, Italy (and most likely, land use controls in that region would no doubt prohibit installation of such a fence that is nontraditional to that area). Given the somewhat abstract nature of what attributes of landscapes contribute to their values, developing a common set of physical indicators across countries that can serve as proxies for these values is not likely.

It is worth mentioning in closing that no indicator exists that will be more than a imprecise guide for how to distribute the cost of any benefit-sharing fund in an economically efficient fashion. Obviously, the ideal indicator relies on fully observable environmental and economic benefits, and thus increases the possibilities for efficient and equitable distribution of any and all benefit-sharing funds. However, at least having some reasonable indicators available as a guide may reduce the potential for the funds being distributed through an opaque process.

NOTES

1. The views presented herein are those of the authors, and do not necessarily represent the views or policies of the Economic Research Service or the United States Department of Agriculture.

2. If one could design and empower an international institution to intervene for the good of all, then international environmental problems would be easier to redress. However, national sovereignty considerations are generally an effective stumbling block in the design of international institutions with enforcement power. Not only does a successful MEA have to account for the nonexistence of a supranational authority that can address transboundary pollution problems; it must also address the fact that most countries differ considerably with respect to environmental, economic, political and demographic characteristics.

3. For example, Eggers and Mackenzie (2000) discuss how the Cartagena Protocol and the WTO SPS and TBT Agreements take different approaches to similar issues.

4. "Cereals" include wheat, rice, barley, maize, millet, sorghum, as well as other grains. These figures are derived from the FAOSTAT database (*www.fao.org*).

5. See Barton and Christensen (1988), Cooper (2001), Frisvold and Condon (1998), Knudson (1999), and Swaminathan (1996) for discussions of these and other related issues.

6. PGRFAs consist of the diversity of genetic material contained in all domestic cultivars as well as wild plant relatives and other wild plant species and plant matter (germplasm) that are used in the breeding of new varieties—either through traditional breeding or through modern biotechnology techniques.

7. Climate change mitigation presents a parallel literature on developing formulas for making country allocations. In that case the question is what formula should be used for setting greenhouse gas emission reduction targets. Authors in that literature have suggested indicators for making allocations such as GDP, historical emissions, population, and energy use (Cline, 1992; Panayotou, Sachs and Zwane, 2002; Rose *et al.*, 1998).

8. The relative size of VAP with respect to GDP tends to be higher for developing countries than for the industrialized Northern countries. This may decrease the acceptance of VAP as an indicator since some of the larger developing countries, such as China, India, Brazil, and Indonesia will pay more than most OECD countries, which may be viewed as inequitable.

9. Worldwide, the value of seed export turnovers is 15 per cent of the internal commercial seed market value *(www.worldseed.org/~assinsel/stat.htm)*. For the 17 countries for which it was possible to construct these ratios, Japan had the lowest percentage (1.6 per cent) and The Netherlands the highest (206.7 per cent). Other examples include the US at 15.7 per cent and Chile at 62.5 per cent.

10. Note that WTO rules require signatories to WTO to also be members of UPOV.

11. Note that Table 7.1 refers to relative equity among the measures. The first three measures are all equitable in the sense that countries with greater values pay more, but developing countries pay relatively more with indicators 1 and 3 than with 2.

12. Of course, environmental indicators can be important in the domestic policy setting as well. For example, in the US, the Environmental Benefits Index (EBI) uses environmental indicators to help prioritize land for inclusion into the Conservation Reserve Program.

13. See *www1.oecd.org/env/policies/index.htm*.

8. Further considerations

Joseph Cooper[1]

In the long term, the full elimination of global agricultural policy distortions is estimated to result in an annual world welfare gain of $56 billion, which is about 0.2 per cent of global GDP (Burfisher, 2001). These statistics obviously do not convey the whole picture regarding the importance of the agricultural sector, which some may consider to be small enough to suggest that agricultural trade liberalization is not a particularly major issue from a strictly economic standpoint. However, notwithstanding that agriculture represents from 1.5 to 16 per cent of US GDP, its share of total water use is approximately 80 per cent of US consumptive water use and its share of land use around 45 per cent of total US land area (US Department of Commerce, 2002; Edmondson, 2001; ERS, 2000b; FAO, 2002).[2] These figures are in the same ballpark for other OECD countries. Hence, changing agricultural production levels could have notable environmental effects.

Agricultural trade liberalization under a post-Doha trade liberalization scenario is likely to affect the environment in a variety of ways, some positive, and others negative. Our empirical simulation results suggest that for the US as a whole, the environmental impacts stemming from the hypothesized trade shocks are probably within normal seasonal variation as well, as least for the types of environmental impacts examined. This general characterization of the results aside, it should be noted that the estimated changes in commodity production and the environmental impacts are not uniform across the country, with increases in agricultural production and the environmental indicators in some regions and decreases in others. The model in Chapter 3 can place monetary values on only a few of the environmental indicators examined in the analysis, and of course, the model does not have all possible environmental indicators. The value of the aggregate damages to the environment for our narrow set of externalities exceeds $16 million, and represents approximately 1 per cent of the expected net change in gross producer receipts and gross consumer expenditures for agricultural products. While interpreting these results, one should bear in mind that the trade liberalization scenario discussed here is an upper limit on whatever levels of liberalization will actually take place in the near future; both the changes in production and in the environmental impacts will likely be smaller in actuality, especially when the pace of liberalization is incremental and gradual.

At this point we cannot economically value the change in supply of agricultural amenities (that is, desirable environmental by-products of agriculture) associated with the trade liberalization scenario, nor can we estimate the changes in the supplies of the amenities themselves, given that a precise definition of these amenities and their relationship to production is not presently available (Chapter 2). However, the predicted overall expansion of the US agricultural sector does suggest that agricultural trade liberalization will likely help to conserve the "working agricultural landscape" in the US.

In the introduction, we discussed the environmental Kuznets curve (EKC), which claims that beyond a certain income point at least, increasing income is associated with decreasing negative environmental consequences, given that increasing incomes results in increasing demands for environmental services. However, the predicted global welfare gain attributable to agricultural trade liberalization, at 0.2 per cent, may not be large enough to translate into the environmental effect suggested by the EKC.[3] That being said, this single number may mask some notable regional impacts on income, particularly in some developing country regions that are net agricultural exporters, where agriculture tends to make up a greater proportion of GDP than for developed countries.

While the full elimination of global agricultural policy distortions may not increase total global agricultural production by much, analysis of trade shifts can be of interest, especially given that this elimination may increase the total volume of trade by 15 per cent (Diao, Somwaru and Rowe, 2001). Agriculture (including processed food products) accounts for 5 per cent of the GDP of developed countries (DCs) and 15 per cent of the GDP of less developed countries (LDCs) (*ibid.*). Residents of rural areas that can benefit economically from agricultural trade liberalization may increase their demand for environmental amenities. However, national level effects of trade reform are likely to be small in proportion to the benefits received by rural households (*ibid*). Hence, one may question whether an increase in the demand for environmental amenities within a rural area will be sufficient to induce (in the long run) increasingly stringent domestic environmental regulations and enforcement at the national level.

While the existing theoretical and empirical literature about the environment, international trade, and economic development suggests that the economic development fostered by trade liberalization offers the prospect of substantial improvement in the environment over the long run, we cannot test this assertion beyond what we discussed above. In the short run, world agricultural trade liberalization is likely to have a combination of positive and negative effects on the environment, as producers select alternative techniques of production, increase or decrease the scale of production, and modify the crop and animal composition of their agricultural activities. By coordinating trade and environmental policy, countries can help to preserve the economic gains from trade liberalization while mitigating potential adverse environmental impacts.

NOTES

1. The views presented herein are those of the authors, and do not necessarily represent the views or policies of the Economic Research Service or the United States Department of Agriculture.

2. The low end estimate of the share of GDP represents the value at the farm level while the upper bound encompasses the whole food and fiber system, that is, the producers of goods and services required to assemble, process, and distribute raw farm products to US and foreign consumers.

3. Chapter 1 does discuss some means that are not explicitly tied to income growth for achieving gains in environmental standards.

Glossary

Agriculture Agreement. Part of the Uruguay Round Agreement covering issues related to agriculture (for example, market access, export subsidies, and internal support). Under the Agreement, domestic support measures with minimal impact on trade (known as "green box" policies) are allowed and are excluded from reduction commitments—they are listed in Annex 2 of the Agreement. Among them are expenditures under environmental programs, provided that they meet certain conditions. The exemption enables governments to capture "positive environmental externalities."

Article 20. Negotiated as early as 1947, GATT Article 20 on General Exceptions lays out a number of specific instances in which WTO members (originally GATT "contracting parties") may be excepted from GATT rules. These include two sets of circumstances for environmental protection: (1) necessary to protect human, animal or plant life or health; (2) relating to the conservation of exhaustible natural resources if such measures are made effective in conjunction with restrictions on domestic production or consumption. These two exemptions are designed to allow WTO members to adopt policy measures that would normally be inconsistent with GATT, when "necessary" to protect human, animal or plant life or health (which together can be taken to mean "environment"), or if related to the conservation of exhaustible natural resources. However, the opening paragraph (the "chapeau") of Article 20 is designed to ensure that the GATT-inconsistent measures do not result in arbitrary or unjustifiable discrimination and do not constitute disguised protectionism.

Commission for Environmental Cooperation (CEC). The CEC is an international organization created by Canada, Mexico and the United States under the North American Agreement on Environmental Cooperation (NAAEC). The CEC was established to address regional environmental concerns, help prevent potential trade and environmental conflicts, and to promote the effective enforcement of environmental law. The Agreement complements the environmental provisions of the North American Free Trade Agreement (NAFTA).

Committee on Trade and Environment (CTE). The CTE is the principal forum in the WTO for discussing environmental issues in the trade context. Membership in the CTE consists of all WTO members.

EU (European Union). Established by the Treaty of Rome in 1957 and known previously as the European Economic Community and the Common Market. Originally composed of six European nations, it has expanded to 15. The EU attempts to unify and integrate member economies by establishing a customs union and common economic policies, including the CAP (Common Agricultural Policy). Member nations include Austria, Belgium, Denmark, Germany, Greece, Finland, France, Ireland, Italy, Luxembourg, the Netherlands, Portugal, Spain, Sweden, and the United Kingdom.

Executive Order 13141 and The Environmental Review Process. Recognizing the beneficial relationship between trade liberalization and environmental protection, President Clinton signed Executive Order 13141, "Environmental Review of Trade Agreements," on 16 November, 1999 (64 Fed. Reg. 63169, Nov. 18, 1999). The Executive Order demonstrates the US Government's commitment to the inclusion of ongoing environmental assessment and evaluation procedures in bilateral, multilateral, and natural resource sector free trade agreements. Under the direction of the US Trade Representative and the Council on Environmental Quality, the effects of free trade agreements are to be evaluated, and when deemed appropriate, established in a written Environmental Review. The environmental review mechanism aims to "contribute to the broader goal of sustainable development" and "help identify potential environmental effects of trade agreements, both positive and negative." The Order establishes the fundamentals of the environmental review process, including essential elements of the process such as interagency collaboration, public participation, and transparency. To implement the Executive Order effectively, the President directed the United States Trade Representative and the Chair of the Council on Environmental Quality, in consultation with relevant foreign policy, environmental, and economic agencies, to develop Guidelines for the Environmental Review of Trade Agreements ("Guidelines"). These Guidelines, released in December 2000 (65 Fed. Reg. 79442, December 19, 2000), provide a detailed outline of the environmental review evaluation process and focus on the primary steps to complete an effective and timely environmental review. The Guidelines are centered on an ongoing and thorough scoping process, which serves as the keystone of the review. Throughout the scoping process, domestic, transboundary, and global environmental impacts of the free trade agreement are identified and analyzed, both qualitatively and quantitatively, as appropriate, in consultation with private and public entities.

GATT (General Agreement on Tariffs and Trade). Originally negotiated in Geneva, Switzerland, in 1947, among 23 countries, including the United States, GATT is an agreement to increase international trade by reducing tariffs and other trade barriers. The Agreement provides a code of conduct for international commerce and a framework for periodic multilateral negotiations on trade liberalization and expansion.

NAFTA (North American Free Trade Agreement). A trade agreement involving Canada, Mexico, and the United States, implemented on 1 January, 1994, with a 15-year transition period. The major agricultural provisions of NAFTA include (1) the elimination of nontariff barriers—immediately upon implementation, generally through their conversion to tariff-rate quotas or ordinary quotas; (2) elimination of tariffs—many immediately, most within ten years, and some sensitive products gradually over 15 years; (3) special safeguard provisions; and (4) country-of-origin rules to ensure that Mexico does not serve as a platform for exports from third countries to the United States.

Nontariff trade barriers. Regulations used by governments to restrict imports from, and exports to, other countries, including embargoes, import quotas, and technical barriers to trade.

Nontrade Concerns. The Agriculture Agreement provides significant scope for governments to pursue important "nontrade" concerns such as food security, the environment, structural adjustment, rural development, poverty alleviation, as embodied in the "multifunctionality of agriculture" concept, for example. Article 20 says that negotiations have to take nontrade concerns into account.

OECD (Organization for Economic Cooperation and Development). An organization founded in 1961 to promote economic growth, employment, a rising standard of living, and financial stability; to assist the economic expansion of member and nonmember developing countries; and to expand world trade. The member countries are Australia, Austria, Belgium, Canada, the Czech Republic, Denmark, Finland, France, Germany, Greece, Hungary, Iceland, Ireland, Italy, Japan, Luxembourg, Mexico, the Netherlands, New Zealand, Norway, Poland, Portugal, Spain, Sweden, Switzerland, Turkey, the United Kingdom, and the United States.

Round. Refers to one of a series of multilateral trade negotiations held under the auspices of GATT for the purposes of reducing tariffs or other trade barriers. There have been eight trade negotiating rounds since the adoption of GATT in 1947.

Tariff. A tax imposed on commodity imports by a government. A tariff may be either a fixed charge per unit of product imported (specific tariff) or a fixed percentage of value (ad valorem tariff).

Tariff-rate quota. Quantitative limit (quota) on imported goods, above which a higher tariff rate is applied. A lower tariff rate applies to any imports below the quota amount.

UR (Uruguay Round) Agreement. The Uruguay Round of multilateral trade negotiations, conducted under the auspices of GATT, is a trade agreement designed to open world markets. The Agreement on Agriculture is one of the 29 individual legal texts included in the Final Act under an umbrella agreement establishing the WTO. The negotiation began at Punta del Este, Uruguay, in September 1986 and concluded in Marrakesh, Morocco, in April 1994.

WTO (World Trade Organization). Established on 1 January, 1995, as a result of the Uruguay Round, the WTO replaces GATT as the legal and institutional foundation of the multilateral trading system of member countries. It provides the principal contractual obligations determining how governments frame and implement domestic trade legislation and regulations. It is the platform on which trade relations among countries evolve through collective debate, negotiation, and adjudication.

References

Abler, D., "A Synthesis of Country Reports on Jointness Between Commodity and Non-Commodity Outputs in OECD Agriculture," presentation at Workshop "Multifunctionality: Applying the OECD Analytical Framework Guiding Policy Design", OECD, Paris, 2–3 July, 2001, *www1.oecd.org/agr/mt*, accessed April 2002.

Abler, D. and J. Shortle, "Environmental and Farm Commodity Policy Linkages in the US and the EC," *European Review of Agricultural Economics*, Vol. 19, No. 2, 1992: 197–217.

Abler, A. and J. Shortle, "Decomposing the Effects of Trade on the Environment," in Shortle and Abler (eds), *Environmental Policies for Agricultural Pollution Control*, CABI Publishing: Oxon, UK, 2001.

Anania, G., "Modeling Agricultural Trade Liberalization: A Review," paper presented at the annual meeting of the American Agricultural Economics Association, Chicago, 5–8 August, 2001.

Anderson, K. (1992a), "Agricultural Trade Liberalisation and the Environment: A Global Perspective," *World Economy*, Vol. 15, No. 1, January 1992: 153–71.

Anderson, K. (1992b), "The Standard Welfare Economics of Policies Affecting Trade and the Environment," Chapter 2 in *The Greening of World Trade Issues*, University of Michigan Press: Ann Arbor, 1992.

Anderson, K. (1992c), "Effects on the Environment and Welfare of Liberalizing World Trade: The Cases of Coal and Food," in Kym Anderson and Richard Blackhurst (eds), *The Greening of World Trade Issues*, The University of Michigan Press: Ann Arbor, 1992: 145–72.

Antweiler, W., B. Copeland and M. S. Taylor, "Is Free Trade Good for the Environment?" *American Economic Review*, September 2001: 877–908.

ASSINSEL (International Association of Plant Breeders), "ASSINSEL: Position on Access to Plant Genetic Resources for Food and Agriculture and the Equitable Sharing of Benefits Arising from their Use," ASSINSEL: Nyon, Switzerland, 5 June, 1998.

Association of University Technology Managers, Inc. (AUTM), "AUTM Licensing Survey: Fiscal Years 1991–1993," 1993.

Babcock, B., "The Effects of Uncertainty on Optimal Nitrogen Applications," *Review of Agricultural Economics*, Vol. 14, No. 2, July 1992: 271–81.

Barnard, C. H., G. Whittaker, D. Westenbarger and M. Ahearn, "Evidence of Capitalization of Direct Government Payments into US Cropland Values," *American Journal of Agricultural Economics,* Vol. 79, No. 5, 1997: 1642–50.

Barrett, Scott (1994a), "Strategic Environmental Policy and International Trade," *Journal of Public Economics*, Vol. 54, No. 3, 1994: 325–38.

Barrett, Scott (1994b), "Self-Enforcing International Environmental Agreements," *Oxford Economic Papers*, Vol. 46, No. 0 (Supplement), October 1994: 878–94.

Barton, J.H. and E. Christensen, "Diversity Compensation Systems: Ways to Compensate Developing Countries for Providing Genetic Material," in J. R. Kloppenburg (ed.), *Seeds and Sovereignty: the Use and Control of Plant Genetic Resources*, Duke University Press: Durham, NC, 1988.

Batabyal, Amitrajeet A. (ed.), *The Economics of International Environmental Agreements*, International Library of Environmental Economics and Policy, Aldershot: Ashgate, UK, 2000.

Batie, S., "Green Payments as Foreshadowed by EQIP," Staff paper 99-45, Department of Agricultural Economics, Michigan State University, 1999.

Baumol, W. and W. Oates, *The Theory of Environmental Policy*, Cambridge University Press: Cambridge, 1988.

Beghin, John, Sebastien Dessus, David Roland-Holst and Dominique van der Mensbrugghe, "The Trade and Environment Nexus in Mexican Agriculture. A General Equilibrium Analysis," *Agricultural Economics*, Vol. 17, No. 2–3, December 1997: 115–31.

Bernstein, J., J. Cooper and R. Claassen, "Agriculture and the Environment," in M. Normile (ed.), "EU-US Comparison Report," Economic Research Service, USDA, 2004.

Bhagwati, Jagdish, "Diversity of Environmental Standards," in J. Bhagwati and R. Hudec (eds), *Fair Trade and Harmonization: Prerequisites for Free Trade?* MIT Press: Cambridge, Massachusetts and American Society of International Law: Washington, DC, 1996.

Bhagwati, J., A. Panagariya and T. Srinivisan, *Lectures on International Trade*, Second edition, MIT Press: Cambridge, 1998.

Bohman, M., J. Cooper, D. Mullarkey, M.A. Normile, D. Skully, S. Vogel and C. E. Young, "The Use and Abuse of Multifunctionality," Economic Research Service, USDA, November 1999, *http://www.ers.usda.gov/briefing/wto/PDF/multifunc1119.pdf*

Bohman, M. and P. Lindsey (1997a), "Divergent Environmental Regulations and Trade Liberalization," *Canadian Journal Agricultural Economics*, Vol. 45, December 1997: 17–38.

Bohman, M. and P. Lindsey (1997b), "Harmonization of Environmental Policies of Agriculture under NAFTA," *Canadian. Journal of Agricultural Economics*, Vol. 45, December 1997: 383–91.

Braathen, Nils Axel, "Model Simulations for OECD's Environmental Outlook: Methods and Results," Discussion paper, Fourth Annual Conference on Global Economic Analysis, Purdue University, 27–29 June, 2001.

Browning, E. K., "On the Marginal Welfare Cost of Taxation," *American Economic Review*, Vol. 77, No. 1, 1987: 11–23.

Burfisher, M. (ed.), "Agricultural Policy Reform in the WTO—The Road Ahead," Agricultural Economics Report No. 802, USDA, Economic Research Service, May 2001, *http://www.ers.usda.gov/publications/ aer802/aer802.pdf*

Burfisher, M. and J. Hopkins (eds), "Decoupled Payments: Household Income Transfers in Contemporary US Agriculture," USDA, Economic Research Service, Agricultural Economic Report No. 822, February 2003.

Burfisher, M. E., R. M. House and S. V. Langley, "Effects of a Free Trade Agreement on US and Southern Agriculture," *Southern Journal of Agricultural Economics*, Vol. 24, 1992: 61–78.

Cahill, C., "The Multifunctionality of Agriculture: What Does it Mean?," *EuroChoices*, Vol. 1, No. 1, 2001.

Carraro, C. (ed.), *International Negotiations: Strategic Policy Issues*, Edward Elgar Publishing: Cheltenham, UK, and Northhampton, Massachusetts, 1997.

Carraro, C. and D. Siniscalco, "Strategies for the International Protection of the Environment," *Journal of Public Economics*, Vol. 52, 1993: 309–28.

Chichilnisky, Graciela, "North–South Trade and the Environment," *American Economic Review*, Vol. 84, No. 4, 1994: 851–74.

Claassen, R. and R. Horan, "Environmental Payments to Farmers: Issues of Program Design," *Agricultural Outlook*, Vol. AO-272, 2000, 15–18.

Claassen, R., R. Heimlich, R. House and K. Wiebe, "Estimating the Effects of Relaxing Agricultural Land Use Restrictions: Wetland Delineation in the Swampbuster Program," *Review of Agricultural Economics*, Vol. 20, 1998: 390–405.

Claassen, Roger, LeRoy Hansen, Mark Peters, Vince Breneman, Marca Weinberg, Andrea Cattaneo, Peter Feather, Dwight Gadsby, Daniel Hellerstein, Jeff Hopkins, Paul Johnston, Mitch Morehart and Mark Smith, "Agri-Environmental Policy at the Cross-Roads: Guideposts on a Changing Landscape," Agricultural Economic Report No. 794, USDA, Economic Research Service, January 2001.

Cline, W., *The Economics of Global Warming*, Institute for International Economics: Washington, DC, 1992.

Cole, M., A. Rayner and J. Bates, "Trade Liberalisation and the Environment: the Case of the Uruguay Round," *The World Economy*, Vol. 21, No. 3, 1998: 337–47.

Commission of the European Communities (CEC), "Communication from the Commission to the Council and the European Parliament: Mid-term Review of the Common Agricultural Policy," COM(2002) 394, Brussels, 10 July 2002, *http://europa.eu.int/comm/agriculture/mtr/index_en.htm*, accessed Oct. 2002.

Commission on Genetic Resources for Food and Agriculture (CGRFA), "Report of the Eighth Extraordinary Session of the Commission on Genetic Resources for Food and Agriculture," CGRFA-8/99/4, April 19–23, 1999, Food and Agricultural Organization of the United Nations, Rome.

Commission on Genetic Resources for Food and Agriculture, "Item 2 of the Draft Provisional Agenda: Third Inter-Sessional Meeting of the Contact Group," CGRFA/CG-3/00/2. April 2000, Food and Agricultural Organization of the United Nations, Rome.

Convention on Biological Diversity (CBD), "Sustaining Life on Earth: How the Convention on Biological Diversity Promotes Nature and Human Well-Being," August 2002 update, *www.biodiv.org/doc/publications/guide.asp?id=action-int*

Cooper, J., "The Application of Nonmarket Valuation Techniques to Agricultural Issues," USDA/ERS Staff Paper, No. 9503, 1995.

Cooper, J., "The Economics of Public Investment in Agro-Biodiversity Conservation," chapter in R. Evenson, D. Gollin and V. Santaniello (eds), *Agricultural Values of Plant Genetic Resources*, CABI International: Wallingford, UK, 1998.

Cooper, J. (2001a), "Construction of a Fund for the Sharing of Benefits from the Utilization of Plant Genetic Resources for Food and Agriculture," *Environment and Development Economics*, Vol. 6, February 2001, 47–62.

Cooper, J. (2001b), "Economic Valuation of the Environmental Externalities of Agriculture," paper presented at the *Workshop on Socio-Economic Analysis and Policy Implications of the Roles of Agriculture in Developing Countries*, FAO, Rome, March 2001, *www.fao.org/es/ESA/Roa/ROA-e/EMP.htm*

Cooper, J., M. Peters and R. Johansson, "Environmental Issues in the FTAA," chapter 9 in M. Burfisher (ed.), "US Agriculture and the Free Trade Area of the Americas," USDA, Economic Research Service, AER/AIB, forthcoming, 2004.

Copeland, Brian R. and M. Scott Taylor, "North-South Trade and the Environment," *The Quarterly Journal of Economics*, Vol. 109, Issue 3, No. 438, August 1994: 755–87.

Costanza, R., R. d'Arge, R. de Groot, S. Farber, M. Grasso, B. Hannon, S. Naeem, K. Limburg, J. Paruelo, R.V. O'Neill, R. Raskin, P. Sutton and M. van den Belt, "The Value of the World's Ecosystem Services and Natural Capital," *Nature*, Vol. 387, 1997: 253–60.

Crutchfield, S., J. Cooper and D. Hellerstein, "The Benefits of Safer Drinking Water: The Value of Nitrate Reduction," USDA, Economic Research Service, Agricultural Economics Report, No. 752, 1997.

Dasgupta, Susmita, Benoit Laplante, Hua Wang and David Wheeler, "Confronting the Environmental Kuznets Curve," *Journal of Economic Perspectives*, Vol. 16, No. 1, 2002: 147–68.

Darwin, Roy, Kevin Ingram and John Sullivan, "FARM's Land and Water Resources Database: Project Plan," Documentation Draft, USDA, Economic Research Service, December 2001.

Darwin, Roy, Marinos Tsigas, Jan Lewandrowski and Anton Raneses, "World Agriculture and Climate Change: Economic Adaptations," Agricultural Economic Report No. 703, US Department of Agriculture, Economic Research Service, Washington, DC, 1995, *www.ers.usda.gov/publications/ aer703*

Darwin, Roy, Marinos Tsigas, Jan Lewandrowski and Anton Raneses, "Land Use and Cover in Ecological Economics," *Ecological Economics*, Vol. 17, 1996: 157–81.

Diao, Xinshen, Agapi Somwaru and Terry Roe, "A Global Analysis of Agricultural Reform in WTO Member Countries," Agricultural Policy Reform in the WTO—The Road Ahead. Agricultural Economic Report No. 802, USDA, Economic Research Service, May 2001.

Drake, L., "The Non-Market Value of the Swedish Agricultural Landscape," *European Review of Agricultural Economics*, Vol. 19, 1992, 351–64.

Duffy, P. A., C. R. Taylor, D. Cain and G. J. Young, "The Economic Value of Farm Program Base," *Land Economics*, Vol. 70, 1994: 318–29.

Economic Research Service (ERS), (2000a), "Briefing Room on Global Climate Change," USDA, Economic Research Service, December 2000 update. *http://www.ers.usda.gov/Briefing/GlobalClimate/Questions/ Ccmqa4.htm#lewandrowsk*

Economic Research Service (2000b), "Briefing Room on Irrigation and Water Use: overview." *http://www.ers.usda.gov/Briefing/wateruse/overview.htm #this%20research*, accessed May 23, 2002.

Economic Research Service, "Briefing Room on Conservation and Environmental Policy," USDA, Economic Research Service, December 2001 update, *www.ers.usda.gov/briefing/ConservationAndEnvironment/Questions/ consenvwq2.htm* and *www.ers.usda.gov/briefing/ConservationAnd Environment/Questions/consenvwq1.htm*

Economic Research Service (2002a), "ERS Analysis: Conservation Programs," ERS Briefing Room, June 2002, *www.ers.usda.gov/features/farmbill/ analysis/conservationoverview.htm*, accessed 26 April, 2003.

Economic Research Service (2002b), "WTO: Technical Barriers to Trade," ERS Briefing Room, March 2002, *www.ers.usda.gov/briefing/WTO/ tbt.htm*, accessed 1 October, 2002.

Edmondson, W., "Food and Fiber System Share of GDP Remains Robust," Rural America, USDA, Economic Research Service, Vol. 16, May 2001, *www.ers.usda.gov/publications/ruralamerica/ra161/ra161i.pdf*

Edwards, Sebastian, "Trade Orientation, Distortions, and Growth in Developing Countries," *Journal of Development Economics*, Vol. 39, No.1, 1992: 31–57.

Eggers, B. and R. Mackenzie, "The Cartagena Protocol on Biosafety," *Journal of International Economic Law*, Vol. 3, No. 3, September 2000: 525–43.

Environmental Protection Agency (EPA), "Report to Congress: Nonpoint Source Pollution in the US," Washington, DC, 1984.

Environmental Protection Agency "National Water Quality Inventory: 1998 Report to Congress," EPA841-R-00-001, Washington, DC, 1998, *www.epa.gov/305b/98report/* , accessed November 5, 2002.

Esty, D. and B. Gentry, "Foreign Investment, *Globalisation, and the Environment*," in T. Jones (ed.), *Globalization and the Environment*, OECD: Paris, 1997.

European Commission, "State of Application of Regulation (EEC) No. 2078/92: Evaluation of Agri-Environment Programmes," DGVI Commission Working Document VI/7655/98, 1998, *http://europa.eu.int/comm/agriculture/envir/ programs/evalrep/text_en.pdf* and *http://europa.eu.int/comm/agriculture/ envir/programs/index_en.htm*, accessed August 2002.

European Commission (2000a), "EC Comprehensive Negotiating Proposal," World Trade Organization: Committee on Agriculture, Special Session, G/AG/NG/W/90, December 2000.

European Commission (2000b), "'Greening the CAP' together with the Commission's replies," Special Report No 14/2000, Official Journal C353, 08/12/2000, Community Legislation in force, Document 300Y1208(01), 2000.

European Commission, Directorate General for Trade, "Informal Discussion Paper: The Non-Trade Impacts of Trade Policy—Asking Questions, Seeking Sustainable Development," 8 January, 2001.

Faeth, P., *Growing Green: Enhancing the Economic and Environmental Performance of US Agriculture*, World Resources Institute: Washington, DC, 1995.

Feather, P. and J. Cooper, "Strategies for Curbing Water Pollution," *Agricultural Outlook*, Vol. AO-224, November 1995.

Feather, P., D. Hellerstein and L. Hansen, "Economic Valuation of Environmental Benefits and the Targeting of Conservation Programs: The Case of the CRP," Agricultural Economic Report No. 778, USDA, Economic Research Service, April 1999.

Ferris, R. and J. Humphrey, "A review of potential biodiversity indicators for application in British forests," *Forestry*, Vol. 72, No. 4, 1999: 313–28.

Food and Agricultural Organization of the United Nations (FAO), "State of the World's Plant Genetic Resources for Food and Agriculture," background documentation prepared for the International Technical Conference on Plant Genetic Resources, Leipzig, Germany, 17–23 June, 1998, FAO, Rome.

Food and Agricultural Organization of the United Nations, *FAO Statistical Databases*, Rome, 2002.

Frankel, J. and A. Rose, "Is Trade Good or Bad for the Environment? Sorting Out the Causality," NBER Working Paper No. 9201, September 2002, *http://ksghome.harvard.edu/~.jfrankel.academic.ksg/*, accessed October 2002.

Fredriksson, Per G. and Daniel Millimet, "Is There a Race to the Bottom in Environmental Policies? The Effects of NAFTA," paper presented at the Commission for Environmental Cooperation's North American Symposium on Understanding the Linkages between Trade and Environment, Washington, DC, 11–12, October 2000, *www.cec.org/programs_projects/ trade_environ_econ/pdfs/Fredrik.pdf*

Frisvold, G. B., Personal Communication from Prof. George Frisvold, University of Arizona, 2002.

Frisvold, G. B. and P. T. Condon, "The Convention on Biological Diversity and Agriculture: Implications and Unresolved Debates," *World Development*, Vol. 26, No. 4, April 1998: 551–70.

Fry, S., *The Hippopotamus*, Soho: New York, 1994.

Gehlhar, Mark and Frederick Nelson, "Treatment of Domestic Agricultural Support and Implications for Reductions: The Case for the United States," Discussion paper, Fourth Annual Conference on Global Economic Analysis, Purdue University, 27–29 June, 2001.

Grossman, Gene M. and Alan B. Krueger, "Economic Growth and the Environment," *The Quarterly Journal of Economics*, Vol. 110, No. 2, May 1995: 353–77.

Hagem, C. and H. Westskog, "The Design of a Dynamic Tradable Quota System under Market Imperfections," *Journal of Environmental Economics and Management*, Vol. 36, 1998: 89–107.

Hansen, LeRoy, Vince Breneman, Cecil Davison and Chris Dicken, "The Cost of Soil Erosion to Downstream Navigation," *Journal of Soil and Water Conservation*, Vol. 57, No. 4 July/August 2002: 205–12.

Harrison, Ann, "Openness and Growth: A Time-Series, Cross-Country Analysis for Developing Countries," *Journal of Development Economics*, Vol. 48, No. 2, 1996: 419–47.

Heimlich, R. and R. Claassen, "Agricultural Conservation Policy at a Crossroads," *Agricultural and Resource Economics Review*, April 1998: 95–107.

Heimlich, R., K. Wiebe, R. Claassen and R. House, "Recent Evolution of Environmental Policy: Lessons from Wetlands," *Journal of Soil and Water Conservation*, Vol. 52, 1997: 157–161.

Hellerstein, D. and V. Breneman, "Estimating the Effects of Changes in Estuarine Water Quality on Outdoor Recreation: A First Order Gravity Model," manuscript, US Department of Agriculture, Economic Research Service, December 2000.

Hellerstein, D., C. Nickerson, J. Cooper, P. Feather, D. Gadsby, D. Mullarkey, A. Tegene and C. Barnard, "Farmland Protection: the Role of Public Preferences for Rural Amenities," USDA, Economic Research Service, Agricultural Economic Report No. 815, 2002.

Hertel, T. W. (compiler), "Short Course in Global Trade Analysis: July 1993," Department of Agricultural Economics, Purdue University, West Lafayette, IN, 1993.

Hertel, Thomas (ed.), *Global Trade Analysis: Modeling and Applications*, Cambridge University Press, 1997.

Horner, G., S. Hatchett, R. House and R. Howitt, "Impacts of San Joaquin Valley Drainage-Related Policies on State and National Agricultural Production," in *National Impact of Drainage-Related Policies*, University of California and San Joaquin Valley Drainage Program, 1990.

House, R., M. Peters, H. Baumes and W. Disney, "Ethanol and Agriculture: Effect of Increased Production on Crop and Livestock Sectors," Agricultural Information Bulletin 667, US Department of Agriculture, Economic Research Service, Washington, DC, 1993.

House, R., H. McDowell, M. Peters and R. Heimlich, 1999, "Agriculture Sector Resource and Environmental Policy Analysis: an Economic and Biophysical Approach," in *Environmental Statistics: Analyzing Data for Environmental Policy*, John Wiley and Sons: New York, 1999: 243–61.

ICF Consulting, "North American Trade and Transportation Corridors: Environmental Impacts and Mitigation Strategies," paper prepared for the North American Commission for Environmental Cooperation, 21 February, 2001, *www.cec.org/programs_projects/pollutants_health/trinational/corridors-e.pdf*

Johansson, R. and J. Kaplan, "Manure Stew—US Ingredients: Carrots, Sticks, and Water," selected paper presentation, American Agricultural Economics Association Meeting, Montreal, Canada, 27–30 July, 2003.

Josling, T., "New Farm Programs in North America and their Treatment in the WTO: Discussion," *American Journal of Agricultural Economics*, Vol. 82, August 2000: 775–77.

Kada, R., Untitled presentation, at Workshop "Applying the OECD Analytical Framework Guiding Policy Design," OECD, Paris, 2–3 July, 2001, *www1.oecd.org/agr/mf*, accessed April 2002.

Kaplan, J. and R. Johansson, "When the !%$? Hits the Land: Implications for US Agriculture and Environment when Land Application of Manure is Constrained," selected paper presentation, American Agricultural Economics Association Meeting, Montreal, Canada, 27–30 July, 2003.

Kellogg, R. L., C. H. Lander, D. C. Moffitt, and N. Gollehon, "Manure Nutrients Relative to the Capacity of Cropland and Pastureland to Assimilate Nutrients: Spatial and Temporal Trends for the United States," Natural Resource Conservation Service and Economic Research Service, USDA, Washington, DC, 2000.

Kline, J. and D. Wichelns, "Measuring Public Preferences for the Environmental Amenities Provided by Farmland," *European Review of Agricultural Economics*, Vol. 23, No. 4, 1996: 421–36.

Knudson, Mary, "Agricultural Diversity: Do We Have the Resources to Meet Future Needs?" in G. Frisvold and B. Kuhn (eds), *Global Environmental Change and Agriculture: Assessing the Impacts*, New Horizons in Environmental Economics, Edward Elgar: Cheltenham, UK and Northampton, Massachusetts, 1999, pp. 43–86.

Kreuger, A., "Growth, Distortions and Patterns of Trade Among Many Countries," International Finance Section: Princeton, NJ, 1977.

Krissoff, B., N. Ballenger, J. Dunmore and D. Gray, "Exploring Linkages Among Agriculture, Trade, and the Environment: Issues for the Next Century," AER No. 738, Economic Research Service, US Department of Agriculture, Washington, DC, May 1996.

Krugman, Paul, "What Should Trade Negotiators Negotiate About?" *Journal of Economic Literature*, Vol. 35, March 1997: 113–20.

Leamer, E. E., "Paths of Development in the Three Factor, n-Good General Equilibrium Model," *Journal of Political Economy*, Vol. 95, No. 5, October 1987: 961–99.

Leetmaa, S. and M. Smith, "The Conservation Reserve Program: Implications of a Reduced Program on US Grain Trade," selected paper presented at the annual meetings of the American Agricultural Economics Association, San Antonio, TX, 31 July, 1996.

Lemétayer, J. M., "Discours de clôture du Président LEMÉTAYER," Rassemblement des Élus Locaux de la FNSEA, Palais des Sports de la Porte de Versailles, 27 February, 2002, *www.fnsea.fr/actu_suite.asp?IdArticle=2321*, accessed August 2002.

Leonard, Jeffrey, *Pollution and the Struggle for the World Product*, Cambridge University Press: Cambridge, 1998.

Leuck, D., S. Haley, P. Liapis and B. McDonald, *The EU Nitrate Directive and CAP Reform: Effects on Agricultural Production, Trade, and Residual Soil Nitrogen*, Foreign Agricultural Economic Report No. 255, USDA, Economic Research Service, Washington, DC, January 1995.

Lopez, R., "The Environment as a Factor of Production: The Effects of Economic Growth and Trade Liberalization," *Journal of Environmental Economics and Management*, Vol. 27, No. 2, September 1994: 163–84.

Lopez, R., Personal communication from Prof. Ramon Lopez, Department of Agricultural and Resource Economics, University of Maryland, 2002.

Lynch, S. and K. R. Smith, *Lean, Mean, and Green...Designing Farm Support Programs in a New Era*, Henry Wallace Institute for Alternative Agriculture: Greenbelt, MD, 1994.

Mahé, L. P. and F. Ortalo-Magné, *Politique Agricole, un Modèle Européen*, Presses de Science-Po: Paris, 2001.

McCarl, B. and T. Spreen, "Price Endogenous Mathematical Programming as a Tool for Sector Analysis," *American Journal of Agricultural Economics*, Vol. 62, No. 1, 1980: 86–102.

McDowell, H., R. Kramer, A. Randall and M. Price, "An Analysis of US Farm Income Policies: Historical, Market-Determined, and Sector-Wide Stabilization," *Southern Journal of Agricultural Economics*, Vol. 21, No. 2, 1989: 1–11.

Miltz, D., J. B. Braden and G. V. Johnson, "Standards Versus Prices Revisited: the Case of Agricultural Non-point Source Pollution," *Journal of Agricultural Economics*, Vol. 39, No. 3, 1988: 360–68.

Mitchell, G., R. Griggs, V. Benson and J. Williams, "EPIC Documentation," Texas A&M University, 1998, *www.brc.tamus.edu/epic/documentation/index.html*

Mitsch, W. J., J. W. Day, Jr., J. W. Gilliam, P. M. Goroffman, D. L. Hey, G. Randall and N. Wang, *Reducing Nutrient Loads, Especially Nitrate-Nitrogen, to Surface Water, Groundwater, and the Gulf of Mexico*, Topic 5 Report for the Integrated Assessment of Hypoxia in the Gulf of Mexico, US Department of Commerce, National Oceanic and Atmospheric Administration, Silver Spring, MD, 1999.

Mullarkey, D., J. Cooper and D. Skully, "Multifunctionality of Agriculture: Do Mixed Goals Distort Trade," *Choices*, First quarter, 2001.

Nadal, Alejandro, "Maize in Mexico: Some Environmental Implications of the North American Free Trade Agreement," in *Assessing Environmental Effects of the North American Free Trade Agreement (NAFTA): an Analytic Framework (Phase II) and Issue Studies*, Communications and Public Outreach Department, Commission for Economic Cooperation Secretariat, 1999, *www.cec.org/pubs_info_resources/publications/pdfs/english/engmaize.pdf*

Nakashima, Y., "Multifunctionality: Applying the OECD framework. A Review of Literature in Japan," presentation at Workshop "Multifunctionality: Applying the OECD Analytical Framework Guiding Policy Design," OECD, Paris, 2–3 July, 2001, *www1.oecd.org/agr/mf/*, accessed April 2002.

Nelson, F., "Aligning U.S Farm Policy With World Trade Commitments," *Agricultural Outlook*, January–February 2002: 12–6.

Nelson, G. C., T. Josling, D. Bullock, L. Unnevehr, M. Rosengrant and L. Hill, *The Economics and Politics of Genetically Modified Organisms in Agriculture: Implications for WTO 2000*, Bulletin 809, College of Agricultural, Consumer and Environmental Sciences, University of Illinois at Urbana-Champaign, November 1999, *http://web.aces.uiuc.edu/wf/ GMO/GMO.pdf*

Nimon, W., J. Cooper, and M. Smith, "NAFTA, Agricultural Trade, and the Environment," chapter in Steven Zahniser and John Link (eds), *Effects of North American Free Trade Agreement on Agriculture and the Rural Economy*, USDA, Economic Research Service, Agriculture and Trade Report No. WRS0201, July 2002.

Organization for Economic Cooperation and Development (OECD), "Report on the OECD Workshop on Agri-Environmental Indicators," COM/AGR/CA/ENV/EPOC(98)136, November, 1998.

OECD, "Background Information on Future OECD Work on Agri-Environmental Indicators," COM/AGR/CA/ENV/RD(2000)131, Paris, 27 March, 2000.

OECD (2001a), "Key Environmental Indicators," Paris, 2001.

OECD (2001b), "Multifunctionality: Towards an Analytical Framework," Paris, 2001, *www.oecd.org/oecd/pages/documentredirection?paramID=5180& language=EN&col=OECDDCoreLive*, accessed December 2002.

OECD (2001c), "Environmental Indicators for Agriculture, Volume 3: Methods and Results," Paris, 2001, *www.oecd.org/agr/env/indicators.htm*.

OECD, "Agri-Environmental Indicators: Progress Report and Planning Joint Working Party on Agriculture and Environment," COM/AGR/CA/ENV/EPOC(2002)34, Paris, 21 March, 2002.

Padgitt, M., D. Newton, R. Penn and C. Sandretto, "Production Practices for Major Crops in US Agriculture, 1990-97," Statistical Bulletin No. 969, US Department of Agriculture, Economic Research Service, Washington, DC, September 2000.

Panayotou, T., J. Sachs and A. Zwane, "Compensating for Meaningful Participation in Climate Change Control: A Modest Proposal and Empirical Analysis," *Journal of Environmental Economics and Management*, Vol. 43, No. 3, May 2002: 437–54.

Peters, M., H. McDowell and R. House, "Environmental and Economic Effects of Taxing Nitrogen Fertilizer," selected paper presented at the annual meetings of the American Agricultural Economics Association, 27–30 July, Toronto, 1997.

Peters, M., J. Lewandrowski, R. House and H. McDowell, "Economic Impacts of Carbon Charges on US Agriculture," *Climatic Change*, 50, 2001: 445–73.

Randall, A., "Valuing the Outputs of Multifunctional Agriculture," *European Review of Agricultural Economics*, Vol. 29, 2002: 289–307.

Regione Siciliana, Assessorato Agricoltura e Foreste, "Piano di Sviluppo Rurale Regione Sicilia ["Plan for Rural Development"], 2000–2006", undated, *www.regione.sicilia.it/Agricolturaeforeste/Assessorato/d3/default.htm*

Ribaudo, M., "Reducing Soil Erosion: Offsite Benefits," Agricultural Economic Report No. 561, USDA, Economic Research Service, September 1986.

Ribaudo, M., "Water Quality Benefits From the Conservation Reserve Program," USDA, Economic Research Service, Agricultural Economics Report No. 606, February 1989.

Ribaudo, M., D. Colacicco, L. Langer, S. Piper and G. Schaible, "Natural Resources and Users Benefit from the Conservation Program," USDA, Economic Research Service, Agricultural Economic Report No. 627, January 1990.

Ribaudo, M., R. Heimlich, R. Claassen and M. Peters, "Least-cost Management of Nonpoint Source Pollution: Source Reduction vs. Interception Strategies for Controlling Nitrogen Loss in the Mississippi Basin," *Ecological Economics*, Vol. 37, 2001: 183–97.

Ribaudo, M., R. Horan and M. Smith, "Economics of Water Quality Protection from Nonpoint Sources: Theory and Practice," USDA, Economic Research Service, Agricultural Economic Report No.782, 1999.

Rose, A. and B. Stevens, "Will a global warning agreement be fair to developing countries?" *International Journal of Environment and Pollution*, Vol. 9, No. 2/3, 1998: 157–78.

Rose, A., B. Stevens, J. Edmunds and M. Wise, "International Equity and Differentiation in Global Warming Policy: An Application to Tradeable Emission Permits," *Environmental and Resource Economics*, Vol. 12, July 1998: 25–51.

Runge, C. Ford and Glenn Fox, "Feedlot Production of Cattle in the United States and Canada: Some Environmental Implications of the North American Free Trade Agreement," in *Assessing Environmental Effects of the North American Free Trade Agreement (NAFTA): An Analytic Framework (Phase II) and Issue Studies*, Communications and Public Outreach Department, Commission for Economic Cooperation Secretariat, 1999, *www.cec.org/pubs_info_resources/publications/pdfs/english/engfeed.pdf*

Russell, C., "A Note on the Efficiency Ranking of Two Second-Best Policy Instruments for Pollution Control," *Journal of Environmental Economics and Management*, Vol. 13, 1986: 13–17.

Seki, M., "Streamlining National Reporting," United Nations Environmental Programme (UNEP), *Synergies*, Vol. 2, April 2000.

Sierra Club and Sheila Holbrook-White, "NAFTA Transportation Corridors: Approaches to Assessing Environmental Impacts and Alternatives," paper presented at the "North American Symposium on Understanding the Linkages Between Trade and Environment," Washington, DC, 11–12 October, 2000, *www.cec.org/programs_projects/trade_environ_econ/pdfs/sierra.pdf*

Smith, V. K., "Environmental Costing for Agriculture: Will it be Standard Fare in the Farm Bill of 2000?," *American Journal of Agricultural Economics*, Vol. 74, February 1992: 1076–88.

Stern, David, Michael Common and Edward Barbier, "Economic Growth and Environmental Degradation: The Environmental Kuznets Curve and Sustainable Development," *World Development*, Vol. 24, No. 7, 1996: 1151–60.

Strutt, Anna and Kym Anderson, "Will Trade Liberalization Harm the Environment? The Case of Indonesia to 2020," *Environmental and Resource Economics*, Vol. 17, 2000: 203–32.

Sullivan, John (ed.), "Environmental Policies: Implications for Agricultural Trade," USDA, Economic Research Service, Agricultural and Trade Analysis Division, Foreign Agricultural Economic Report No. 252, June 1994.

Swaminathan, M., "Compensating Farmers and Communities Through a Global Fund for Biodiversity Conservation for Sustainable Food Security," *Diversity*, Vol. 12, 1996: 73–75.

Tobey, J., "The Effects of Environmental Policy Towards Agriculture on Trade: Some Considerations," *Food Policy*, April 1991: 90–94.

UNEP (United Nations Environment Programme), *Environment and Trade—A Handbook*, International Institute for Sustainable Development: Winnipeg, Canada, 2000, *www.iisd.org/pdf/envirotrade_handbook.pdf*

UPOV (International Union for the Protection of New Varieties of Plants), "Plant Variety Protection Statistics for the Period 1990–1994," document number C/27/7, Geneva, Switzerland, October 1995.

US Congress, Office of Technology Assessment, *Agriculture, Trade, and Environment: Achieving Complementary Policies*, OTA-ENV-617, US Government Printing Office: Washington, DC, May 1995.

US Department of Agriculture (USDA), "Food and Agricultural Policy: Taking Stock for the New Century," Washington, DC, 2001, *www.usda.gov/news/pubs/farmpolicy01/fpindex.htm*

US Department of Agriculture, Agricultural Research Service, "EPIC—Erosion Productivity Impact Calculator, 1. Model Documentation," TB-1768, Sept. 1990.

US Department of Agriculture, Farm Service Agency, Conservation Reserve Program—Long-Term Policy; Final Rule, 1997, *www.nhq.nrcs.usda.gov/OPA/FB96OPA/CRPfrul.html*

US Department of Agriculture, Foreign Agricultural Service, "Agreement on Agriculture," 2000, *www.fas.usda.gov/itp/policy/gatt/ag_text.html*

US Department of Agriculture, National Agriculture Statistics Service (NASS), "Census of Agriculture—1997," 1997, *www.nass.usda.gov/census/*

US Department of Agriculture, Soil Conservation Service, "Land Resource Regions and Major Land Resource Areas of the United States," AH-296, Washington, DC, 1981.

US Department of Agriculture, Soil Conservation Service, "Summary Report, 1992 National Resources Inventory," Washington, DC, 1994.

US Department of Agriculture, World Agricultural Outlook Board, "USDA Agricultural Baseline Projections to 2007," Staff Report WAOB-98-1, US Department of Agriculture, Office of the Chief Economist, Washington, DC, 1998.

US Department of Commerce, Bureau of Economic Analysis, "Table 3.—Price Indexes for Gross Domestic Product and Gross Domestic Purchases," *Survey of Current Business* August 2000, *www.bea.doc.gov/bea/ARTICLES/NATIONAL/NIPA/2000/0800gdp.pdf*

US Department of Commerce, Bureau of Economic Analysis, "Gross Domestic Product by Industry in Current Dollars, 1994–2001," October, 2002, *www.bea.doc.gov/bea/dn2/gpoc.htm#1994-2001*

US Department of Commerce, Bureau of the Census, "Census of Agriculture (1987)—Volume 3: Related Surveys, Part 1, Farm and Ranch Irrigation Survey (1988). Use in General Circulation Climate Models," 1990.

US Environmental Protection Agency (EPA), *Inventory of US Greenhouse Gas Emissions and Sinks: 1990–1998*, EPA 236-R-00-001, April 2000.

US Environmental Protection Agency, *National Water Quality Inventory: 1996 Report to Congress*, EPA841-R-97-008, Office of Water, April 1998.

US Environmental Protection Agency, "National Water Quality Inventory: 1998 Report to Congress," EPA841-R-00-001, Washington, DC, 1998, *www.epa.gov/305b/98report/*, accessed 5 November, 2002.

US Environmental Protection Agency, "Report to Congress: Nonpoint Source Pollution in the US," Washington, DC, 1984.

US, Government of (1999a), "Linkages Between Trade and Environmental Policies: Statement of the United States," WTO High Level Symposium on Trade and Environment, 15–16 March, 1999, *www.ustr.gov/environment/statements.shtml*

US, Government of (1999b), "Synergies Between Trade Liberalization and Sustainable Development," WTO High Level Symposium on Trade and Environment, 15–16 March, 1999, *www.ustr.gov/environment/statements.shtml*

US International Trade Commission, "Cattle and Beef: Impact of the NAFTA and Uruguay Round Agreements on US Trade," Investigation No. 332-371, Publication 3048, US Government Printing Office, Washington, DC, July 1997.

US Trade Representative (USTR), "Draft Environmental Review of the proposed US-Chile Free Trade Agreement," undated, *www.ustr.gov/environment/environmental.shtml*, accessed 15 April, 2003.

US Trade Representative (USTR), "FTAA—Free Trade Area of the Americas, Draft Agreement, Chapter on Agriculture," FTAA.TNC/w/133/Rev.1, 3 July, 2001, *www.ftaa-alca.org/ftaadraft/eng/ngag_e.doc*

US Trade Representative (2000a), "Environmental Review of Trade Agreements Draft Guidelines: E.O. 13141 implementation," July 11, 2000, *www.ustr.gov/environment/environmental.shtml*

United States Trade Representative (2000b), "Report of the Quantitative Analysis Working Group to the FTAA Interagency Environment Group," October 2000, *www.ustr.gov/environment/environmental.shtml*

Valluru, S. R. K. and E. W. F. Peterson, "The Impact of Environmental Regulations on World Grain Trade," *Agribusiness*, Vol. 13, 1997: 261–72.

Van Sickle, J., C. Brewster and T. Spreen, "The Impact of Methyl Bromide Ban on the US Vegetable Industry," University of Florida, Food and Resource Economics Department Staff Paper SP 99-11, October 1999.

Van Tongeren, Frank, Hans van Meijl and Yves Surry, "Global Models Applied to Agricultural and Trade Policies: A Review and Assessment," *Agricultural Economics*, Vol. 26, 2001: 149–72.

Vasavada, U. and S. Warmerdam, "Green Box Policies and the Environment," Briefing Room, Economic Research Service, USDA, 1998, *www.USDA.ERS.gov/briefing/wto/issues/environm.htm*

Vatn, A., "Multifunctional Agriculture: Some Consequences for International Trade," *European Review of Agricultural Economics*, Vol. 29, 2002: 309–27.

Wheeler, David and Paul Martin, "Prices, Policies, and the International Diffusion of Clean Technology: the Case of Wood Pulp Production," in P. Low (ed.), *International Trade and the Environment*, World Bank Discussion Paper, World Bank, Washington, DC, 1992.

Williams, J., C. Jones and P. Dyke, "The EPIC Model: EPIC-Erosion/Productivity Impact Calculator, model documentation," in A. Sharpley and J. Williams (eds), *EPIC-Erosion/Productivity Impact Calculator 1. Model Documentation*, USDA Technical Bulletin No. 1768, Washington, DC, 1990: 3–92.

Williams, Shon P. and C. Richard Shumway, "Trade Liberalization and Agricultural Chemical Use: United States and Mexico," *American Journal of Agricultural Economics*, Vol. 82, No.1, February 2000: 183–99.

Wood, Stanley, Kate Sebastian and Sara Scherr, *Pilot Analysis of Global Ecosystems: Agroecosystems*, a joint study by the International Food Policy Research Institute: Washington, DC and the World Resources Institute: Washington, DC, 2000.

World Bank, "GNI per capita 1999, Atlas method and PPP," table from *2001 World Development Indicators Database*, 11 April, 2001, *www.worldbank.org/data/databytopic/GDP.pdf*

World Bank, *Greening Industry: New Roles for Communities, Markets, and Governments*, World Bank Policy Research Report, Oxford University Press, Inc.: New York, 1999.

World Bank (2000a), "Total GDP 1999," table from *2000 World Development Indicators database*, 2 August, 2000, *www.worldbank.org/data/databytopic/GDP.pdf*

World Bank (2000b), "Population 1999," table from the *2000 World Development Indicators database*, 2 August, 2000, *www.worldbank.org/data/databytopic/POP.pdf*

World Trade Organisation (WTO) (2001a), "Framework for Conducting Environmental Assessments of Trade Negotiations: Communication from Canada," WT/CTE/W/183, Geneva, 15 March, 2001.

WTO (2001b), "Legitimate Non-Trade Concerns: Submission by Argentina (Item 6 of the Work Programme)," WT/CTE/W/188, Geneva, 25 April, 2001.

WTO (2001c), "Committee on Trade and Environment's (CTE) Meeting on June 27–28, 2001," Trade and Environment News Bulletins TE/036, 6 July, 2001, *www.wto.org/english/tratop_e/envir_e/te036_e.htm*, accessed 22 November, 2002.

WTO (2002a), "Doha WTO Ministerial 2001: Briefing Notes. Intellectual Property (Trips) Negotiations, Implementation and TRIPS Council Work," 17 January, 2002, *ww.wto.org/wto/english/thewto_e/minist_e/min01_e/brief_e/brief08_e.htm*, accessed 31 September, 2002.

WTO (2002b), "WTO Agriculture Negotiations: The Issues, and Where We are Now," 8 April, 2002, *www.wto.org/english/tratop_e/agric_e/negs_bkgrnd23_ph2envir_e.htm*, accessed October 2002.

World Wildlife Federation, "Balanced Process, Balanced Results: Sustainability Assessments and Trade," WWF—World Wildlife Fund for Nature, Gland, Switzerland, 2001, *www.balancedtrade.panda.org*

Xu, X., "Do Stringent Environmental Regulations Reduce the International Competitiveness of Environmentally Sensitive Goods? A Global Perspective," *World Development*, Vol. 27, No. 7, July 1999: 1215–26.

Young, C. E. and C. T. Osborn, "The Conservation Reserve Program: An Economic Assessment," USDA, Economic Research Service, Agricultural Economic Report No. 626, February 1990.

Appendices

Appendix 1. Graphical representation of linkages between trade and the environment

This appendix presents a conceptual approach for analyzing environmental and trade issues under alternative policy measures. In Figure A1.1, we show the linkages between trade and environmental concerns. It shows a traditional trade framework (exporter, importer or Rest of World (ROW), and world market determining an equilibrium price). Lines D_e and D_m are domestic demands in the exporting and importing countries, respectively. Lines S_0 and S_m are domestic supplies in the exporting and importing countries, respectively. For prices above the point where D_e and S_0 intersect, producers represented by the country graph on the left would produce more than domestic consumers will buy. Thus, in the middle graph, one can trace out the excess supply line ES_0 for that country. For below the point where D_m and S_m intersect, consumers represented by the country graph on the right would demand more than domestic producers will produce. Thus, in the middle graph, one can trace out the excess demand line ED for that country. At equilibrium price, P^0, produced at the intersection of ES_0 and ED, production in the exporting country, is QX^0.

Extending the system of functions, a relationship is mapped between production by the agricultural sector and pollution by the line F_0. A linear relationship is shown for ease of illustration. The pollution axis could relate to a single environmental concern or objective, such as nutrient loss or erosion, or the probability of threat to an endangered species, or it could reflect a weighted index of several environmental concerns. For a given level of production QX^0 from the sector, there is an associated amount of pollution or environmental harm (Z_x^0) at a national level that results from a given mix of land, land use, and applied technologies used in production (for example, land cultivated, relative crop mix, and production practices).

Some of the difficulty policymakers face when attempting to achieve an environmental target can now be shown. Suppose, given the fixed production–pollution relationship represented by F_0, government sets a pollution-reduction goal, T, and institutes a policy to meet it. The policy results in a shift in the supply schedule from S_0 to S_1 resulting in a decline in production. However, the shift in the domestic supply function causes the excess supply schedule to shift up and

Figure A1.1 Linkages between trade and the environment

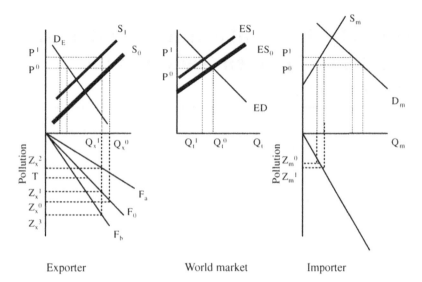

world prices to increase to P^1. The higher world price induces greater production (slippage) which causes pollution ($Z_x^{\ 1}$) to exceed the policy goal.

Relaxing the assumption of a fixed production–pollution relationship recognizes the probability that producers will adopt alternative practices in response to policy measures. F_a represents a more environmentally friendly set of practices such that for a given amount of production, less pollution results than with the original set of practices (F_0). For example, in response to a fertilizer tax to reduce nitrogen losses, producers may increase the use of crop rotations or substitute land for fertilizer. However, the set of alternative practices would yield a higher marginal cost schedule than current practices, which would shift the excess supply schedule, and yield a higher world price. In Chapter 5 for example, the instruments for lowering nitrogen use (Chapter 5, Table 5.1) lower production and trade volume, and consequently are likely to yield a higher world price. As illustrated, production would fall in response to the policy measure by an amount that is more than necessary and the goal would be more than met ($Z_x^{\ 2}$). This might occur if policymakers were to use too stringent a measure to achieve a goal. However, it is also possible that producers may adopt more environmentally harmful practices (F_b) such that for the same amount of production, the goal is not met ($Z_x^{\ 3}$). An example of this latter scenario would be if, in response to a pesticide ban, producers adopted use of a more harmful pesticide or intensified their use of other chemicals or tillage.

A comparison of alternative policies and their effects on trade is illustrated in Figure A1.2. For purposes of comparison across policy instruments, we assume that policymakers are able to set alternative policy measures in such a way that the environmental goal is met. The initial equilibrium occurs at world price P^0, resulting in exporter's production of Q_x^0, traded quantities of Q_t^0, and pollution of Z_x^0.

In response to a uniform input tax to reduce pollution to T, one would expect the supply schedule to shift from S^0 to S^1, yielding exporter production of Q_x^1 and traded quantities of Q_t^1, both below the Q_x^0 and Q_t^0. With a tax, not only does each firm face a higher marginal cost schedule, but because the tax also increases average costs as well it encourages exit from the sector (Baumol and Oates, 1988). At the same time the relationship between production and pollution shifts from F_0 to F_1 as the mix of input use, cultivated land, crop mix, and production practices that producers may adopt to achieve the policy goal reduces amount of pollution per given level of production.

With an agri-environmental payment or subsidy for reducing input use firms will face the same shift in their marginal cost schedules, but because the agri-environmental payment reduces average costs exit from the sector will be less than would occur with the tax policy, if not reversed (Baumol and Oates, 1988).[1] Two of the hypothetical agri-environmental programs in Chapter 6 that use subsidies actually slightly increased crop production. With a subsidy, the

Figure A1.2 Relative policy effects to achieve an environmental goal

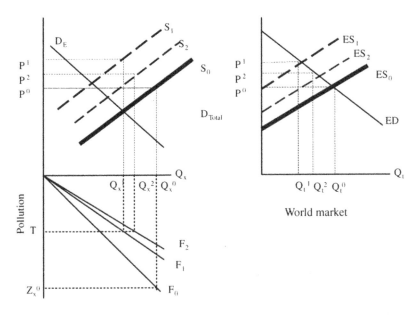

World market

payment rate needed to reach the same environmental target will be higher than the tax. The higher payment rate will induce the adoption of less pollution-intensive land uses than adopted under a tax, resulting in a mix of production practices represented by F_2, indicating that pollution per quantity of output is less than for F_1. Production (Q_x^2) and quantity traded (Q_t^2) will be higher than under the tax policy, while prices will be lower.

The production and trade effects of a uniform regulatory policy relative to that of an input tax are not necessarily determinate from theory. Miltz *et al.*(1988) and Russell (1986) show that the relative efficiency of a uniform tax and a uniform regulatory policy will depend on characteristics of pollution sources (that is, marginal cost of abatement, relative contribution of pollutant to the media of concern). Specifically, if pollution sources with a high marginal abatement cost affect the environmental indicator of interest more than do sources with low marginal abatement cost sources, then "the uniform charge will be more expensive than a uniform reduction, unless the difference in effects on environmental quality is sufficiently small to overbalance the difference in marginal costs" (Russell, 1986, p. 16). Hence, it is possible that for a given quantity of pollution reduction that reductions in production and exports would be less under a uniform regulation than under uniform input tax, as is the case in Chapter 5 for the nitrogen reduction scenarios (Table 5.1, Chapter 5).

The relative efficiency of land retirement for reducing pollution will depend on the marginal costs of uniform prevention relative to that of targeted prevention and remediation. Obviously, if land retirement were applied uniformly as a preventative measure it could be no more efficient than a uniform input tax or subsidy since land retirement is an option under both. If lands to be retired were targeted for their remediation capacity or for their high vulnerability to pollution so as to allow more productive areas to maintain production, then the net costs could be less than for the uniform policies. If, however, a relatively large extent of land were required, then substantial economic costs would result. Hence, the relative production and trade effects of a land retirement policy could be severely contractionary, or relatively small.

While we have discussed a theoretical comparison of how alternative policies designed to achieve an environmental goal, how they may actually compare is an empirical question, and is addressed in Chapters 5 and 6. Factors that will be important are the correlation between the policy instrument and the environmental target, producers' ability to alter their production technologies and the extent to which entry and exit occur.

NOTES

1. An agri-environmental payments policy is defined here as a payment to reduce a targeted input use or to employ a management practice appropriate to achieve the policy goal. Such an agri-environmental payment is not a payment to reduce emissions, the reduction of which is difficult to quantify for nonpoint sources.

Appendix 2. Different instruments for environmental protection

Agri-environmental policy in the US and the EU generally consists of a combination of voluntary instruments (subsidies) and involuntary instruments (taxes and regulatory requirements) in order to promote the use of environmentally sound farm practices.[1] Cross-compliance is another agri-environmental policy instrument that is sufficiently different from the instruments above to merit a separate discussion in this appendix.

Agri-environmental taxes are per-unit (either on an emission or on an input) charges designed to serve as a disincentive to using environmentally unsound practices. Total tax payments depend on the farmer's behavior; the further from the environmental goal, the higher the payment. The advantages of environmental tax policies are that they are consistent with the "polluter pays" principle, which states that the public owns environmental resources, and those who pollute these resources must pay compensation to the public (Krissoff et al., 1996). In addition, taxes do not promote expansion of environmentally damaging activities. On the other hand, taxes have a negative impact on farm income. Taxes do not play a significant role in the agri-environmental policies of either US Federal policy or EU-wide policy.

An agri-environmental subsidy pays the farmer to adopt environmentally sound practices or to retire land from production. The advantage of subsidies, such as those sharing the costs of adoption of environmentally benign management practices or paying farmers to set aside land, is that they increase the likelihood that farmers will adopt the desired practices or retire land. The disadvantage of subsidies is that achieving desired levels of adoption of environmentally benign management practices or of land retirement may be costly for taxpayers. Subsidies can also have the effect of expanding production by the farm, or increasing entry into the sector so even if the disamenities produced by each farm (or on each field) decrease, more farms (or fields) now produce disamenities.

Regulatory requirements, or standards, represent involuntary participation approaches that establish standards that all targeted actors must adhere to. The ban on the production and application of the chemical DDT is one such example. Unlike policy choices in which farmer participation is uncertain, regulations simply require that all farmers participate. This feature is particularly important if the consequences of not changing are drastic or irreversible. On the other hand, regulatory requirements can be the least flexible of all policy instruments, requiring that producers reach a specific environmental goal or adopt specific practices. Producers are not free to determine their own level of participation, based on their costs. Unless regulators know farm-specific costs and can use this information to establish farm-specific regulations, agri-environmental effort is not necessarily directed toward producers who can makes changes (achieve gains) at the lowest cost. Consequently, regulation can be less flexible and less efficient than economic incentives such as taxes and subsidies. Regulatory requirements are rare within traditional agri-environmental policy in both the EU and the US, but the regulatory environment is becoming increasingly complex.

Cross-compliance requires a basic level of environmental compliance as a condition for farmer eligibility for other government programs that farmers may find economically desirable, such as those that provide producer payments. Technically, cross-compliance is a voluntary instrument, but as it represents a standard for receiving an existing subsidy, in practice it may not strictly be voluntary, particularly when the existing subsidy represents an important share of total farm income. It is difficult for a farmer to for go cross-compliance when the value of the existing subsidies exceeds the farmer's costs of adopting the mandated practices.[2] In this circumstance, loss of these payments is dramatically different from foregoing an *additional* subsidy that is offered as compensation for adopting conservation practices. An advantage of cross-compliant programs is that less government outlay is required than with subsidies to address environmental problems. Disadvantages are that it will have lower capacity for impact on farms that are not traditional clients of Federal farm payment programs or in situations when program payments are low.

While some agri-environmental instruments tend to be more cost-effective than others in producing environmental benefits, the cost-effectiveness of any specific program depends greatly on the details of implementation.[3] For example, significant variation in climate, soils, crops, and proximity to environmental resource (for example, rivers or lakes) means that the ability to produce environmental benefits (or reduce environmental damage) can vary widely among farms, particularly in a national program. Highly erodible soils, located near a major river in an area of high rainfall intensity are likely to deliver significantly more sediment to the river than less erodible land located farther from the river or in an area of lower rainfall intensity. The cost-effectiveness of specific policy instruments can vary widely depending on the extent to which this type of variation is recognized and accommodated within the program. This and other potential variations in implementation (for example, the level of flexibility accorded producers) make it difficult to rank the cost-effectiveness of instruments irrespective of other program details.

In practice, however, both the US and EU try to use environmental programs to support farm price, income, or both as well as increase environmental amenities or reduce pollution. Agri-environmental policies often have the dual objective of environmental protection *and* farm income support, at least implicitly. The fact that some agri-environmental policies are trying to fulfill the twin objectives, in part explains their structure. It also raises the question of whether these policies are truly environmental programs or income support programs.

NOTES

1. Only a brief overview is provided here; for a more detailed overview of the economic instruments pertaining to US agri-environmental policy, see Claassen *et al.* (2001). See *http://europa.eu.int/comm/agriculture/envir/programs/evalrep/text_en.pdf* for more detail on EU agri-environmental programs.

2. In recent years, government payments have accounted for a large share of farm income, particularly in grain-producing states. Moreover, farm commodity programs have been in place for sufficient lengths of time in both the EU and the US—more than 65 years in the US—and payments are largely capitalized into the value of land (Barnard *et al.*, 1997; Duffy *et al.*, 1994) and are generally built into producers' financial calculations. For many producers, the ability to purchase land or pay cash rent depends significantly on farm program payments.

3. See Claassen *et al.* (2001) for a more detailed discussion of these issues.

Appendix 3. Agricultural sector models used in the analysis in the text

Three models of the agricultural sector are used in the simulation analyses in this book. The world price and production shocks resulting from an elimination or reduction of agricultural policy distortions are modeled using both the Economic Research Service/Penn State University trade model (Chapter 3) and with GTAP in the FARM model (Chapter 4). The US Regional Agricultural Model (USMP) models estimates detailed US domestic production and environmental impacts (Chapters 3, 5 and 6). The ERS/Penn State, USMP, and GTAP models are briefly described below.

Partial Equilibrium (PE) and Computable General Equilibrium (CGE) are the major modeling options used to investigate the impacts of trade policy (for an overview see Van Tongeren, van Meijl and Surry, 2001 and Anania, 2001). The USMP and ERS/Penn State trade models have a PE framework while the FARM has a CGE framework. PE is essentially a supply and demand framework either for a single good, or for a set of goods, or even for a set of goods across countries. CGE models simultaneously represent multiple sectors in the national (world) economy to account for the sectoral (international) flows of goods and services and their consequent effects on domestic (world) prices and consumption.

Specifically, in a PE model such as the one used in our analysis, the US agricultural sector (primary and secondary product supply, consumption and trade) is independent of other the US economic sectors (for example, manufacturing and service). PE models could also link several sectors, for example, agriculture and energy, together. Regardless, a defining feature of a PE model is that price and income impacts are limited to only those that occur between sectors in the model. In a CGE representation of the US agricultural sector, the other US sectors would be included on both the supply and demand sides. While a CGE model would seem favorable because it can account for changes in one industry impacting other industries, its overall complexity requires a rather simplistic representation of the various economic sectors. Furthermore, if the industry of interest has little potential for impact on other industries, then the advantages of CGE approaches are lessened. In general, PE models allow for a much greater level of sophistication when modeling a specific industry and regional environmental effects, such as changes in agricultural production resulting from trade policy.

1.   ERS/PENN STATE TRADE MODEL[1]

The ERS/Penn State trade model is an applied partial equilibrium, multiple commodity, multiple-region model of agricultural policy and trade. It is a non-spatial model—meaning that it does not distinguish a region's imports by their source or a region's exports by their destination. It is a gross trade model that accounts for exports and imports of each commodity in every region.

The model is dynamic in that it allows for lags in adjustment over time in crop area, livestock production, dairy product production, and oilseed crushing. In this way, the model can trace a time path of adjustment to alternative trade liberalization scenarios. The model can also be used to compare different options for phasing in reductions in tariffs, export subsidies, or other agricultural trade policies.

Country and Commodity Coverage

The version of the model used in our analysis contains four countries/regions: the United States (US), European Union (EU-15), Japan, and the Rest of World (ROW). There are currently 21 commodities in the model: seven crops (rice, wheat, corn, other coarse grains, soybeans, other oilseeds, tropical oils, sugar), four oilseed products (soybean oil and meal, other oilseed oil and meal), four livestock products (beef and veal, pork, poultry, raw milk), and five processed dairy products (butter, cheese, nonfat dry milk, fluid milk, and other dairy products). The "other coarse grains" aggregate is primarily barley, sorghum, millet, and oats. The "other oilseeds" aggregate consists primarily of rapeseed and sunflower. The "other dairy products" aggregate includes ice cream, yogurt, and whey. In the model, raw milk, fluid milk, and other dairy products are nontraded commodities. Raw milk is used domestically in the production of the model's five processed dairy products. The other 18 commodities are all traded internationally.

Policy Coverage

A wide range of policies is incorporated into the model. The core set of policies for all countries includes both specific and ad valorem import and export taxes/subsidies, tariff-rate quotas (TRQs), and producer and consumer subsidies. In the case of the US, the model also includes loan rates for crops and marketing orders for dairy products. For Japan, the model includes "mark ups" that are very high for rice and wheat.

Policy coverage for the EU is particularly extensive. The model includes intervention prices (which entail government purchases and then export subsidies), variable import levies, compensatory payments, acreage set-asides, and base area bounds (which limit the total area of grains and oilseeds by cutting off payments if the base area bound is reached). The EU component of the model also includes production quotas for raw milk and sugar.

Data and Base Year

The base year used in our analysis is 2000. Baseline data on area, yields, production, consumption, stocks, and trade are drawn from USDA and country sources, including USDA's Production, Supply, and Distribution (PS&D) database. Tariffs, TRQs, and world prices are drawn from the Agricultural Market Access Database (AMAD).

Model Structure and Parameters

The model is a reduced-form economic model in which the behavior of producers, consumers, and other economic agents is represented by elasticities and other model parameters. The behavioral equations in the model are largely constant-elasticity in nature. Constant-elasticity functions were selected because of their ease of interpretation and well behaved properties (provided the elasticities are chosen appropriately). The structure of the behavioral equations is the same for all countries in the model. The parameters of the equations and the values of variables in these equations vary from one country to another.

In assembling the parameter values for the model, the model draws on parameters in other trade models, including the European Simulation Model (ESIM), the ERS baseline projections model, the Food and Agricultural Policy Simulator (FAPSIM), AGLINK, SWOPSIM, as well as other sources in the trade literature. Adjustments were made to parameters in the process of testing the model when the test results did not appear reasonable. A number of restrictions were imposed on the model's elasticities to ensure that requirements of economic theory were satisfied.

2. US MATHEMATICAL PROGRAMMING MODEL (USMP)

To consider the effects of alternative environmental policies on traded volumes, market prices and agriculture's environmental performance, as well as the effects of trade liberalization on the latter, we employ USMP, a regional model of the US agricultural sector. USMP is a comparative-static, spatial and market equilibrium model of the type described in McCarl and Spreen (1980). The model incorporates agricultural commodity, supply, use, environmental emissions and policy measures (House *et al.*, 1999). The model has been applied to study various issues, such as design of agri-environmental policy

(Claassen *et al.*, 2001), regional effects of trade agreements (Burfisher *et al.*, 1992), climate change mitigation (Peters *et al.*, 2001), water quality (Johansson and Kaplan, 2003; Kaplan and Johansson, 2003; Peters *et al.*, 1997; Ribaudo *et al.*, 2001), irrigation policy (Horner *et al.*, 1990), ethanol production (House *et al.*, 1993), wetlands policy (Claassen *et al.*, 1998; Heimlich *et al.*, 1997), and sustainable agriculture policy (Faeth, 1995).

USMP estimates equilibrium levels of commodity price and production at the regional level, and the flow of commodities into final demand and stock markets. Geographic units consist of 45 model regions within the United States based on the intersection of the 10 USDA Farm Production Regions and the 25 USDA Land Resource Regions (USDA, SCS, 1981). Within each region, highly erodible land (HEL) is distinguished from non-HEL. Twenty-three inputs (for example, nitrogen fertilizer, energy, labor) are included as are 44 agricultural commodities (for example, corn, hogs for slaughter) and processed products (for example, soybean meal, retail cuts of pork). Crop production systems are differentiated according to rotation, tillage, and fertilizer rate. Production, land use, land use management (HEL, non-HEL, crop mix, rotations, tillage practices), and fertilizer applications rates are endogenously determined. Substitution among the production activities is represented with a nested constant elasticity of transformation function. Parameters of the nested-CET function are specified so that model supply response at the national level is consistent with supply response in the USDA's Food and Agriculture Policy Simulator (McDowell *et al.*, 1989) an econometric estimated national level simulation model of the US agriculture sector. The version of the model used in the analysis has the same elasticities as the ERS/Penn State Model.

Of special relevance to Chapter 5, note that USMP explicitly models producer risk with respect to selection of nitrogen fertilizer application rate. Producer selection of nitrogen fertilizer application rates will depend on the expected returns and producers, perception of risk to those returns. Producers' perceptions of risk are represented in USMP with a risk premium that increases exponentially with the reduction in nitrogen fertilizer application rates from the base application rate. While reducing nitrogen fertilizer application rates will reduce the variation in net returns it may also reduce the yield attainable under good growing conditions. Producers, however, are likely to be more concerned with making sure that yields are not constrained by lack of nitrogen to the plant under good growing conditions than they are with the costs associated with overapplication of nitrogen fertilizer under poor growing conditions. Consequently, producers will likely view the reduction of their nitrogen fertilizer application rates below that needed to achieve maximum yields under good growing conditions as risky, and will require a premium above that of the expected return for reducing their fertilizer application rates below what they believe to be needed to assure maximum yields under good growing conditions.

Major government agricultural programs, chiefly the Flexibility Contract Program (FCP), the Conservation Reserve Program (CRP), and conservation compliance are also represented. The most important of these for this analysis is conservation compliance, which limits expansion of production onto HEL by requiring producers to forego FCP and CRP payments when bringing new HEL into production without implementing an approved conservation system.

On the demand side, domestic use, trade, ending stocks and price levels for crop and livestock commodities and processed or retail products are determined endogenously. Trade is represented with excess demand and supply curves, with the assumption that there is no policy response by Rest of World to US environmental policies. Hence, trade volumes respond to changes in prices. USMP allocates production practices regionally based on relative differences in net returns among production practices by region.

With data from US Department of Agriculture (USDA) production practice surveys (Padgitt *et al.*, 2000), the USDA Long-Term Agricultural Baseline (USDA, WAOB, 1998), the National Resources Inventory (USDA, SCS, 1994), and the Environmental Policy Integrated Climate model, or EPIC (formerly known as the Erosion Productivity Impact Calculator) (Williams, Jones and Dyke, 1990), USMP is used to estimate how changes in environmental or other policies affect US input use, production, demand, trade, world prices, and environmental indicators.

Environmental indicators include soil erosion, losses of nitrogen and phosphorous to ground and surface water, volatilization and denitrification of nitrogen, nitrogen runoff damage to coastal waters and erosion damage.[2,3] Environmental emissions for each crop production activity were obtained from simulations of the production activities using EPIC. EPIC utilizes information on soils, weather, and management practices, including specific fertilizer rates, and produces information on crop yields, erosion, and chemical losses to the environment. For the simulations management practices and initial fertilizer application rates were set consistent with agronomic practices for the 45 regions as reported in the USDA's Cropping Practices Survey (a predecessor of the Agricultural Resource Management Survey). Yield and environmental indicators—such as, nitrogen losses and erosion—were then estimated by running each of the cropping systems represented in USMP through EPIC. Take, for example, the process of constructing USMP's erosion indicator. In the first step, yields were obtained by running EPIC for seven years for each crop in the rotation with erosion rates set at zero and the distribution of rainfall and temperature set to match reported rainfall and temperatures for the seven-year period 1989–1995 for each region. Erosion rates were set at zero to ensure that the yields were a function of weather and not of losses in soil productivity. Average yields by crop for each region were calculated from NASS county data for this same time period and used to evaluate EPIC's performance in simulating crop growth. EPIC-based average yields by crop and region came within 10 per cent of average reported yields for these crops and regions over the seven-year period. The environmental indicators were then obtained by running the systems through EPIC with erosion rates set at zero for a period of 60 years. This permitted the systems to be run through two complete cycles of the weather distribution, removing the effect of particular weather patterns on the results. For the estimation of nitrogen losses, a similar two-step process was repeated for nitrogen application rates representing 10, 20, 30 and 40 per cent reductions from their initial values.

Assigning monetary values to these production and environmental changes is necessary to assess the costs and benefits of agri-environmental policies. However, there are relatively few assessments of the value (monetized or non-monetized) of environmental impacts of agricultural activities. In USMP, market and nonmarket economic values have been linked to regional net returns in the cropping and livestock sectors and to several of the environmental indicators. The onsite cost, the soil depreciation indicator, is the discounted monetary value of long-term yield changes due to this loss, and is based on current output prices. Of course, wind and soil erosion produce offsite economic costs as well. In USMP, changes in upstream erosion are linked to downstream economic costs through a hydrologic model based on annual dredging cost data from all 400 Army Corps of Engineers dredging sites in the continental US (Hansen *et al.*, 2002). Costs of offsetting erosion—in this case, the dredging of sediment by the Corps of Engineers—represents the public's efforts to offset direct (for example, flooding, the forced use of smaller vessels, downtimes, and repair) and indirect costs (human and environmental health impacts, such as the environmental costs of fuel and cargo leaks that results from groundings) of erosion (Claassen *et al.*, 2001; Hansen *et al.*, 2002; Ribaudo, 1986). Dredging costs per ton of sediment vary by location in the model, for example, cost is a function of the distance needed to haul the sediment for disposal.

Travel cost analysis was used to estimate the relationship between recreational waterfowl hunting trips nationwide and sediment and nitrogen concentrations in waterbodies at the recreational sites (Feather, Hellerstein and Hansen, 1999; Hellerstein and Breneman, 2000). The resulting coefficients reflect the negative correlation between recreational value and pollutant discharge and enable us to link changes in these agri-environmental environmental impacts to changes in consumer surplus associated with fresh water-based recreation, navigation, and estuary-based boating, swimming, and recreation. The set of monetized environmental impacts is by no means an exhaustive list of all activities affected by sediment and nitrogen runoff, let alone that the impacts of other environmental indicators remain to be monetized. Hence, the monetized estimates of offsite damage calculated by USMP are presumably a lower bound on total offsite damages.

3. THE FUTURE AGRICULTURAL RESOURCES MODEL (FARM)

The Future Agricultural Resources Model (FARM) was developed at the US Department of Agriculture's Economic Research Service to evaluate impacts of global climate change on the world's agricultural system (Darwin *et al.*, 1995). FARM is composed of a geographic information system (GIS) and a CGE economic model. The GIS links climate variables with land and water resources in FARM's environmental framework. In FARM's economic framework (see Figure A3.1), the CGE model links land, water, and other primary factors with production, trade, and consumption of 13 commodities in eight regions.

FARM's environmental framework is dominated by climate. Broad differences in land productivity are obtained by dividing each region's land into classes based on length of growing season, a measure highly correlated with primary production. Length of growing season is defined as the longest continuous period of time in a year that soil temperature and moisture conditions support plant growth. Growing season lengths were computed from monthly temperature and precipitation data.

FARM's economic framework consists of a multiregion, multisector CGE model. The CGE model explicitly accounts for all domestic and international money flows for 1990. Households are assumed to own the four primary factors of production (land, water, labor, and capital). They use the revenue from the sale of these factors to purchase consumer goods and services from the producing sectors in domestic and international markets. Accounting for this circular flow enables CGE models to provide comprehensive measures of economic activity.

FARM's CGE model is an aggregation and extension of the Global Trade Analysis Project (GTAP) model (Hertel, 1993). GTAP provides researchers with a well documented global database and modeling structure. FARM's major extensions to GTAP are the inclusion of land as a primary input in all producing sectors, the introduction of water as a primary input in the crops, livestock and service sectors, and the modeling of crop production as a multioutput sector. Including land as a primary input in all producing sectors allows simulated changes in land use.

A region's primary factor endowments of land, water, labor, and capital are determined exogenously and are region-specific. That means one region's primary factors cannot be used by another region's sectors. Water, labor, and

Figure A3.1 FARM's environmental framework

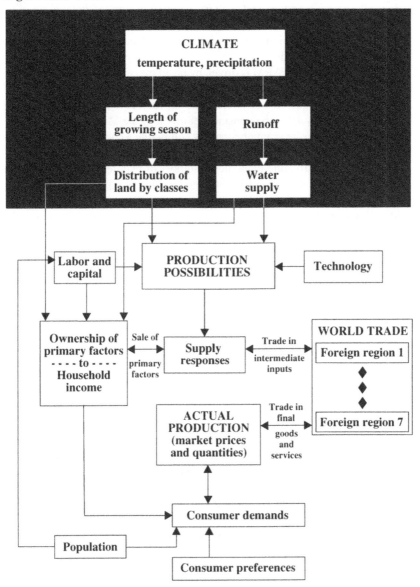

capital are homogenous, so within regions these factors are perfectly mobile across all economic sectors, and each has one regional price. Water is supplied to the crops, livestock, and services sectors. Land, labor and capital are supplied to all sectors. Regional demands for water, land, labor, and capital are sums of sectoral demands.

Producer behavior in FARM is driven by profit maximization assuming competitive markets. The land-intensive sectors—crops, livestock and forestry—are composed of subsectors, one for each land class. Technology in each sector is assumed to be constant returns to scale. A commodity is produced from a composite input obtained by combining a composite primary factor with 13 composite commodity inputs in fixed proportions.

This production structure embodies a number of realities that are lacking in other CGE models. First, land is heterogenous and is a primary factor in all economic sectors. Second, land is in fixed supply, so cropland cannot increase without reducing land in another category. Third, it is relatively difficult to substitute labor and capital for land in the land-intensive sectors. Also, each region's commodities are treated as separate goods when traded, which helps to maintain product differentiation.

FARM's treatment of land embodies both ecological and economic concepts regarding land's productivity. And because land use and cover is an integral component of the modeling framework, one can track how changes in land use and cover interact not only with the production of goods and services, but also with the ecological resources of a region.

FARM also has data on support and protection as does GTAP. Agricultural policies have been the topic of many measurement efforts. Producer and consumer subsidy equivalents, developed by the Organization for Economic Cooperation and Development and by USDA's Economic Research Service, quantify tariff and nontariff policies for many agricultural products. These two sources estimate the effects that government policies have on producer and consumer prices by type of policy. This makes it possible to separate producer price impacts into border measures and domestic measures. Hence, three measures—import tariffs, export subsidies, and production subsidies—make up the agricultural component of the support and protection data.

For the exercise in this book, we simulate changes in global trade policies by adjusting the wedges between producer and market prices (subsidies) and between domestic and foreign prices (duties and tariffs) of wheat, other grains, nongrain, and livestock commodities. A 30 per cent across-the-board cut in agricultural subsidies, duties, and tariffs is applied in all regions. Trade policy analysis is limited to the agricultural sectors because FARM's CGE model contains the necessary support and protection data for agricultural products in all regions.

NOTES

1. This description is drawn from *http://trade.aers.psu.edu/documentation.cfm*, from which a full description is also available.

2. Denitrification is the process by which nitrogen is released to the atmosphere due to bacterial action in wet and compact soils and volatilization occurs when fertilizer applied releases directly to the environment. The sum of these is the USMP indicator "nitrogen loss to the atmosphere."

3. For information on the environmental impacts of agriculture, please see the ERS Briefing Room on Conservation and Environmental Policy (ERS, 2001) as well as the Briefing Room on Global Climate Change (ERS, 2000a).

Appendix 4. Extracts of URAA text of specific Green Box criteria relevant to environmental programs[1]

1. Domestic support measures for which exemption from the reduction commitments is claimed shall meet the fundamental requirement that they have no, or at most minimal, trade-distorting effects or effects on production. Accordingly, all measures for which exemption is claimed shall conform to the following basic criteria:

   (a) the support in question shall be provided through a publicly-funded government programme (including government revenue foregone) not involving transfers from consumers; and,

   (b) the support in question shall not have the effect of providing price support to producers;

plus policy-specific criteria and conditions as set out below.

2. General services

   Policies in this category involve expenditures (or revenue foregone) in relation to programmes which provide services or benefits to agriculture or the rural community. They shall not involve direct payments to producers or processors. Such programmes, which include but are not restricted to the following list, shall meet the general criteria in paragraph 1 above and policy-specific conditions where set out below:

   (a) research, including general research, research in connection with environmental programmes, and research programmes relating to particular products;

   (b) pest and disease control, including general and product-specific pest and disease control measures, such as early-warning systems, quarantine and eradication;

(c) training services, including both general and specialist training facilities;

(d) extension and advisory services, including the provision of means to facilitate the transfer of information and the results of research to producers and consumers;

(e) inspection services, including general inspection services and the inspection of particular products for health, safety, grading or standardization purposes;

(f) marketing and promotion services, including market information, advice and promotion relating to particular products but excluding expenditure for unspecified purposes that could be used by sellers to reduce their selling price or confer a direct economic benefit to purchasers; and

(g) infrastructural services, including: electricity reticulation, roads and other means of transport, market and port facilities, water supply facilities, dams and drainage schemes, and infrastructural works associated with environmental programmes. In all cases the expenditure shall be directed to the provision or construction of capital works only, and shall exclude the subsidized provision of on-farm facilities other than for the reticulation of generally available public utilities. It shall not include subsidies to inputs or operating costs, or preferential user charges.

10. Structural adjustment assistance provided through resource retirement programmes

   (a) Eligibility for such payments shall be determined by reference to clearly defined criteria in programmes designed to remove land or other resources, including livestock, from marketable agricultural production.

   (b) Payments shall be conditional upon the retirement of land from marketable agricultural production for a minimum of three years, and in the case of livestock on its slaughter or definitive permanent disposal.

(c) Payments shall not require or specify any alternative use for such land or other resources which involves the production of marketable agricultural products.

(d) Payments shall not be related to either the type or quantity of production or to the prices, domestic or international, applying to production undertaken using the land or other resources remaining in production.

12. Payments under environmental programmes

(a) Eligibility for such payments shall be determined as part of a clearly-defined government environmental or conservation programme and be dependent on the fulfilment of specific conditions under the government programme, including conditions related to production methods or inputs.

(b) The amount of payment shall be limited to the extra costs or loss of income involved in complying with the government programme.

NOTES

1. The number paragraphs are extracted verbatim from the URAA's "Annex 2: Domestic Support—the Basis for Exemption from the Reduction Commitments" (*www.wto.org/wto/english/docs_e/legal_e/14-ag_02_e.htm*).

Appendix 5. Theoretical description of basic conditions for a successful MEA

This appendix uses mathematical relationships to illustrate some of the concepts discussed in Section I of Chapter 7. As discussed in that chapter, signing an MEA must be profitable (either on a monetary or nonmonetary basis) for all countries involved in the negotiations process. The stability issue refers to the intrinsic instability of environmental agreements. Namely, some countries may prefer to free ride, that is, to profit from the environmental benefits achieved by the signatory countries (because the environmental benefit is not excludable) without paying the costs. Cooperation is thus unstable unless there is no incentive to free ride (Carraro, 1997). Mathematically, a coalition of countries s is profitable when each country $i \in s$ gains from joining the coalition (with respect to its position when no countries cooperate) that forms the MEA (Carraro and Siniscalco, 1993). Formally, a coalition s is profitable if and only if $P_i(s) \geq P_i(\phi)$, $\forall\, i \in s$ where $P_i(s)$ is country i's payoff when coalition s forms. Adding transfers T_i to the profitability condition above produces $P_i(s) + T_i \geq P_i(\phi)$, $\forall\, i \in s$ (Carraro, 1997). Linking two agreements, such as a trade and an environmental agreement, denoted by subscripts 1 and 2, is profitable for coalition s if $P_{1i}(s) + P_{2i}(s) \geq P_{1i}(\phi) + P_{2i}(\phi)$, $\forall\, i \in s$.

A coalition s if stable if and only if there is no incentive to free ride, that is, $Q_i(s \setminus i) - P_i(s) < 0$ for each country i belonging to s, where $Q_i(s \setminus i)$ is country i's payoff when it defects from coalition s; there is no incentive to broaden the coalition, that is, $P_i(s \cup i) - Q_i(s) < 0$ for each country i which does not belong to s.

Appendix 6. Coordination of domestic agri-environmental policies and trade liberalization

Agricultural support and protection rates are higher in developed than in developing countries (Burfisher, 2001: 29). Reducing agricultural support with trade liberalization will likely decrease the return to agriculture most in those countries with the highest level of support. Diminished profitability then decreases the incentive to apply costly polluting inputs, so environmental stress from pesticide runoff and groundwater contamination would be reduced. Conversely, in countries that are better able to accommodate increased agricultural intensity because pesticide and fertilizer usage historically has been low, one might expect increased rates of chemical application as world prices rise in response to diminished domestic price supports and subsidies. On the other hand, the externalities associated with extensive methods of production may decrease. Thus, one might expect both positive and negative environmental impacts from trade liberalization. This possibility illustrates the potential to coordinate international trade and domestic environmental policies in order to benefit from trade liberalization's environmental improvements and efficiency gains while mitigating its potential to encourage specific negative environmental externalities. In other words, by coordinating domestic environmental policy with trade policy, a "win-win" outcome emerges.

Different countries employ various domestic agri-environmental policies that can combat suspected adverse environmental impacts of production increases that may result from trade liberalization. Some countries, particularly in the EU, employ various domestic agri-environmental policies designed to reduce the loss of desirable environmental by-products of agriculture that may be perceived to be under threat due to agricultural production decreases resulting from trade liberalization. In fact, the WTO recognizes the need for countries to protect their environment and to conserve natural resources. Under the WTO regulations set forth in the Agreement on Agriculture, member nations are required to reduce domestic support levels. However, the WTO allows domestic environmental and natural resource policies that meet certain criteria to be placed under the green box exemption (Appendix 5), and therefore not are not subject to reductions in support. To qualify for the "green box", a program:

- must affect trade and production only minimally;
- must not support prices or increase consumer costs, and;
- must be financed by the government.

The potential use of generic agri-environmental programs, such as agri-environmental payment programs, to reduce the environmental impacts of agricultural production is demonstrated empirically in Claassen *et al.* (2001). However, an important question in terms of trade negotiations is what impacts these programs may have on production. Chapter 5 of this book shows that agri-environmental programs may actually counter some of the production increases due to liberalized trade. Chapter 6 suggests that agri-environmental payment programs have minimal impacts on production.

Current US Federal-level agri-environmental policy spans a wide range of programs, but unlike in the EU, these policies are targeted only at the potential negative consequence of agriculture, although that is changing to some extent with the introduction of the Grassland Reserve Program (GRP) and a revised Farmland Protection Program (FPP) in the 2002 Farm Bill.[1] USDA-administered programs that can be used to counter possible adverse environmental impacts of production increases that may result from trade liberalization include:[2]

- **Environmental Quality Incentives Program (EQIP)**—Through the use of technical assistance, education, cost sharing, and incentives payments, EQIP assists farmers and ranchers in adopting management techniques that reduce nonpoint-source surface and groundwater pollution. Fiscal 2000 expenditures: US$174 million. Funding increases by 450 per cent with the 2002 Farm Bill (comparing the six year period of the 2002 Farm Bill with the six year period of the previous Farm Bill), for around $9 billion in spending over 2002–2011.

- **Conservation Reserve Program (CRP)**—CRP provides rental payments to agricultural producers who retire environmentally sensitive cropland. Fiscal 2000 expenditures: US$1.6 billion. Near $2 billion in funding over 2002–2011 under the 2002 Farm Bill.

- **Farmland Protection Program (FPP)**—FPP allocates funds for purchase of conservation easements and other types of interest in land with prime, unique, or other highly productive soils. Although there were no fiscal 2000 expenditures, the 2001 budget requested US$65 million. Funding of $597 million is mandated for 2002–2007.

- **Wetland Reserve Program (WRP)**—WRP assists landowners in returning farmed wetlands to their original condition through easement payments and restoration cost sharing. Fiscal 2000 appropriations: US$157 million. Near $2 billion in funding over 2002–2007 under the 2002 Farm Bill.

- **Conservation Security Program (CSP)**—Provides payments to farmers in return for their use of a wide range of environmentally benign land management practices. The program will have three "tiers" for participation; higher tiers require greater conservation effort and offer larger payments. Existing practices can be enrolled. This program is new under the 2002 Farm Bill, with $2 billion in funding over 2002–2011 (funding level forecast in 2002).

- **Grassland Reserve Program (GRP)**—Using contracts or easements in conjunction with compensatory payments, up to 2 million acres of grassland will be protected from conversion to other uses. This program is new under the 2002 Farm Bill, with up to $254 million in funding available over 2002–2007.

NOTES

1. Types of state and local programs that can be used to protect the amenities of agriculture are briefly covered in Chapter 2 and are covered in detail in Hellerstein *et al.* (2002).

2. The budget data for these programs are derived from estimates supplied by the USDA's Office of Budget and Program Analysis.

Index